CW00556891

GRAND-PRIX DE L'AVIATION

Henri FARMAN boucle les 1000m sur son aéroplane

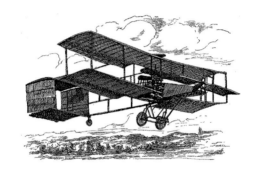

The Right Flyer

Gabriel Voisin, Henry Farman and the archetype of aeroplanes

by Reg Winstone

FOR HÉLOISE AND MILO

Cover: *Hommage à Blériot*, Robert Delaunay, 1914 (detail)
Endpapers: *Grand Prix de l'Aviation,* Ernest Montaut, 1908

ISBN: 978-0-9569811-0-3

faustroll.co.uk

Contents

PROFESSIONAL JEALOUSY.

Icarus (*watching the triumphant flight of Mr. Farman*). "CONFOUND THE FELLOW! WISH
I'D THOUGHT OF THAT!"

Foreword

As 1908 drew to a close, the number of viable aeroplanes in the world could be counted on the fingers of one hand: the three year-old Wright Flyer III, the Wright Model A flown by Wilbur at Le Mans, Orville's similar Fort Myer machine and the two Voisin cellular biplanes belonging to the sculptor Léon Delagrange (his third), and to the celebrated racing motorist Henry Farman.

This is the story of the latter. Partly, because this historic artefact and its creators are undeservedly overlooked in accounts of these epoch-defining innovations. But also because its eventful and fulsomely chronicled two-year lifespan provides a revealing prism through which to examine the social, cultural, financial and political context of the final lap of the race to fly.

These five landmark machines represented two parallel but fundamentally distinct solutions to the problem of flight. As to whether Europe or the United States was the true cradle of heavier-than-air aviation, chronology favours the New World, but mechanical autonomy and design legacy are firmly held boasts of the Old.

Once hotly debated, this controversy is irrelevant today. More interesting is the public discourse prompted by these achievements, and the ideas, passions and relationships involved. This account is therefore less about technical minutiae than the ways in which the zigzag of technological progress was driven by the very different personalities concerned. Their hopes and fears. Their strengths and weaknesses. And so, drawing on contemporary sources, it seeks to establish the facts from the fiction in a way that invests these extraordinary events with some of the gripping immediacy they must have had at the time.

2

Prelude

Henry Farman (*extreme right*) next to Léon Delagrange beside Voisin Farman Nº 1 at Issy-les-Moulineaux in January 1908, with Ernest Archdeacon standing in his Renault.

Although the Wright brothers were unquestionably the first to achieve controlled heavier-than-air powered flight, the original Flyer was not a practical aeroplane. To be so, a flying machine must at least be able to take off unaided under its own power, negotiate a predetermined course and land in a fit state to reascend unassisted; ideally, it should not require exceptional skill to operate. Equally unquestionable is that the first machine officially observed to meet these criteria was the cellular biplane conceived and built in 1907 by Gabriel and Charles Voisin for Henry Farman.

From the bright summer day of its delivery to the triumphant official vindication of its capabilities 18 weeks later, this machine underwent innumerable modifications by the manufacturers and the owner, and many more in the latter's hands during the ensuing year. Like the proverbial axe, few of its original components can have remained by the end of its illustrious career, but what follows is an attempt to chart the evolution of this milestone in aviation history and its impact on the wider world.

Inextricably linked with its story is the question as to whether or not mastery of this world-changing new discipline would confirm the supremacy of European cultural values and technology leadership, as exemplified by France, over the vigorous spirit of market-driven innovation and individual achievement that prevailed on the other side of the Atlantic. The protagonists in both camps were standing on the shoulders of giants, of course. In the closing years of the 19th century, when the Voisin brothers were still teenagers and the Wrights were in their twenties, the older sibling of each pair devoured the published work of pioneers such as Sir George Cayley, Hiram Maxim, Samuel Langley and Horatio Phillips; just as importantly, they also familiarised themselves with the gliding experiments of Percy Pilcher in England and Otto Lilienthal in Germany.

The Wrights built their first test kites and gliders in 1899; Gabriel Voisin claimed that he and his brother had made their first kite a little earlier, inspired by reading about the Australian researcher Lawrence Hargrave *(appendix XIV)*, whose studies of the aerodynamic qualities of box kites and aerofoil sections with thicker leading edges had also informed US thinking. Tethered, the Voisin boys' Hargrave kite apparently remained aloft for days. So impressed were they that Gabriel's first design for a heavier-than-air craft, in May 1900, was for a twin-engined 'Hargrave' with a forward elevator plane similar to Maxim's machine, and a vertical rudder in the tail cell.

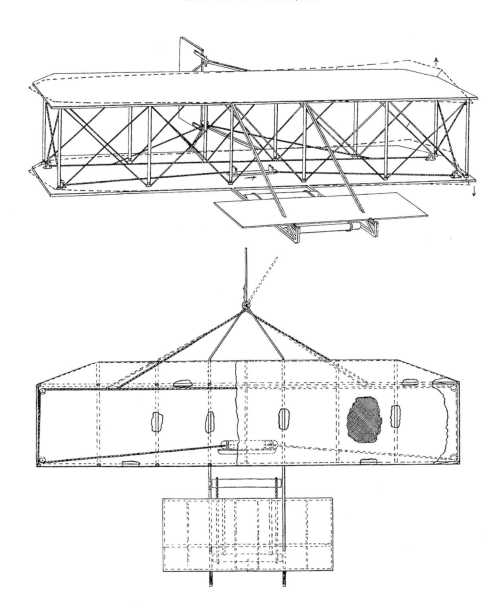

6

Hargrave was admired in France as much for his altruistic approach to the question of intellectual property as for as his aeronautical research. "Workers must root out the idea [that] by keeping the results of their labours to themselves, a fortune will be assured to them," he declared. "Patent fees are wasted money. The flying machine of the future will not be born fully-fledged. [..] Like everything else, it must be evolved gradually. The first difficulty is to get a thing that will fly at all. When this is made, a full description should be published as an aid to others. Excellence of design and workmanship will always defy competition."

This was not a view shared by the Wrights. How they came to make their four short flights at Kill Devil Hills a few days before Christmas 1903 is amply chronicled elsewhere, but it is worth comparing with the state of play in France at the time. They had first come to the attention of the French aeronautical community ten months earlier, when Octave Chanute (*appendix IX*) gave a lecture to the luminaries of the Aéro Club de France on recent developments in aviation research in America. An eminent civil engineer in his adoptive United States, Chanute was known and respected in his native France through his voluminous correspondence with virtually every notable experimenter in the field since the early 1880s, thereby forming an unrivalled worldwide network of flight researchers. It was Chanute who had introduced the Wrights to Lilienthal's pivotal gliding experiments in Germany, which, along with Chanute's experiences with his own cellular gliders, influenced their initial approach to aircraft construction; indeed, their original Flyer was directly inspired by Chanute's 1896 trussed biplane glider, to which Wilbur added his own crucial refinement by bracing the leading and trailing edges without trussing the ends, allowing the planes to warp without sacrificing beam strength.

As the Dayton brothers' closest aeronautical confidant, Chanute recounted their 1902/03 gliding successes in his address to the Aéro Club, which was extensively reported in *L'Aérophile* and other French journals over the following months. The news had a galvanising effect: "Engineers, to your drawing boards!" cried one. "Patrons, sponsors and members of the government, put your hands in your pockets or we shall be beaten!" As far as Paris was concerned, the race was on.

Left, with the help of Colonel Charles Renard, Ernest Archdeacon's first glider was built at the military aeronautical research centre at Chalais Meudon over the winter of 1903/04 by Dargent on the basis of Octave Chanute's rough sketches of the 1901/02 Wright glider.

Below, Archdeacon demonstrates his glider's crude elevator control cord in the grounds of Chalais Meudon. The image was published for the purpose of inspiring other aspiring aeronauts in France to build their own flying machines; he never intended to pilot the glider himself.

That summer, 300 miles away in Neuville, on the banks of the River Saône just north of Lyon, the 23 year-old Gabriel Voisin, released early after only nine months of military service, read one of these articles about Chanute's gliding experiments in a magazine borrowed from a friend who knew of his enthusiasm for the burgeoning new science and its potential for even more sporting thrills than the boats, rifles and cars that Voisin had already built with his younger brother Charles.

Together, they built themselves a Chanute glider. When it proved too unstable to lift either of them, they made what turned out to be a fortuitous discovery. To rectify the instability, Gabriel Voisin tried replacing the diminutive tail with one of the old Hargrave biplane cells they had packed away in a garden shed four years earlier. It worked. The Chanute no longer flew tail down, but adopted a stable horizontal attitude in the airstream – stable enough to lift Gabriel, the lighter of the two, aloft for a few seconds. For Voisin, this minor epiphany hardened into an article of design faith.

Back in Paris, no one had been more disconcerted by Chanute's news of the Wrights' gliding feats than Ernest Archdeacon *(appendix V)*. A Franco-Irish lawyer of considerable private means and a leading light of the Aéro Club community of well-heeled young amateurs, industrialists, financiers and aristocrats, Archdeacon had since 1890 been the most ardent torchbearer for France's leadership in all matters technological. In the absence of any documentary evidence of the Wright glider's claimed capabilities, he determined to replicate the 1902 machine to test it for himself.

With no production resources of his own (having relinquished his bicycle manufacturing company to concentrate on aviation), Archdeacon turned to the most eminent of his Aéro Club colleagues, Colonel Charles Renard. With a distinguished record as the builder of the first true dirigible, Renard had in 1872 also built a 10-winged glider with a streamlined fuselage, cruciform tail and pendulum-actuated self-stabilising planes of the type patented five years earlier by Matthew Boulton. As head of the army's aeronautical research establishment at Chalais Meudon, Renard was ideally placed to execute the commission. He entrusted the task to his assistant Dargent, a veteran pattern maker and model builder. Guided by Chanute's sketchy and substantially inaccurate plans of the Flyer, Dargent started work, innocent of the rapid progress being made on the other side of the Atlantic.

Archdeacon's first glider being displayed in the grounds of the Aéro Club at Saint-Cloud in late January 1904.

With a 7.4m span and a chord of 1.44m, it was two-thirds of the size of the original, bereft of wing warping or any other form of roll control, and had main planes of a constant radius section. It sported a tall central rudder at the rear, with an adjustable front elevator plane of modest size mounted above the foremost extremity of the landing skids. The mortise joints of the delicate ash airframe were screwed together (misguidedly, as it turned out) to allow easy disassembly for transportation purposes. The ensemble weighed 34 kilos.

Meanwhile, having decided to move to Paris, Gabriel Voisin disembarked at the magnificent new Gare de Lyon to move in with Claudius Genevrier, a school friend then working as a hack on the right-wing Paris daily *Le Matin*. He had 265 francs in his pocket, a case of drawing instruments and little else but a gleam in his eye. Certainly, he had no contacts in the élite world of the Aéro Club.

Serendipity intervened in the guise of a friend of his flatmate's: Armand Lézy, an ambitious young fellow journalist from Lyon. In this capacity, Lezy was sent on December 29th to report on the inaugural journey of a formidable road train Colonel Renard had developed. While Renard's partner in this enterprise, Edouard Surcouf (of whom more later) drove the elephantine Darracq-built contraption from Chalais Meudon through the streets of Paris, Lézy, on completing his interview with the great man, took the opportunity to suggest a meeting with Voisin. Perhaps distracted by the vivid green gauntlets the dandyish scribe habitually sported, Colonel Renard surprisingly agreed. It was his brother, Commandant Paul Renard, who received Gabriel Voisin at Chalais Meudon in the first week of January 1904. "I was visited in my office by a pleasant looking young fellow who told me that he lived near Lyon but had come to Paris to practice aviation," he recalled 20 years later. "As he enthusiastically explained his ideas and outlined the project he planned to undertake, I soon saw that he had fire in his belly." Voisin showed Renard photographs and notes of his gliding experiments at Neuville with the Chanute modified with a Hargrave rear cell, and expounded his own ideas on propeller design and the critical relationship between centres of pressure and gravity.

"I wanted to encourage him, but in view of the practicalities involved, I asked what he had by way of financial resources with which to realise his ambitions," said Renard.

"'None whatsoever,' he replied. Asked whether he at least had enough to live on until he could profit from his inventions, the young man once again shook his head: 'Unfortunately I only had a modestly paid job in Lyon, which I left in order to come to Paris to work on the conquest of the air.' I pointed out that although things might well change in years hence, there was no hope of making money from aviation at that time. The only advice I could give was that he should return to his job in Lyon until matters improved. 'I'm sure that better days will come,' I said, 'And I promise to let you know as soon as I judge the time to be right.'

"'Impossible!' he cried. "'I've resigned from my post, which has since been filled.' This put me in an awkward position. The last thing I wanted was to discourage this keen and clearly intelligent young man, but on the other hand, how on earth could he hope to survive with no capital behind him? On reflection, I told him that there was perhaps one man in Paris, and one alone, who might be able to help. Go and tell him I sent you. And I gave him a letter of introduction to Ernest Archdeacon."

This was Voisin's big break, for Archdeacon was undoubtedly the most influential figure in the Aéro Club. But it was no shoe-in. Several inconclusive visits followed to Archdeacon's apartments in the 17th *arrondissement* until one day, inter alia, the millionaire mentioned problems with his new Renault. Having built two automobiles of his own and fettled the big Mors his brother had acquired with the proceeds of a modest legacy, Gabriel Voisin was able not only to diagnose the problem - carburetter icing - but to effect a simple cure by contriving a tube to conduct hot air from around the exhaust manifold to warm the offending component. So impressed was Archdeacon by this determined and evidently mechanically competent young man bearing photographs of his kite-flying and gliding experience that he engaged him to help with the first trials of his own new glider, whose planes Dargent was now expensively cladding in extra-fine silk.

In December, Archdeacon had identified a site for the tests at Merlimont on the Channel coast between the seaside resorts of Le Touquet and Berck. It was an ideal venue, with substantial hillocks from which to launch the machine and soft sand on which to land it; with an 80-strong local amateur gliding and kite-flying club, the Société de l'Aéroplane Berckois, there would also be no shortage of experienced helpers.

Then came the bombshell. On January 10th 1904, Ferdinand Ferber *(appendix VI)*, captain of artillery, mathematician, graduate of the elite Ecole Polytechnique and one of France's foremost aeronautical experimenters, received a letter from Orville Wright describing the powered flights made three weeks earlier at Kitty Hawk. A longstanding correspondent of Chanute's, Ferber had for years been the strongest French advocate of Lilienthal's gliding experiments of the early 1890s, and had since August exchanged several letters with the Wrights on the subject. Like Archdeacon, he was in his early forties, and was generally regarded as the only French practitioner with enough experience to lead the Old World's counteroffensive to recent advances by the Americans in general and the Wrights in particular.

In the January edition of *L'Aérophile*, Orville's matter-of-fact account of the momentous flights of December 17th occupied barely more than a page, most of which was spent describing the wind conditions and the terrain of Kill Devil Hills. No fanfare, no triumphalism, but also very little useful information. Nevertheless, the news prompted Archdeacon to swing into patriotic action with renewed vim. To the sound of a stable door slamming, he made an urgent appeal for financial support "in case France gets left behind by the Americans. To inspire people, we must encourage the will to emulate, and we can only do that through competitions and world records."

He proceeded to set out the rules for such a competition. Predictably, the criteria reflected French thinking and practice - and complexity. The inclination of the take-off terrain was related to wing area and the prevailing wind speed, and measures of total weight per second aloft, and so on, all expressed in a splatter of equations footnoted by even more abstruse formulae. The answer turned out to be 47, which was the optimum factor to be achieved, taking into account all the measures involved. Sophisticated it was and looked, but also spectacularly French.

Archdeacon's new glider was completed by January 15th, after which it went on display at the Aéro Club for two weeks, in order to inspire France's would-be aeronauts. He published plans of various glider designs to encourage public participation, along with approximate instructions to build one, right down to the recipe for coating the fabric.

With flight trials impossible in the grim February weather and no gainful employment, Gabriel Voisin returned home, where he attended a conference addressed by Captain Ferber at the Club Aéronautique Lyonnais, an association founded by one of Voisin's earliest aviation mentors, the Lyon dentist Jean-Claude Pompéien-Piraud, who had told him of Lilienthal's work. It was at this event that Voisin met Ferber for the first time (although Ferber later claimed to have introduced Voisin to Archdeacon in Paris the next day). It is inconceivable that they did not discuss the Wrights, since Ferber had just completed a seminal paper entitled *Advances in aviation through gliding experiments since 1891,* with photographs of their 1901 and 1902 gliders, for publication in the March edition of the *Revue d'Artillerie*, in which he credited the Wrights as the first to master aerial control.

Ferber's mathematical credentials saved him from being scorned as a mere empiricist by the French scientific establishment, for whom theory always preceded practice rather than the other way round. But qualifications notwithstanding, Captain Ferber was, like Voisin, a pragmatist at heart: "The most that science can do is follow in the wake of practice and interpret it," he wrote. "This is the progressive method of practical experiment."

If Ferber underestimated the Wrights' theoretical knowledge, the other Aéro Club members had even less idea of the depth of research they had undertaken, or of the calculating seriousness of their intent. When one of their number, the wealthy balloonist Jacques Balsan, who travelled the world buying wool for his family mills, proclaimed that he had ordered a Flyer and would return with one from his imminent trip to the US, no one demurred. It simply stirred Archdeacon to new flights of rhetoric: "We shall soon catch them up!" he cried. "The land of Montgolfier must at all costs never let the glory of the ultimate conquest of the air slip into foreign hands!"

In a bid to accelerate the pace of development in France, Archdeacon declared that the 25,000 francs he had personally offered to reward definitive mastery of heavier-than-air flight was insufficient even to cover the cost of constructing a suitable machine, and solicited benefactors to contribute to a headline-grabbing half million franc prize fund "in the noble cause of the greatest scientific advance for the benefit of mankind."

All this brouhaha meant nothing to the Wrights, of course. At the time, they were engrossed in devising legal strategies for getting their wing warping patent accepted in Germany, where it had been rejected on the grounds that it infringed an existing patent by another disciple of Chanute's, Hermann Moedebeck.

Gabriel Voisin had submitted to the Aéro Club a paper on his own gliding experiences at the same time as Ferber's, which was duly reported in *L'Aérophile* as "the interesting work by Messrs Voisin on their aviation trials executed in 1903 with Lilienthal and Chanute machines". It was the first time the name Voisin had appeared in print. The outsider had become an insider.

Archdeacon and Voisin set out for the coast by train in the third week of February, with the glider neatly packed into two crates. The first trials on the sand dunes between Berck and Merlimont were reported to the Aéro Club committee on February 22nd 1904, having been cut short by stormy weather. It was, however, enough to discover that Dargent's lightweight biplane wing cell flexed alarmingly, and Voisin set about improving its torsional rigidity and adding horizontal bracing members midway between each pair of wing struts. He also redesigned the front elevator control by replacing Dargent's haphazard cord and pulley arrangement with a more accurate rod mechanism.

While Ferber continued his gliding experiments in Nice, the Pas de Calais weather didn't improve enough to allow any more tests until March 15th – this time, at nearby Berck-Bellevue beach rather than Merlimont, which, being closer to the town, was more convenient. To Archdeacon's dismay, Henri Robart, the champion cyclist and experienced gliding enthusiast whom he had initially engaged as the pilot, refused to fly the machine on the grounds that it was too flimsy. Gliding was a dangerous game, after all – as every amateur knew, it had claimed the lives of Pilcher and Lilienthal a few years earlier. Voisin, though, was unfazed. Hungry to learn by experience and anxious to please his new patron, he seized his opportunity, despite what he considered to be the machine's all-important lack of a tail. Lying prone in the centre as four helpers supported the corners of the lower plane ready to launch the machine on Voisin's "*Lachez tout!*", he managed a glide of a dozen metres or so before a painfully maladroit landing.

Above, Gabriel Voisin launching Ernest Archdeacon's first *planeur* from one of the high dunes at Merlimont early in 1904; meanwhile, the Wrights' glider patent was lodged in France on March 22nd.

Right, as it's being hauled up to the summit for yet another attempt, the torsional weakness of the first Dargent-built Archdeacon glider is plain to see. Captain Ferber's confidential report on this craft to Colonel Renard criticised this and other aspects of its construction.

16

Shaken and bruised, he had nevertheless flown, and since the snapshot immortalising the event was taken by the director of the nearby naval hospital, there was at least one medic at hand. Motivated now by self-preservation as much as his aeronautical convictions, Voisin strengthened the glider further still.

The steady sea breeze that prevailed on Easter Sunday a fortnight later, on April 3rd, was ideal for reprising the trials, especially as Captain Ferber had by then arrived from Nice "to instruct Voisin on first principles". Whether as a result of the maestro's words of wisdom or not, Voisin's 15-metre glide in the weak spring sunshine was better controlled than previous attempts; in further flights back at the Merlimont site five days later, the machine rose several metres above the launch point into a strong headwind, although the total distance travelled was only 20 metres or so.

Among the eyewitnesses was the precociously talented 10 year-old Jacques Henri Lartigue, who had been driven from Paris to photograph the flights with his new Spido-Gaumont stereoscopic camera. "Suddenly I spotted little black things moving far away among the dunes," he said. "As we got nearer, I saw that they were men gathered around a big white, almost transparent, kite. Uncle Raymond explained that it was called an aeroplane, and the young man lying face down on it was an inventor. We waited once again. It took a long time, and then just as suddenly, everything started again. The crowd stood back, a man started running and then… straight away the gentleman lying flat on his tummy was flying! He's flying high, maybe three or four metres in the air, and glides down almost the entire length of the dune before landing again."

But although widely reported, the Berck trials were a disappointment. As *L'Aérophile* ruefully admitted: "It would be puerile to imagine that with an untried machine and inexperienced pilots it would be possible to eclipse what has taken the masters of the art, the Wright brothers, months, even years, of experiment to achieve." More tellingly, under the misapprehension that the Archdeacon was an exact replica of the Wright, its indifferent performance fuelled suspicions that the Americans were exaggerating, if not bluffing outright. For Voisin, the experience merely entrenched his faith in the superiority of the Hargrave concept over the Wrights'.

Archdeacon's 1904 gliding experiments on the Channel coast were sufficiently publicised to attract interested spectators from Paris, including the young Jacques Henri Lartigue. This famous shot of Gabriel Voisin in full flight exemplifies the dynamism that characterises the teenage photographer's astonishing visual chronicle of the early years of the century.

18

Robert Esnault-Pelterie *(see appendix XI)*, a longstanding collaborator of Henri Robart, made the same mistake, and reached the same conclusion, the following month. Like reconstructions made from fossil fragments, the Wright copies built in France were approximations based largely on guesswork. At least Esnault-Pelterie's was closer to the size of the original, with a span of 10 metres and an aerofoil section to the main planes, set 1.5 metres apart, but it had no facility for wing warping. Made of lime wood, with zigzag bonds and cast aluminium brackets, it flew even less well than the Archdeacon, being so nose heavy that it dived immediately and landed clumsily after eight metres. Several equally futile attempts later, it was abandoned as too dangerous.

On receiving photos of the Archdeacon from Chanute the following month, Wilbur replied that it looked better suited to kite flying than gliding. Ferber sent a revealing critique of the machine to Colonel Renard a few days after his return from Berck: "The flexible parallelepiped of the main planes adopted a bird-like form, in that they assumed an upward curvature on each side. The vertical members at each extremity bend under load, being too weak. The piano wire used for tensioning the main structure regularly fails at the attachment points, and should be replaced by galvanized steel cable. Likewise, the joints should be secured by being bound with waxed cord rather than screws, which work loose every time the glider lands. The planes have a regular arc section rather than an aerofoil, so that the downward curvature at the trailing edge impedes forward progress by preventing the free escape of the airflow; and as on the Wright, the main wing spar is on the lower surface rather than the upper, where it would allow trapped air to escape more easily. The landing skids are too shallow, risking knee injuries on landing, and should be reinforced; I suggest fitting a harness to support the pilot instead on having to lie across three horizontal bars. The rear rudder should be one and a half times longer than it is at present, and the machine would benefit from a differently shaped front elevator, mounted higher to reduce the risk of damage on nose-heavy landings."

In May, at Col. Renard's invitation, Ferber joined the staff at Chalais Meudon. In a letter to Wilbur asking to buy a Flyer, the captain confided that the Wrights' gliding claims were treated by the French with some scepticism. The Ohioan, who respected Ferber, took comfort from this on the

Fondation Lartigue

Above, although ultimately disappointing, Archdeacon's 1904 trials on the dunes at Merlimont and Berck Plage confirmed Gabriel Voisin's reservations about the Wright replica that wasn't, but nevertheless generated a surprising amount of publicity.

Right, Archdeacon's first glider in its final incarnation, as modified by Voisin in November 1904, tucked away in a cave hewn into the limestone beneath the Tour Duval at the small village of Follainville-Dennemont, high above the banks of the Seine west of Paris. Because of Archdeacon's absence and the unsuitability of the terrain, the planned trials never took place.

grounds that their disbelief "presents the best possible proof of the low state of the art in France at this time, if even our gliding stories are considered too wonderful to be true."

After flying the Archdeacon so many times, Voisin more than anybody recognised the need for the modifications Ferber suggested in his note to Renard (which probably included Voisin's conclusions) and incorporated them into a complete rebuild in May and June. In this sturdier form, with aerofoil section main planes with the spars above rather than below, a new lever-operated front elevator, twin triangular rear rudders and a harness to support the pilot, the glider was photographed in a cavern hewn into the rock beneath the Tour Duval at Follainville, a village 60km west of Paris, in November 1904. On a steep escarpment 100 metres above the meandering Seine, the location was clearly chosen for further trials. Apart from a confused reference in Gabriel Voisin's memoirs to a fruitless month spent alone there, courting local girls in neighbouring Dennemont while waiting for suitable weather, no record remains of such experiments; the profusion of shrubbery, hedges and stone soil retaining walls on the upper slopes would in any case have made short landings perilous.

Voisin suggested to Archdeacon that he commission a second glider – this time, to be built by Voisin himself - which could be towed with a strain meter to determine the tractive effort required for it to sustain powered flight. At the time, this was a vexed question. In France, despite the paltry dozen horsepower the Wrights were said to have at their disposal from the simple four-cylinder unit of their own design at Kitty Hawk, and despite the French experimenters' lack of progress in terms of aerial control with gliders, it was generally believed that the absence of a suitably light and powerful engine was the main impediment to their mastery of the air.

There was no consensus as to the energy required, however. Victor Tatin, the doyen of the French theorists, thought 35 horses, but Ferber, as a Wrightist, only 12; the eminent engineer and balloonist Rodolphe Soreau argued that nothing less than 100 would suffice, as did Renard. Such an enormous disparity of expert opinion discomfited all concerned, and much heated debate ensued as to the value of the critical constant K, which was variously calculated to be anything from 0.065 to 0.66 - a difference of ten orders of magnitude. Nobody knew, in other words.

Edouard Surcouf (1862-1938) was probably the 19th century's largest aeronautical manufacturer, making the rubberised fabric for balloon envelopes as well as many of the most important balloons and dirigibles of the time. As such, at Archdeacon's suggestion, he provided moral support as well as the premises for Gabriel Voisin's first machines.

After a few days' reflection, Archdeacon agreed. To finance the second glider and the subsequent programme of tests, he formed the Syndicat d'Aviation with fellow *sportsmen* of the Aéro Club, all balloonists and dirigible enthusiasts, including two motor car manufacturers: Léonce Girardot, the eponymous co-founder of Automobiles CGV and Louis Turgan of Automobiles Turgan Foy, along with René Loysel, Count Henri de Vogüé, Eugène Maas and Edouard Surcouf, the driver and co-developer of the Renard road train whose inaugural journey Lézy had reported. A balloonist since his first ascent in 1879, at the age of 17, Surcouf had inherited the company of the balloon pioneer Gabriel Yon, with which he proceeded to make his fortune selling a tough rubberised fabric for the envelopes of hydrogen-filled dirigibles, and building the two most important airships of the era: the Lebaudy *Jaune* and both incarnations of Henri Deutsch de la Meurthe's *Ville de Paris*. These men were all heavy hitters, with deep pockets to match.

Archdeacon duly gave Voisin a brisk letter of introduction to Surcouf, remarking that "the bearer seems to me a strapping young fellow with the potential to achieve something." Ten years later, Surcouf recalled the appearance one day in his office of "a young engineer, full of dreams and enthusiasm. All he had to offer was his forthright and straightforward manner and more confidence in the future of heavier-than-air flight than any other man I had ever met. I immediately installed him in one of my workshops."

The workshop in question was in part of Surcouf's sprawling airship and balloon factory at the junction of the rue de Bellevue and rue Couchout, not far from the banks of the Seine in the bustling industrial suburb of Boulogne-Billancourt. Gabriel Voisin was employed on a modest stipend of 190 francs a month to build the syndicate's first two machines: a glider for the tractive power tests and later, a larger, powered aeroplane. Archdeacon had persuaded the oil magnate Henri Deutsch de la Meurthe to match the 25,000 francs he had offered to endow the Grand Prix de l'Aviation for which he had been soliciting contributions all year. The equivalent of £2000 (twice the price of a Silver Ghost or Delaunay Belleville chassis), the combined sum was a substantial carrot. Revised rules were duly published on October 1st, stipulating an officially observed one-kilometre flight over a prescribed course, returning to the point of departure.

In a quiet corner of Surcouf's thriving balloon and dirigible factory in rue de Bellevue in Boulogne-Billancourt, a few hundred metres from the rue de la Ferme, Voisin strikes a pose in Archdeacon's second ill-fated glider, which was built during January and February 1905.

24

Although in no need of such financial inducement, Esnault-Pelterie continued his experiments with a second Wright-based glider, this time complete with wing warping, a less pronounced aerofoil section and no front elevator. Towed behind a stripped 40/50HP Mors at up to 100km/h along the quayside of the Seine at Billancourt, it proved dangerously unstable (not least because the wing warping wires kept snapping under load).

Across the Atlantic, the Wrights were slowly mastering lateral control. Having built a second, heavier and more powerful Flyer at the time of Archdeacon's Berck trials, Wilbur managed to fly a complete circle at Huffman Prairie on September 20th. After Orville damaged the craft trying to replicate the feat in the presence of Chanute in October, no further progress was made until November, when Wilbur flew four circuits in five minutes before he was forced to land because of the engine overheating. In December, Flyer Nº II was dismantled, and the airframe destroyed.

Meanwhile, over the winter of 1904, Voisin was building the first craft for Archdeacon's syndicate, a 7.5-metre glider similar to Archdeacon Nº 1 in its later, Voisin-modified form, but with a more sophisticated front elevator; it may even have incorporated elements of the Berck machine in its final incarnation. At Voisin's insistence, it had two major differences: a pair of substantial sprung landing skids that had the effect of inclining the planes 6° to the horizontal and allowing the pilot to be accommodated in a sitting position rather than prone; and crucially, with design input from Tatin, he added a sizeable tailplane with two triangular vertical fins in a bid to minimise pitch and yaw.

In true Archdeacon fashion, the stability of the new configuration was to be publicly tested at the Aéro Club's inaugural *Concours d'Aviation* for unmanned aircraft of all types. Long discussed, the event was organised in great haste. There was only one indoor venue large enough - the Galerie des Machines, a gargantuan vaulted iron and glass structure built at the Champ de Mars for the Paris Exhibition of 1889. Archdeacon booked it on February 2nd, only ten days before the event. Among the bewildering array of gliders, helicopters and rubber band- and clockwork-powered models entered were two Voisin Archdeacons, one of which was a half-scale model of the new glider.

Above, the parade ground at Issy on March 26th, 1905: the Voisin-built Archdeacon glider N°2 ready on its launch rails. Note the hastily filled bags of ballast in the foreground, with one already in place on the pilot's seat.

Under the aegis of Paul and Charles Renard, Ferber, Henry Kapférer *(appendix VII)*, Gustave Eiffel and police chief Louis Lepine, Surcouf rang a hand bell to launch each competing craft from the 41-metre pylon at one end of this 400-metre building. The Archdeacon Voisin was singled out for its particularly gentle landing – so gentle in fact that it took off again for another 10-metre hop after kissing the ground. This was due, it was said, to the main planes "compressing the air beneath".

Encouraged by this performance, Archdeacon and Voisin decided to press ahead with the manned tractive power tests, for which purpose Archdeacon had managed to obtain permission to use the *champ de manœuvres* at Issy-Les-Moulineaux, the large cavalry drill ground beside the Seine southwest of Paris, just outside the fortified city walls and bordered on the other three sides by residential blocks, factories and allotments. It was the first time access had ever been granted for such a purpose.

In bright sunshine on Sunday March 26th, four days after the death of Jules Verne, whose fictional visions of a technology-enabled future had inspired the French aeronauts along with their entire generation, Voisin assembled the Archdeacon N°II on the Issy drill ground. Following Esnault-Pelterie's example, the glider was to be towed by a motor car, with a dynamometer fitted at the point of attachment to measure the energy required to take off.

At the last minute, Archdeacon bade Voisin alight from the craft and fetched an empty sack, which he suggested filling with 50kg of the sandy ballast underfoot, to substitute for the weight of his wiry pilot. Voisin must have agreed without much persuasion, for the dangers of this experiment were of a different order of magnitude than the Berck trials. The half-scale model had climbed steeply from its launch point in the Galerie des Machines before the successive swoops of its descent, and the hoof-beaten surface of the drill ground was considerably more unyielding than a sandy beach.

A pair of stout 40-metre wooden rails were laid facing the prevailing westerly breeze, and greased to accommodate the glider's skids. The towline was hitched to a new Mors, and at Archdeacon's signal, the loud parp of a bulb horn, the military chauffeur let out the clutch, took up the slack and put his foot down. *The Autocar* described what happened next: "When all was ready, the 60HP automobile set off and unrolled about 30 yards of cable, and the flying machine was released at the word of command.

Right, Archdeacon's second glider climbs dramatically skywards moments before the tail disintegrated and it plunged down onto the *champ de manœuvres*.

Below, sporting his expensive but short-lived Panama hat, Gabriel Voisin tests the elevator control of the float glider he designed and built for Ernest Archdeacon in April/May 1905 on the Seine. This substantial machine was in many ways the prototype for the 10-metre Voisin *biplan à queue*, except that its planes were flat rather than of aerofoil section.

"The first start was not a success and had to be repeated, but the second time the aeroplane got well away and attained a height of 35 yards in four seconds. But the Fates were not propitious, for at the moment of cutting the cable which attached it to the automobile, the suddenness and violence of the effort made by the machine to get free broke one of the panels of the rudder, and the aeroplane, fluttering like a wounded bird, turned several times in the air and broke in falling on the ground, where the pieces were gathered up by the ever-present 'collector'". End of glider, although Voisin's insistence on a tail had at least momentarily been vindicated.

Archdeacon persuaded his fellow Syndicat d'Aviation members to allocate what Voisin described as "a sensational amount" to pursue the tractive effort tests on water (as Esnault-Pelterie had attempted a few months earlier with an insufficiently powerful boat), using a new type of hydro-aeroplane his young engineer had been itching to build for months: the first proper Voisin, in effect. Abandoning the Chanute/Wright approach in all but the three-metre adjustable front elevator, Voisin reverted to the Hargrave configuration he had decided upon three years earlier. As long as it was wide, this archetype of the Voisin cellular biplane consisted of a 10-metre main cell, complete with vertical intermediate and end panes, connected via four widely spaced longerons to a six-metre tail cell incorporating a central rudder and mounted on lightweight 7-metre by 30cm varnished fabric floats made to his design at the Ile de la Jatte. The four innermost wing struts were arranged trapezoidally, being closer together where they joined the upper plane. Big as it was, Archdeacon Nº3 weighed less than 230 kilos.

Halfway through its construction, in May 1905, Surcouf signed the lease on a separate workshop for Voisin to continue working on his growing number of commissions. The amount of patents lodged in France for flying machines had skyrocketed since the beginning of the year, and the consequent demand for manufacturing capacity far outstripped the number of skilled craftsmen able to turn often bizarre ideas into testable machines. With his own large workshops fully occupied building balloons and dirigibles, Surcouf offered Voisin an arrangement whereby, alongside his work for the syndicate, he would have a share of the profits from any other machine he built in the new premises. Thus was born Ateliers Voisin (Anciens Etablissements d'Aviation Surcouf) at 4, rue de la Ferme, an

Charles Voisin and his dog, Stop, outside the gates of the Voisin works in rue de la Ferme. The large 'Delagrange volerà!' sign in Italian on the gable suggests that the photograph was taken in April/May 1908.

undistinguished side street five minutes' walk away from Surcouf's factory. The site consisted of a sturdy 150m² hangar attached to a two up/two down cottage giving onto a small courtyard.

Work resumed with the help of Henri Métayer, a 35 year-old former boatbuilder who remained with Voisin for the rest of his working life. Starting at six every morning and often continuing until midnight, they gradually finished the big glider. Voisin later remembered the sheer laboriousness of the task: "Building aeroplanes in those days was far from lucrative and not at all easy. To begin with, you'd be stumped by some tricky design problem that would provoke endless argument among the tooth-sucking know-alls who gathered to proffer their counsel, and then, once you'd finished drawing up all the plans and making the blueprints, there'd be endless sawing, cutting, routing, nailing, painting – all the innumerable tasks required to edify the monster in its final form. The result was cumbersome and uncomfortable, and its capabilities worryingly uncertain; nevertheless, a few weeks later, on the quayside at Billancourt, I assembled the first *biplan à queue*."

Nor was it the only craft Voisin built in what must have been a frenetic few weeks. Soon after the move to the rue de la Ferme, Ferber invited Voisin to meet Louis Blériot *(appendix XII)*, whose prosperous acetylene lighting and electrical automobile accessory business had brought him great wealth and prestige. Eight years Voisin's senior and famously brusque, Blériot's first foray into aeronautics had been in 1902, with an ill-conceived ornithopter of his own design. As Voisin later recalled, "Blériot led Ferber and me into a secret workshop where the unfinished monster revealed its hideous skeleton. A piston driven by compressed air transmitted its motion to two valves; open when rising, closed when falling. [..] Conversation was difficult…"

Voisin must have concealed his scepticism well, however, because Blériot turned up at the rue de la Ferme soon afterwards and remained for three hours picking his brains while inspecting work in progress on the Archdeacon. After a restless night, the great man returned the next day to commission a similar aircraft to the Archdeacon. Voisin referred him to Surcouf, with whom Blériot duly placed his order for a fixed-wing machine with a pronounced curvature to the planes, and which would be capable of motorisation once a suitably light power unit became available.

Above, accompanied by the Aéro Club launch, Gabriel Voisin sets off on his triumphant 600-metre towed glide along the Seine in the Archdeacon III in June 1905.

Left, the same machine on the river bank beside the ill-fated Blériot glider shows the differences in size as well as wing profile. Looking as if they've escaped from Seurat's *La Grande Jatte*, the spectators wait patiently for the craft to be dragged into the water.

Blériot being Blériot, he wanted to be directly involved in the design and was disinclined to defer to such expertise as Voisin had acquired. Voisin agreed to set up a drawing board next to his own, and for weeks the two men worked side by side during the few hours every evening that Blériot could spare from running his company. Unlike Voisin, who had since his architectural days regarded draughtsmanship as the cardinal engineering skill, Blériot was unused to expressing his design ideas on paper. Although his new client had taken great pains to immerse himself in aviation theory, Voisin found him frustratingly slow to grasp the practical technicalities he had himself learned by experience. He could not, for example, dissuade Blériot from the high aerofoil section he insisted on to achieve maximum lift, despite the deleterious effect that Voisin insisted that such a profile would have on lateral stability. Worse still, Blériot wanted a much smaller wingspan than the Archdeacon's, with angled end panes connecting the upper plane to an even stubbier lower plane.

The Archdeacon was ready first, early in June 1905. To provide the motive power for the trials along the Seine, Archdeacon had engaged the rising star of the powerboat fraternity, Alphonse Tellier, and his latest racer, *La Rapière*. Built the year before, this eight-metre hull boasted the same giant 100HP Panhard four-cylinder that powered the latest Gordon Bennett cars, allowing a speed of 21 knots on flat water. On paper at least, it had the grunt to do the job – indeed, Alberto Santos-Dumont *(appendix X)* had used Tellier's machine for the same purpose three months earlier to tow his unmanned N°.11 monoplane glider.

There was no question as to who would be the test pilot; with Ferber occupied testing his sixth aeroplane, Gabriel Voisin was the only choice. By then, Archdeacon had complete faith in his young protégé: "My excellent pilot and engineer, Voisin, light in weight, adroit and a skilled mechanic, has acquired all the necessary skills in the difficult manoeuvring of the aeroplane," he declared with characteristic optimism before the testing began after lunch on Thursday June 8th. The chosen site was a nearby stretch of the Seine between the Pont de Sèvres and the Pont de Billancourt, where it bifurcated around the Île Saint Germain. Although relatively little used by river traffic (which is presumably why official permission was eventually granted) it was a relatively narrow channel with a pronounced curve.

Nevertheless, the first attempt augured well. As the Aéro Club officials bobbed about in a flotilla of small boats, and with a wind speed indicator and strain gauge on the 30-metre towline, Tellier let out the clutch, and despite the enormous drag of the long stepless floats, the Archdeacon rose majestically into the air from the choppy wake of *La Rapière*. Alarmingly high it soared towards the Pont de Sèvres, before a hair-raisingly steep but ultimately safe descent onto the water some 150 metres downstream. The instruments recorded a strain on the towline of between 50 and 60 kilos, and a speed of nearly 40km/h. It was the first time in the world a flying machine had taken off from water.

The *Brooklyn Daily Eagle* described the Archdeacon as "a sort of magnified kite, whose surface offers enough resistance to overcome gravity. It is intended eventually to have a device that will generate enough power to lift it off the ground and give it the start a boy gets for his kite when he takes a run before setting it aloft." The fanciful account which follows suggests that the reporter may have over-imbibed at lunch before filing his copy: "Mr Voisin quickly freed the fastening that bound it to *La Rapière*, and rose free of everything. He shot up into the air diagonally to a height of about three hundred yards, and then he cut a series of remarkable maneuvers, turning quickly, going higher, going in gradually widening curves and taking all sorts of sudden shoots. After an exhibition that lasted a matter of an hour and proved conclusively that he had the machine under perfect control, Voisin gradually let it descend till it rested gently on the bosom of the river."

Buoyed by this success (even though it had lasted seconds, much less an hour), a second attempt was made as soon as Voisin had thoroughly rechecked the integrity of the aeroplane. This time, the plan was to jettison the towline on reaching sufficient altitude in order to undertake a sustained glide. It was not to be – in mid take-off, one float disintegrated and the other took on water, which, combined with a strong sideways gust, had the effect of ejecting the hapless young pilot into the river and damaging the lower plane. It could have been much worse; still on an adrenal high, Voisin jokingly bemoaned the loss of the 14.95-franc Panama hat to which he had treated himself for the occasion. A week later, he received a personal invitation from the cinematography pioneer Léon Gaumont to see the multi-camera newsreel footage of his exploit, during which, by Voisin's own admission, he experienced for the first and only time an *émotion sportive*.

Bobbing on the Seine opposite the Île St Germain on July 18th 1905, the ill-fated seven-metre float glider that Gabriel Voisin constructed for Louis Blériot in Surcouf's new workshop at the rue de la Ferme at the same time as the Archdeacon III. Blériot specified a 1:13 ratio for the main and tail planes, and it weighed only 175 kg.

A young Alphonse Tellier surveys the helm of *La Rapière* at the 1905 Monaco powerboat meeting, where its most celebrated victories were accomplished.

Towed by *La Rapière,* Gabriel Voisin soars westwards along the Seine from the Pont de Billancourt on June 8th, 1905.

In a later letter to Frank Lahm, Wilbur Wright's assessment of Archdeacon's gliding experiments was withering: "He says that he, Captain Ferber, Tatin, and Renard together can produce a flying machine inside of three months. For a man who has just undergone four years of failure in attempting to equal our first year's gliding experiments, he seems rather sanguine."

The next five weeks were spent completing the Blériot and repairing the big Archdeacon. By July 18th, it had been fitted with sturdier floats and both gliders were towed through the streets of Billancourt once again to the banks of the river for further trials. In the absence of Tellier, the launch vessel was provided by Léon Levavasseur (*appendix XIII*) – the second of his *Antoinette* powerboats, with a state-of-the-art 8-metre Pitre hull, fitted with the revolutionary lightweight V8 he had originally developed in 1902/3 with funding from Colonel Renard's military research establishment. An out-and-out racer, it had neither clutch nor throttle: it went at full tilt or not at all.

At 11 o'clock, with the glider pointing in the direction of the sluggish current and against the prevailing breeze, the *Antoinette* moved into position as best it could, and at Archdeacon's signal, let rip. The slack on the towline was taken up so brutally that the tailplane took on water, and the ensuing short flight consisted of bouncing several times a few metres into the air off the boat's violent wash and crashing down onto the turbulent water again. After further checks and adjustments, the second attempt at three o'clock was more successful, the machine rising more than five metres despite Voisin wrestling with the elevator to prevent it climbing further, and gliding for some 300m before landing on the river again.

For Voisin, the test proved that the glider's angle of flight depended on the location of its attachment point, which was too far aft; a powered version would therefore need the centre of gravity further forward, which he reasoned would be best achieved by means of a central fuselage containing the pilot and engine and extending to the front elevator. The test also yielded enough data for a rough calculation to be made as to the power required for the machine to sustain flight: 28HP without the weight of an engine and an estimated 35HP for a powered version weighing 550 kilos. These estimates were duly published "for the benefit of tomorrow's aviators".

The day was not yet over. There was still the stubby Blériot to test. Given his reservations about the design, Voisin must have climbed onto the rearmost spar of the lower main plane with some trepidation. Justifiably so, as it turned out. Although it had a Hargrave tail cell, the unstable Blériot was even more seriously disturbed by the wash from the powerboat than the Archdeacon, and

40

The helmsman of Levavasseur's brutal *Antoinette*, the fastest powerboat in Europe, watches helplessly as Gabriel Voisin struggles to free himself from the wreckage of Blériot's float glider.

Before and after: the stubby float glider that Gabriel Voisin built for Louis Blériot nearly cost him his life on July 18th 1905.

oscillated wildly from side to side as it struggled to become airborne. Before it could do so, the tip of the lower left-hand plane caught the water and the machine cartwheeled, ending up inverted and semi-submerged, to gasps of horror from the curious spectators now lining the banks. Of the pilot there was ominously no sign. The roaring Antoinette wheeled around and joined the flurry of boats racing to the scene. Struggling to free himself from the tangle of bracing wires, a bedraggled and frightened Voisin eventually gasped to the surface. To everyone's relief, he was hauled to safety – by one Albert Descarmes, a local handyman, part-time pimp and petty felon to whom Voisin showed his gratitude by employing him for the rest of his life.

The tests had certainly highlighted the desirability of a wider and more suitable stretch of water. Tellier had introduced Archdeacon to Ernest Cuénod, a wealthy Swiss banker and founder of the Swiss Automobile Club. A Martini agent and powerboat enthusiast, he offered his 40HP *Martini I* for further tests on Lac Léman, at Amphion-les-Bains. Voisin was kept fully occupied during August and September 1905 rebuilding his two patrons' floatplanes in preparation for these trials.

While the Wrights were plodding ahead at Huffman Prairie, where Wilbur had flown his first figure of eight early in October, the Amphion tests proved to be a step backwards for the French. The Archdeacon, now sporting no fewer than eight vertical panes and with the chord of the main and tail planes almost doubled, never once left the choppy waters of the lake. Even with the vertical panes removed, the *Martini* was too weak. Voisin had rebuilt the Blériot with the lower wing lengthened to match the upper plane and vertical panes between. Unlike the Archdeacon, the main struts on either side of the pilot were parallel, but it proved no keener to become airborne.

Back in Paris in November, the frustrated Voisin started work on another project for Surcouf, a model for Francesco Filiasi, an aristocratic Neapolitan musicologist. A float plane version of the Italian's elegant, fully enclosed wing-warping monoplane of 1902, with twin tractor propellers substituted for the original pushers, the concept was hailed in the press as "very ingenious" when displayed at the *Salon Aéronautique* in December, where, along with Levavasseur's Antoinette engine, it won a medal.

Above, one of the few photographs of Voisin testing the modified Archdeacon III at Amphion-les-Bains on Lake Geneva.

Below, preparing the Archdeacon alongside Cuénod's *Martini I* near the boatyard of the naval architect who had built the hull, François Celle - a friend of Tellier's, whom he had recommended to Voisin and Archdeacon in their search for a stretch of calm water large enough for them to attempt trials directly into the wind.

How dispirited they must all have been in November, when *L'Aérophile* published a letter from the Wright Cycle Company, in which the Daytonians dryly described how they had beaten their own 4.5-kilometre record with a 17-kilometre flight in September, increasing the distance in almost daily increments and culminating in 39- and 35-kilometre flights in as many minutes on October 4th and 5th. Satisfied, the Wrights replied at last to Ferber's written request to buy a Flyer, with the offer of a special price to the French government for a machine with a proven 100-kilometre range: a cool one million francs ($200,000). Like high rolling poker players (which they resembled in no other way), the Wrights knew they had a strong hand, and they played it with calculating audacity. In stark contrast to the French, for whom the technology race was framed by the romance of the air and an altruistic idealism, their approach was rooted in cold *realpolitik*. In his reply to Ferber, Wilbur lost no time in drawing attention to the expansionist ambitions of the Kaiser and the current political turmoil in Austria and Russia, with the probability of armed conflict that implied. With the US government lukewarm in its support for aviation since Langley's disappointing public failure in 1904, Wilbur went for the hard sell. No longer the meek scientific researcher, this was the bicycle salesman writ large. He gave three reasons for proposing such a low price: out of respect for France's role as the pioneer nation in matters aeronautical; because the French had a greater sympathy with, and understanding of, aviation than his compatriots; and finally – the clincher – that France was on front line of any potential conflict eastwards, and by implication, would therefore need the best possible defence capability.

Ferber referred the offer to the Ministry of War, on the basis of a 50-kilometre demonstration flight of less than an hour. Archdeacon urged the Wrights to donate their machine to their own government, on the grounds that going down in history as one of humanity's greatest benefactors and basking in the glow of approbation from a grateful country would be far more gratifying than money. *L'Aérophile* was genuinely puzzled. The offer couldn't be a bluff, they reasoned, because of the Wrights' scientific background and undisputed gliding achievements; it made no sense for such authoritative experimenters to indulge in a deception so easily unmasked. If the claims were true, a million would be a small price to pay. No, their incredulity was based on market economics.

Atelier Turgan 1905 – construction de l'aéroplane Voisin 60m² reads the caption for this previously unpublished family album photograph. As can be seen from the fabricated Tatin-type propeller and the provision made for transverse members between the main planes to support the propeller axes, this is the machine shown overleaf, rather than an Archdeacon or Blériot float glider. Its exact place in the early evolution of the 10-metre Voisin remains a matter of conjecture.

46

If indeed the Wright promised such a keen military advantage, why did no venture capitalist in the land of entrepreneurship and technological progress snap up the profit opportunity?

Aéro Club member Robert Coquelle went to Dayton late in December. Although not shown the new Flyer, he reported that he believed it had flown. Frank Lahm, the club's only American member, read out Mr Weaver's eyewitness testimony of the Huffman Prairie flights. Predictably, Archdeacon would have none of it, insisting that the flight claims were exaggerated, and that the Wrights were simply holding out for the million to finance the development of a more airworthy machine.

Nevertheless, the news further increased the pressure to motorise flight experiments. One such was the mysterious second aeroplane Voisin built for Archdeacon's syndicate, probably in April 1905. Its story is hard to trace. The only two remaining photographs show the engineless airframe under construction in the well-equipped premises of Syndicat d'Aviation member Louis Turgan in Levallois-Perret, northwest of Paris – a comparatively large company, which had been manufacturing motor cars and giant road trains like Colonel Renard's since 1899. With a span of some 10 metres, and sturdily designed to accommodate the stresses of driving a pair of contra-rotating tractor propellers, the wing cell was more substantially constructed than the Archdeacons. Although the general layout was similar to that of Archdeacon N°2, with the pilot seated above bentwood landing skids (at a shallower angle), the machine sported a proportionally larger front elevator, with no tail at all. Even more so than the Wrights, it was a tail-first *canard*. No record of the engine survives, but in the only image of the machine published at the time, it's captioned as the Archdeacon 16CV. Turgan cars of the time were mostly powered by a compact air-cooled flat twin whose unusual configuration would seem to have been suitable for such a craft: each cylinder was connected to its own vertical crankshaft, both of which were geared at the top to a vertical drive shaft running at half engine speed, with a large horizontal flywheel at the base that also served as a fan. The largest of these units, however, was only 8HP. Its designer, the co-founder of Turgan Foy, Joseph Filtz, did produce a conventional straight four rated at 16HP, and a radial steam engine besides, but, whichever was planned, it's far from obvious where any power unit would have been mounted. It was apparently run *in situ* at the Turgan works, but proved unsatisfactory.

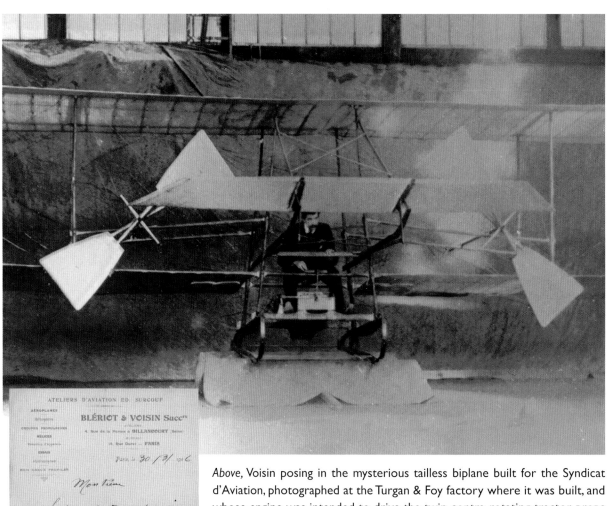

Above, Voisin posing in the mysterious tailless biplane built for the Syndicat d'Aviation, photographed at the Turgan & Foy factory where it was built, and whose engine was intended to drive the twin contra-rotating tractor props by long belts. The design of the landing skids is very similar to those of the second Archdeacon glider, and the main elements differ only slightly from the Archdeacon float glider; the curious broad-bladed propellers, by contrast, bear no resemblance to any other Voisin airscrew.

Left, with several projects to fulfil and only one employee, Gabriel Voisin summoned his Lyon contemporary and fellow aviation enthusiast Maurice Colliex to join the fledgling Blériot-Voisin company on March 30th, 1906.

It has been said that the craft was originally ordered from Surcouf by Achille Bertelli, a prominent pharmacist and aviation pioneer from Brescia who had several patents for rotary wing craft to his credit, at least one of which was built by Surcouf in Paris and left the ground in Rome in 1904. The Bertelli machine which Voisin helped to build as an associate of Surcouf's was the *Aerostave*, a balloon-cum-aeroplane consisting of overlapping curved planes which could be tilted to determine the direction of flight, with the pilot in a wicker basket and the ensemble being suspended beneath an ovoid balloon and powered by a 22HP Antoinette engine driving a pusher propeller. Although the idea of testing the dynamics of a fixed wing craft beneath a balloon was reprised the following year by Santos-Dumont, there seems to be no connection between this eccentric machine and the Voisin-built *canard* in Turgan's workshop. In any case, the Turgan never flew. It may, however, have been recycled into a far more significant machine, of which more later.

Disheartened, with meagre resources and nothing much to occupy him in Paris, Voisin returned home to Neuville in December 1905, where he spent several weeks building a broad-beamed sailing boat (tellingly christened *Pourquoi Pas?*). On his return to the capital in March 1906, realising that Surcouf's promised share of the profits would never materialise from projects that made none, he must have welcomed Blériot's suggestion of a joint venture. Surcouf, content to have made a return from the little rue de la Ferme workshop, accepted Blériot's 6000-franc cheque for the remaining lease and the equipment it contained. Blériot also allowed his young partner to move into the cottage on site, to save the time wasted on commuting from his dingy digs near Montparnasse. With only Métayer to rely on, Gabriel Voisin sent for his former school friend Maurice Colliex (*appendix IV*), an engineering graduate, to join the new enterprise.

The ensuing Blériot-Voisin partnership frittered away most of remaining year to no purpose. Just as Voisin was convinced that the twin Hargrave configuration with a central nacelle, or fuselage, held the secret to stable flight, Blériot had his own ideas. He was also vain enough not to wish to seem to be copying Archdeacon - and as paymaster, the senior partner always had the last word. Voisin nevertheless gradually succeeded in mitigating Blériot's more outlandish ideas. At his insistence, the vast cylindrical wings that the older man advocated were flattened into two ellipses, bisected

Lac d'Enghien, September 1906: the fruitless trials of Blériot-Voisin N° 3-bis, with its useless inflatable floats. The addition of large Blériot headlamps on the front struts allowed tests to be conducted early and late in the day.

by a fixed vertical stabiliser at the rear and with a wide biplane elevator between the upper and lower surfaces directly in front of the pilot, who perched behind the transversely-mounted 24HP Antoinette driving a pair of large, counter-rotating tractor propellers via a complex transmission system weighing some 110kg. Instead of rigid floats, the machine rode on six long, inflatable buoyancy bags. Interestingly, the front ellipse was bisected on each side by an interlinked foot-operated interplane for changing direction in the air - ailerons, in effect. At the end of May, this contraption was reassembled and launched onto the lake at Enghien-les-bains, 15 kilometres north of Paris. With Blériot's head mechanician Louis Peyret at the helm, it barely succeeded in dragging itself across the water. Most of the summer was lost trying various modifications – they even tried a high speed winch from the shore in a bid to increase its take-off velocity. It must have been a particularly frustrating time. Despite public scepticism around the Wrights' claimed feats in the US as well as in France (where Minister of War Eugène Etienne had in February 1906 secretly authorised an option until August on the million-franc Wright contract for 25,000 francs), progress seemed painfully slow – after all, two years had passed since Archdeacon's Grand Prix had been announced, for which there were as yet no serious contenders.

All hopes turned to Santos-Dumont. On July 22nd 1906, he began testing his 14-bis, a full *canard* with a 12-metre span of Hargrave cell main planes set at a steep dihedral and a fully articulated box rudder at the end of a long front fuselage, all made of bamboo and silk, including the propeller. The diminutive Santos stood in a wicker balloon basket immediately in front of a 24HP Antoinette directly driving the pusher airscrew. At 260 kilos, it was very light indeed for such a large machine. Although there is a widespread misconception that Gabriel Voisin was involved in making the wing cells, he consistently denied it - and he was not a man shy of taking credit. According to Orville Wright, the aeroplane was built under the supervision of Santos's chief engineer, Albert Chapin, by Mr Simon and his father-in-law Mr Pontzen, an engineer at the Rothschild coachbuilding company.

Santos began by adopting Bertelli's idea, suspending the startling new craft from his latest hydrogen dirigible, the 16HP Peugeot-powered Nº14, whose spindly gondola had provided the main fuselage of 14-bis. With this arrangement, at the aerodrome he had prepared in the grounds of his Paris

Above, Santos Dumont's improbable 14⁻ᵇⁱˢ suspended beneath his Nº·14 balloon in the park of Neuilly St James. *Below*, the wing cells of 14⁻ᵇⁱˢ en route to the Bois de Boulogne. Note the balloon basket in which the pilot stood.

chateau in Neuilly St James, he set out to study his new aeroplane's behaviour in safety, without having to worry about sustaining it the air. Looking like a giant wounded swan in the clutches of a bulbous alien predator, the effect was visually dramatic but practically useless. There followed a series of experiments for the same purpose, this time with 14-bis suspended from 60 metres of 16mm steel cable descending from 13.5 to seven metres. It was drawn back to the top after each test by an ass. Called Kuigno. Had they known, how the Wrights would have chortled.

In August, 14-bis was strengthened and its silk propeller replaced by a forged steel and rivetted aluminium screw made by Levavasseur. In this form it was tested, with no buoyancy aids, on the lawns of the Bagatelle polo ground in the Bois de Boulogne. The feeble 24HP Antoinette was replaced by a 50HP unit that Louis Breguet had ordered for his helicopter, which had yet to be completed. At daybreak on September 3rd, it made its first taxiing trials across the sward. These continued with various mishaps over the next ten days, with broken elevators, disintegrating airscrews and engine malfunctions. Meanwhile, on the parade ground at Issy, the Romanian lawyer-cum-engineer Traian Vuia was conducting equally fruitless trials. Towards the end of October though, Santos managed a hop of more than 50 metres in his newly rebuilt, and now varnished, 14-bis before a thousand-strong crowd. The great prize was all but won, enthused Archdeacon; from now on, things would progress "at a giant's pace".

They certainly weren't on Lac d'Enghien, where the new Blériot Voisin was on test. Having demonstrated the inadequacy of the twin-ellipse concept, Voisin had persuaded his partner to adopt more of his own ideas. This time, although the seven-metre tail cell housing the rudder remained elliptical, the ten-metre main cell was a classic Hargrave on which was mounted a wide cradle containing two 24HP Antoinettes, each driving a broad-bladed two-metre mahogany pusher propeller at crankshaft speed. The six inflatable floats were replaced by two long rigid ones as on the Archdeacon, and a large adjustable biplane front elevator cell carried two metres in front was complemented by ailerons half-way between the trailing edges of the outer main planes, as per its elliptical wing predecessor. The result was more Voisin than Blériot, but there remained enough Blériot for it not to work. The cumbersome elliptical tail was inefficient and heavy, and the former at least could be said of the two Antoinettes and the angle of the propeller blades they drove.

54

Above and left, the Blériot-Voisin in its penultimate form at Lac d'Enghien, with twin planes and mid-mounted interplanes - ailerons, in effect - replacing the elliptical main cell, and rigid floats in place of the inflatable ones. Temperamental at the best of times, the two 24HP Antoinettes proved impossible to synchronise. The large elliptical tail cell appears to have been built with no aerofoil profile, and therefore simply to assure longitudinal stability rather than to provide lift. Note the diminutive rudder.

Dwarfed by the vast elliptical tail cell, the brace of 24HP Antoinettes, each driving a mahogany-bladed 2m propeller, was mounted on a hefty transverse subframe carried aft of the main planes of the unsuccessful Blériot-Voisin floatplane. The engine's ability to run equally well in both directions allowed the props to counter-rotate without intermediary gearing. Note central crank handle (*right*).

Having by this stage invested a substantial sum in Levavasseur's Antoinette company in return for a directorship, Louis Blériot had first call on the firm's power units, for which demand far exceeded supply.

Charles Voisin's return from three years' military service in October 1906 prompted a rethink. Having run its course, the Blériot-Voisin partnership had for both men become an obstacle to realising their ambitions more than the means of doing so. Voisin couldn't cultivate his clientèle of wealthy amateurs on his own account, and Blériot was frustrated at not having his ideas enacted unquestioningly. The venture was dissolved amicably. Blériot decamped to his new workshop in Neuilly; in return, Voisin had to agree not to sell aeroplanes under his own name for three years, and to pay a royalty on any he made. Thus it was that Appareils d'Aviation Les Frères Voisin was founded on November 5th, 1906 – the first company in the world to be established for the purpose of manufacturing aeroplanes for sale.

Before their ways parted, there remained the land trials of Blériot IV. As Santos seemed to be making progress on grass, it was decided to replace the floats with tricycle undercarriage in November so as to join him at Bagatelle. At dawn on the 12th, the Blériot and 14-bis (75kg lighter, at 375kg, and now sporting crude ailerons) were assembled on the lawns of the polo ground, where more than 100 parked cars testified to the public's high hopes, for Santos had registered his intention to go for the kilometre prize. The big *canard* was manhandled towards the wind by Charles Voisin and the balloonist Jacques Faure. With Charron driving his CGV alongside, from which Faure dropped dinner plates to mark every ascent and touchdown, 14-bis managed two 40m hops before bending the axle, which was repaired during lunch. The Blériot-Voisin's Antoinettes, however, proved impossible to synchronise. When Métayer fouled the airscrews on a gully while taxiing, the engines were wrenched from their mountings and the main cell collapsed. But just before five, in the fading light, Santos made a final run into the wind and somehow remained airborne for 220 metres before landing heavily on his right wing while attempting a turn. It was enough, however, to win the 1500-franc Aéro Club prize for the first heavier-than-air flight of more than 100 metres.

Among those present was the celebrated 33 year-old champion cyclist and racing motorist, Henry Farman *(appendix II)*, whose interest in heavier-then-air flight had initially been kindled by seeing 14-bis on the same turf four months earlier: "I took no special interest in balloons, and Santos-Dumont's first voyage in an airship over Paris did not arouse me to any particular enthusiasm – it seemed to me quite natural," he recalled.

Above, the Blériot Voisin collapsed on striking a concealed gulley at the Bagatelle polo ground on November 12th 1906.

Left, on the same spot an hour later, Santos remained airborne for 220 metres in 14-bis. According to an eyewitness, "the machine left the ground much as an automobile does when it strikes at high speed a ridge in the road, and when it came to earth it was smashed irreparably."

Although biographies of Santos attest that Voisin helped to design and construct the machine, he had no hand in it whatsoever.

"It was not until I watched Santos-Dumont turn his energies to experiments with aeroplanes that I began to take a real interest in the heavier-than-air type of apparatus. I watched him make his plucky flight after numerous trials, and at once resolved to experiment on my own account."

Therein lies Santos's importance to the history of aviation: emblematic rather than technical. Because he conducted his experiments in such a public manner, the modest feat of 14-bis, although aeronautically inconsequential, proved a great psychological boost to the French pioneers.

Even the Wrights, understandably convinced of their own unassailable lead over the French, were interested enough for Wilbur to write to Ferber for a detailed description and drawings of 14-bis. Apart from the brevity of its flight, though, they were unimpressed by the autonomy conferred by wheeled landing gear: "We deduce from the fact that the airplane rests on three wheels that Santos-Dumont, in order to effect his start-off, has first to make a run over a long level field. With the aid of the starting-off pillar that we use, Orville and I speedily go right up into the air in a much more practical fashion."

Pleading that the "two poor Dayton mechanics" couldn't afford to come to France, he added that "if French experts desire to come to Dayton, we will give them a demonstration of the machine in the neighbouring field, flying for five minutes in a complete circle and let them have an option of the performance and release of the machine for $50,000, cash down." The price was falling.

Although he pretended otherwise in his public pronouncements, Archdeacon knew perfectly well how far ahead the Wrights were. Robert Gastambide later recalled Archdeacon's reaction when Ferber showed him the Wrights' letter: "I told you their flying machine would fall on our heads sooner or later. They want to come too soon, unfortunately, and we must at all costs delay their arrival till much later. Just imagine the effect of these two Americans coming over and winning my Grand Prix!"

"If you read the letter carefully, you'll see that their machine can't leave the ground unaided, since it can only do so via their launch derrick system, something the regulations of your prize specifically prohibit. To be in contention, the machine has to take off by its own means," replied Ferber.

The back of the unprepossessing premises in the rue de la Ferme after the addition of the makeshift second hangar. Some 100 metres long and 14.5 metres wide, the plot could barely accommodate one assembled machine - not as much of a handicap as it seems, since the craft were assembled on the flying ground.

"Even so," Archdeacon continued, "Five minutes of seeing a few aerial turns by the Wrights across the plains of France would unleash such extraordinary public enthusiasm that the flutterings of our unhappy aviators would be completely forgotten. We must therefore do our utmost to make sure one of them flies a closed circuit kilometre within six months, just as the Wrights apparently can. In the meantime, write to Wilbur saying that $50,000 is prohibitive, and that in any case, no French aviation commission can visit America before the summer. Tell him that Santos-Dumont is just a loner, a mere amateur whose experiments are of no great import; and advise him to perfect their machine before they bring it over to show the unusually intelligent, discriminating and artistic French public."

"All the same," said Ferber, "However uncomprehending the inhabitants of the United States may be of these matters, the scales will surely fall from their eyes one day. And when they realise that they have amongst them the world's foremost aviators, they'll be so determined to keep their lead that it won't be $50,000 they offer the Wrights to complete their conquest of the air, but hundreds of thousands."

"And that is precisely why, my dear Ferber, I implore you to make sure we get to work as quickly as possible. Since endowing the prize, I can no longer fund nor commission any sort of flyer myself. Having beaten the bass drum for this enterprise, all I can do now is play the cymbals, which I'll willingly do. But you, my dear friend, have to make sure an aeroplane is built that's capable of winning the prize, no matter whether it's yours, or Voisin's, Blériot's, Esnault-Pelterie's or even that egregious eccentric who goes by the name of Levavasseur. But act quickly. Go and see them all, the Wright letter in hand, and whip them into shape. And once you've spurred them on, bring me at long last a flying machine with which we can complete the circuit on some plain in France!"

Back in the rue de la Ferme, without Blériot's capital, the fledgling Voisin firm had few resources beyond the rudimentary hand tools and two employees it had inherited – Métayer and a cabinet maker called Brost – and a line of credit at the local bistro, supplemented by regular food parcels from Aimée, the elder Voisin sister. Despite the recent failures, however, the Seine trials of 18 months earlier were still fresh enough in the memory that the tiny concern was nevertheless well placed to capitalise on the ever-growing enthusiasm for flying machines.

The first order for Les Frères Voisin in 1906 was for this elegant ornithopter for Jean Florencie, although this was not the craft he entered for the Deutsch-Archdeacon Grand Prix. Florencie was the third contender, after Santos-Dumont and Delagrange, to register for the competition. The newly completed machine is seen here in the cobbled yard of the rue de la Ferme, where the second workshop was soon to be built. "We had two types of client in the early days: amateur 'inventors' incapable of even sketching their ideas, and buyers who accepted our proposals without further discussion," recalled Gabriel Voisin. According to Ferber, "[Voisin's] motley clientèle of inventors attracted by the publicity surrounding the prospect of flight listened to no one, and didn't want to imitate anything else. Most of them turned up with ideas for helicopters, ornithopters and other devices far too complicated to succeed."

So it must have been with both relief and impatience that, hardly before the paint was dry on the signwriting that replaced 'Appareils d'Aviation Blériot-Voisin' on the big wooden gates, Gabriel Voisin greeted their first paying customer, Jean Florencie. He arrived bearing plans for a glider-cum-ornithopter of his own design - and crucially, a quarter of the agreed price up front, in cash. Within three short weeks, it was completed and paid for. The next was a Russian émigré, Prince Chelminski, for whom they constructed the large spiral airscrew for a hare-brained 100HP helicopter.

Although the new firm had been set up with the express purpose of building flying machines to order in this way, Voisin was determined to pursue the configuration that the Seine trials had convinced him offered the best combination of stability and control: two Hargrave cells connected by a simple open airframe, retaining the substantial biplane forward elevator. All he had to do was to persuade someone to finance its construction. The easiest way to do that within the terms of his contract with Blériot was to offer in return the kudos of naming each machine after its owner.

Late in November, while the Florencie prototype was being finished, Voisin approached the noted airship pilot Henry Kapférer at the monthly Aéro Club dinner – the first he had been invited to attend. He knew 'Kap', the favourite nephew of oil magnate Henri Deutsch de la Meurthe, as an associate of Surcouf's; indeed, he had worked for him earlier in the year making the propeller, the rudder, the biplane stabiliser planes and parts of the 35-metre nacelle of his uncle's giant dirigible, the second *Ville de Paris*, which Surcouf had built at the astronomical reported cost of some $400,000. Although Kapférer had his own ideas (having conducted his own towed glider experiments behind a motor car in 1905), not only did he allow himself to be talked into ordering a 10-metre cellular biplane of the type Voisin so persuasively advocated, but soon after he brought the successful and popular sculptor Léon Delagrange to the rue de la Ferme – a glamorous art world acquaintance who, like many others, had been spurred into action by the prospect of winning the Deutsch-Archdeacon prize and the celebrity this would entail. While work began on the Kapférer machine in the final weeks of 1906, Voisin cajoled Delagrange into ordering a similar craft instead of building the fanciful confection the artist had initially suggested. This was science, not art.

Above, the first Voisin powered cellular biplane, built for Henry Kapférer (in bowler hat). Seen here at Sartrouville in 1906, its 11-metre upper plane was set closer to the 10-metre lower plane than on later machines

Below left, mounted at the rear of the nacelle, the tiny Buchet is dwarfed by its ignition arrangements

Below right, the tail cell of Delagrange's Voisin being towed to the Bois de Boulogne.

Into these two aeroplanes, and without external interference, Gabriel and Charles Voisin distilled all they had learned so far from their own experiments and building the Archdeacon and Blériot machines, and the Turgan prototype. Both the Kapférer and the Delagrange boasted elegant tapering wing struts, with the main elements of the airframe connected to each other via neat aluminium castings rather than mortised joints, for ease of dismantling and reassembly. Their power units differed, however: from the few available options, Kapférer chose the small but exquisitely engineered air-cooled eight-cylinder Buchet, which Voisin later described as being "as remarkable for its appearance as it was for its lack of power."

The Kapférer was therefore extremely light - reports mention 250 kg - but it was too large, and its propeller too inefficient, to have any hope of flying. Delivered in late February 1907, the only time it left the ground was when it was being manhandled over bollards alongside the airship hangar in nearby Sartrouville, where it was kept. But when Delagrange finally placed his order in December 1906 (also for February delivery), he took Voisin's advice and specified Levavasseur's costly 50HP Antoinette. The contract with Delagrange stipulated a 12,000-franc deposit, which, at a time when the brothers were preparing their own meals on the workshop stove and had but one overcoat between them, paid for a much-needed Panhard band saw.

On February 28th, by which time Delagrange had joined Florencie, Santos-Dumont and Jules Collomb in registering for the Deutsch-Archdeacon prize, Delagrange Nᵒ·1 was carted the six kilometres to Bagatelle on a caravanserai of three trucks accompanied by a posse of excited young boys. Once there, it took no more than an hour to assemble, and Gabriel Voisin managed to taxi it across the polo ground at some 15km/h. After further modifications were made, the machine was tested again on March 7th at Vincennes with Charles at the controls, but the delicate airframe once again broke its back on traversing a rut.

Equipped with beefier longerons a week later, it took off but was forced to land immediately when errant spectators rushed towards its alarmingly unpredictable flight path. And so the month went on, with further trials of a twin-rudder version at Vincennes on the 21st, when the lower main plane and

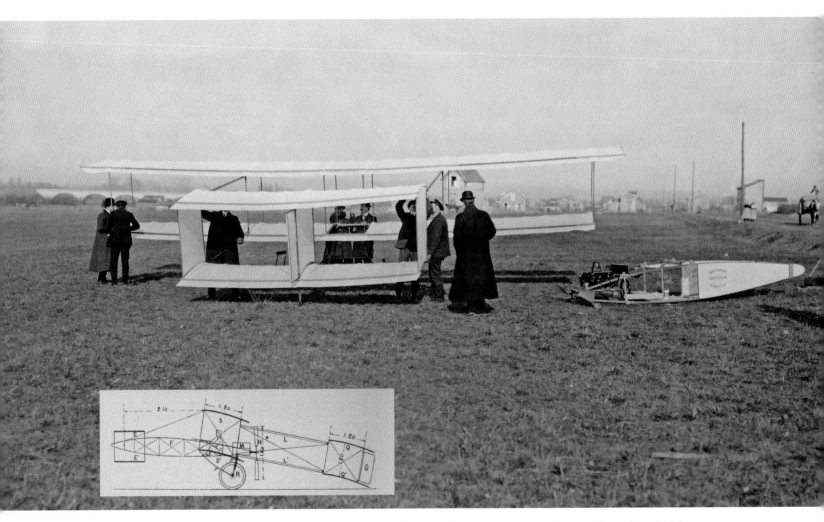

Above, Kapférer (to the right of the tail cell), overseeing the airframe being assembled at Sartrouville early in 1907.
The nacelle containing the tiny Buchet V8 (*right*) has yet to be installed.

Above, Kapférer on the far side of the main plane, with Charles Voisin at the extreme right. Unlike the later customer aeroplanes, the client's name does not appear on the tail cell - only the maker's, on the nacelle.

Above, the fragile Delagrange I breaks its back during its initial trials at Vincennes on February 28th 1907, with Gabriel Voisin at the helm.

Right, snapped just as the terrified photographer abandoned his tripod and fled, Charles Voisin executes a barely-controlled hop in the same machine at the Bois de Boulogne in March. Blériot also rose briefly into in his Type V *canard* monoplane at the same place during March and April before destroying itself..

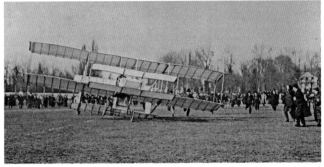

nacelle were damaged. While Esnault-Pelterie, Ernest Zens and Vuia were testing their machines at various locations around Paris, Blériot was back, testing his stubby *canard* monoplane at Bagatelle. Finally, Charles Voisin managed a 60-metre flight on the afternoon of March 30th, after a two-kilogram copper weight had been added to the right wing to mitigate its disconcerting tendency to veer leftwards.

Meanwhile, having deferred commissioning a flying machine of his own until he could secure a light engine of sufficient power, Henry Farman spent March and April immersing himself in the theory of flight and testing models he built from paper, wood and wire in the workshop of the Farman brothers' great motor emporium, Le Palais de l'Automobile.

"I must have built at least 20 different models of all sorts and sizes," Farman recalled two years later. "Many worked splendidly indoors, but directly I took them out into the open air they all went wrong. I rebuilt them, with various alterations and modifications, upon a larger scale and took them down to the Goulet, near Vernon, where I experimented by throwing them from a hill some 240 feet in height. These models were between six and seven feet in width. I purposely attached weights to them in the wrong places – in fact, in all sorts of impossible positions, in order to discover the real centres of gravity and pressure. I likewise placed the steering apparatus in front, so as to counteract the lack of equilibrium of the fall when the rapidity of movement had become sufficiently great. In this way I succeeded in throwing one of my model machines with a bag of stones weighing ten pounds from the top of the hill, and in making it alight on the ground 240 feet below without damage. I resolved without further delay to build a full-sized model, to which I would fit a motor. The form selected was that which had so far given the best results, and which Santos-Dumont had used – in fact, the only form of heavier-then-air machine which had ever flown. This is the cubic cellular form. I had discovered in the course of experiments with my models that in an aeroplane of this description the tail was everything, the front portion being of much less importance. The question is one which will require a great deal of study and practice before an ideal aeroplane is built, but so far as I have gone, I have discovered to my own satisfaction that the essential portion of an aeroplane built on the cubic cellular plan is the tail end."

Above: Little is known about this intermediate machine, which almost certainly dates from the summer of 1907. Although fitted with floats similar to the previous year's Blériot Voisin, the main planes now carry a dihedral and the tail cell is of the type first fitted to Farman's machine; a single Antoinette provided the (obviously insufficient) grunt. With no client's name on the tail and Voisin having no resources to build such a craft on his own account, it was presumably paid for by Archdeacon.

Right: This shot of Farman about to launch a monoplane glider from the Châlons observation tower towards the end of 1908 illustrates the continuing role of large scale models in evaluating the flight characteristics of various designs.

This preference for a cellular *biplan à queue* along the lines Voisin had always advocated may have been retrospective; certainly, none of the surviving photographs of Farman's models show a cellular configuration. One article of the time declared that Farman was initially planning an *aviette* – effectively a winged bicycle, the front wheel laced with canvas as a rudder, which he intended to pedal down the long downhill straight of the côte de Gaillon until he achieved take-off speed.

More credibly, *Aeronautics* reported that Farman proposed to build a tractor device powered by a 20HP engine, with a lifting area of $30m^2$ and weighing some 250 kilos – about half the size and weight of the Voisin. On balance, it seems likely that Farman was easily persuaded of the virtues of the Voisin configuration. At any rate, the racer's mind was made up, and he had the confidence of a man accustomed to early success. The stage was set for Europe's first proper aeroplane to take its bow. But as with any great première, there was the small matter of rehearsing the performance first...

May 26th, 1907 - the Voisin brothers and Colliex (*in white sweaters*) take Farman (*crouching left*) and Delagrange to practice their gliding skills at Le Touquet's Paris Plage.

№ 1

The modest premises of the world's first aeroplane factory, at 4 rue de la Ferme, Boulogne-Billancourt, after the second hangar (*left*) had been hastily erected in July, 1907. The house-cum-office was occupied by Gabriel and Charles Voisin, seen standing by the front door. At only 40m by 14.3m, the site was barely large enough to assemble airframes with a 10m wingspan, which had to be dismantled and trailered by road for the flight tests. On the waste ground at the far side can be seen the edge of the quarry pit beside which Charles Voisin posed with the Le Touquet glider (*inset*).

78

Whatever the nature of Farman's proposal, it was once again Archdeacon who in May 1907 effected the introduction to Les Frères Voisin, where a second wooden hangar was planned for the courtyard of the rue de la Ferme premises to cope with the steady influx of new orders. Like a long-awaited wave taking too long to break, France's conquest of the air was by now much overdue, and the resulting atmosphere of febrile expectation was contagious. Dozens of aspiring birdmen were exercising their contraptions, and news of the imminent arrival of Wilbur Wright from London, soon to be followed by Orville, had galvanised the tight-knit Parisian aeronautical community.

Farman arrived at the rue de la Ferme at a hectic time. Gabriel Voisin, who had just returned from Rome, where he had overseen flight trials at Forte Pietralata of a Chanute-type glider they had built to the order of Mario Calderara for the Italian government, privately shared Farman's concerns about the lack of a light engine of sufficient power. In an unpublished letter to Ferber on May 2nd, Voisin wrote that the 28 horsepower he estimated the Antoinette of Delagrange Nᵒ1 to be producing allowed the 490-kilo machine to reach no more than 10.9 metres a second (some 24mph). Not enough, of course – but he didn't let on to Farman, who agreed to commission an improved version of the Delagrange and Kapférer craft, specifically to win the Deutsch-Archdeacon Grand Prix.

Having achieved such conspicuous success on two wheels as well as four, mechanically skilled and highly competitive by nature, Farman was the perfect client for this purpose. While the Voisin brothers were cynically neglecting Delagrange in a devious ploy to buy back his machine cheaply so as to compete for the great prize themselves, work duly began at the rue de la Ferme on Farman Nᵒ1 on Monday May 20th, although the order was formally placed ten days later.

By way of initiation, Gabriel and Charles Voisin and their deputy Maurice Colliex took Farman and Delagrange to Paris Plage, near le Touquet, on Sunday May 26th, to practise their control skills on a seven-metre Chanute glider of the type Voisin had just delivered to the Italians. The chain-smoking Farman doggedly hauled it up the dunes, time after time; by the Monday, he and Colliex were gliding for some 40 metres at altitudes of up to 15 metres. The experience must have convinced Farman that he was dealing with people who knew what they were doing, as he handed over the first cheque

Left, with his hands on the front elevator control bar, Voisin Frères' famous new customer inspects work in progress on the bare nacelle of his machine with Charles Voisin at the rue de la Ferme worshop in July 1907, with the unwieldy six-metre tail cell in the background.

Above, Farman and Gabriel Voisin stand partly obscured behind the nacelle of the newly completed machine on the drill ground at Issy in late August 1907, showing its low-mounted biplane front elevator and the disproportionate size of the original six-metre tail cell, with its extended trapezoidal side panels and rudder mounted at the leading edge. Note too the horizontal bar bracing the inner front struts in front of the pilot, and the fact that the suspension uprights were initially configured to be parallel with the struts.

Right, Charles Voisin's 1907 order for Reissner's Antoinette V16.

to Charles Voisin in the train on the return journey. Back in Billancourt, not to be outdone by the apparently fearless Charles, Farman even launched himself into the six-metre deep quarry pit on the waste ground behind the workshops with another Chanute glider. The new client was as brave as he was determined.

With three phase payments, Farman's contract stipulated that the 12,000 francs for the airframe depended on the machine flying one kilometre (as opposed to the 50 metres required by the equivalent agreement with Delagrange). But the hand-to-mouth finances of Les Frères Voisin meant that the contract with Farman necessarily excluded the most expensive component: the engine. Farman agreed to pay a deposit for six months' use of the 13,000-franc Antoinette, in return for allowing it to be lent back temporarily for fitment to other Voisin machines if required. As it turned out, this condition was never acted upon for the simple reason that whenever conditions were propitious for flight attempts over the next four months, Farman was making them.

Working from plans drawn up by Colliex, who later received from the Aéro Club a gold medal struck by Delagrange for his contribution, Farman's Voisin took 80 days to complete. This was partly because yet another order had arrived, for a highly unconventional one-off biplane with adjustable main and rear biplane cells and a large gondola housing a V16 version of the Antoinette. This curious and ungainly machine was built in five weeks during August and September for the eminent Berlin quantum physicist and aerodynamics guru Professor Hans-Jacob Reissner, who took the machine back to his laboratory at the University of Aachen for further development with Hugo Junkers.

From the start, Farman decided to find a more suitable site for testing his new machine than the Bois de Boulogne, so as to avoid having to dismantle it and tow it through the streets every time. Alternatives were not easy to come by, since Prefect of Police Louis Lepine, although an aviation enthusiast, had understandable concerns for public safety, as the aeronauts were attracting increasingly large crowds of spectators with little idea of the attendant dangers. Gaining permission for any attempt at the Bagatelle polo ground involved days of form filling, countersigning and rubber-stamping before a permit for a few hours was granted, within which time the aeroplane also had to be assembled and dismantled. Farman therefore followed Archdeacon's example with Voisin's

A schoolboy shields his ears from the bark of the Antoinette's octet of exhaust stubs as Gabriel Voisin squats in the cockpit beside the up-ended pilot's bench, verifying either the trembler coil or the variable fuel pump. By late summer 1907, there was more frustration in the air than there were flying machines. Although Farman was taxiing around the parade ground almost every day, Fernand Charron and the Marquis de Dion felt confident enough to bet Archdeacon and Delagrange 5000 francs that no aeroplane would achieve sustained flight in the next six months. They lost.

second glider experiments of two years earlier and, with Lepine's help, sought permission to use the *champ de manœuvres* at Issy-les-Moulineaux. Since the drill ground was still used for exercises by the 13th Dragoons and 1st Hussars, permission was only forthcoming when Farman applied a little bureaucratic sophistry himself. There was a precedent, he claimed: kite flying had been allowed on the site since the late 1880s, and by the authorities' own reckoning, his machine was just a kite that would never fly under its own power…

So it was agreed that when the weather looked promising, the Commissaire de Police would be phoned and 18 francs 50c (three days' wages for a labourer) paid for a two-hour permit on the following day. Farman therefore rented a plot among the rag and bone merchants and market gardens on waste land just outside the perimeter wall of the drill ground, where despite a carpenters' strike, a timber hangar was built in late July and early August identical to the extension recently erected at the rue de la Ferme.

It was to this shed that the nacelle and both wing cells were towed over the Seine from Billancourt on Saturday August 17th. As assembled on the following Tuesday, Farman's Voisin sported a main cell spanning 10 metres (some reports quoted 10.8) and a chord of two metres. The planes were set 1.5 metres apart by four pairs of struts on each side (as opposed to three on Delagrange No.1), and carried a slight dihedral. Sturdier ribs to the main planes allowed the horizontal members bracing the front and rear wing struts beneath the upper plane on the earlier machines to be dispensed with. The tail cell, trapezoidal in elevation, had a span of six metres, with a central rudder mounted in line with the leading edge, and extended side panels inscribed HENRI FARMAN No.1 beneath the (much smaller) manufacturer's name.

The nacelle that enclosed the pilot and the engine was a third shorter than those of the Kapférer and Delagrange No.1, and the five-metre biplane front elevator was similar to that fitted to the two unsuccessful prototypes Voisin built for Blériot in 1906. This elevator was the only part of the Voisin that can be said to have been Wright-inspired, although Voisin vehemently denied any such influence. This may well have been true, as Hiram Maxim had used a similar arrangement a decade earlier, and the design of the Voisin elevator was quite different from the Wrights'.

Above: Henry Farman stands beside the tail of his newly delivered machine on the *champ de manouevres* while Gabriel Voisin fettles the Antoinette. Note the radiator of thin copper tubes diagonally traversing the nacelle, and the pair of steps used to climb into the cockpit.

Citing the Archdeacon glider trials along the Seine the previous year, together with a cache of design drawings "that will make you tremble with excitement day and night if you judge me capable of realising them," Voisin insisted somewhat disingenuously in a letter to Ferber in November 1906: "I am an *arriviste* in these matters, it is true, but I have never once copied others, not even the Wrights."

Wright-inspired or not, the elevator's angle of inclination was controlled by a transverse wooden bar connected to a system of cables and pulleys; the rear rudder was operated by cable from a centrally pivoted horizontal bar by the pilot's feet. As on the Delagrange, two pointed cylindrical brass tanks – one for fuel and the other, a radiator header tank – were mounted atop the nacelle directly in front of the pilot. Their roles, however, were now reversed. On the earlier machine, the tanks were on the same side as the corresponding pump on the engine, with fuel to the left and water to the right. By contrast, the fuel system on Farman's was pressured by a small hand pump, so the tanks were reversed to bring the fuel reservoir and its pump within easy reach of the pilot's right hand.

For the first three months, the nose of the nacelle also housed a simple lightweight radiator consisting of 12 thin-walled small bore copper tubes extending diagonally downwards from the top of the front of the cockpit to the tip, just behind the elevator. The slender longerons (of ash or spruce – reports differ) connecting the front and rear cells were set far enough apart to accommodate the 2.1-metre aluminium-bladed Voisin propeller. Given the repeated failure of these members on Delagrange N°1, they were of sturdier section and better reinforced. The ensemble was braced by steel wires threaded through holes drilled in the heads of purpose-made bolts that passed through the timber, and were looped and split-pinned against washers and tensioned by turnbuckles. Although some contemporary reports describe the planes as being initially covered in varnished raw silk (apart from the nacelle, which was at first left uncovered), Voisin himself recalled 50 years later that the material used was Percaline, a lightly glazed fine cotton bookbinding fabric, sealed by a coat of wallpaper paste.

Imposing in size and brilliant in white, Farman's Voisin measured 13.5 metres from elevator to tail and weighed considerably more than its two flimsier antecedents: 530 kilos, ready to fly. This was in part due to its being equipped with far more sophisticated undercarriage than on either of the

earlier Voisins, or indeed any other flying machine of the time. Not only did it incorporate long-travel coil springs on tall suspension uprights rising either side of the pilot, but also castering wheels front and rear, of 70cm and 40cm diameter respectively. Both the Kapférer and Delagrange machines had been suspended far more simply; at the rear, the former made do with a skid, while the latter had a precariously small central wheel under the wide tail cell.

Despite its substantial drag and sheer heft – Voisin later estimated the landing gear assembly weighed 70 kilos – this sturdy undercarriage gave the Voisin team a decisive advantage during the critical three months of trials before the closed circuit kilometre attempt. Robust triangulation distributed the main stresses into the strongest part of the airframe, and combined with generously sprung castering wheels (courtesy of Monsieur Colin, owner of the bicycle workshop almost opposite the rue de la Ferme works) allowed repeated take-offs and landings without so much as buckling a spoke – a routine cause of landing accidents on all but the flimsiest competitor machines.

For most of their rivals, every landing usually entailed a partial or complete rebuild of the entire airframe, let alone the wheels; indeed Blériot, who survived more than a dozen crashes during the latter half of 1907 with no more than cuts and bruises, made a virtue of the shock absorbing qualities of his airframes' progressive collapse. By contrast, Farman's Voisin, although larger and heavier, made more than 100 returns to earth of varying severity before a wheel eventually failed.

The Voisin undercarriage also allowed pilots to familiarise themselves with their mount by taxiing across the ground before taking to the air – indeed, this was basically all that pilot training consisted of before the advent of two-seaters. In a Wright, the trainee's first experience of conducting the machine was the adrenaline-fuelled moment when it was catapulted from the launch rail.

At Voisin's insistence, Farman resisted entreaties from his motor racing cronies to provide the motive power. At a meeting of the Panhard and Levassor board, René de Knyff reported that Farman had rejected their offer of a 100HP engine because of its weight, and that in the dire state of the automobile market, they could not accede to his request to develop a lighter unit. Farman's friend

As if to emphasise the value of Voisin's hefty landing gear, the lack of robust undercarriage cost Blériot dear in 1907-8, during which his bewildering succession of experimental machines were often damaged beyond repair, including N°V in March 1907 *(top left)*, N°VI in July *(below)*, N°VI^{-bis} in September *(opposite above)* and N°VIII in July 1908 *(opposite below)*.

Immaculate in his usual tweeds, Farman checks the coolant reservoir while Voisin kneels by the upturned wooden seat attending to the fuel pump of the compact Antoinette, squatting in its spindly cage of wire and wood, devoid of its later protuberances by way of intake trumpets, condenser tanks and control paraphernalia. The array of thin radiator tubes in the nose is clearly visible, as are the copper riveted aluminium blades of the directly-driven Voisin propeller and the castering front wheels of the robust landing gear, with its tall suspension uprights. Despite the commendable slimness of the members, the airframe proved sturdy enough to survive thousands of hours of punishing experimentation over the bumpy terrain of the Issy parade ground without any serious breakage.

94

Louis Renault, for whom he had only the month before piloted a Type AK in the Grand Prix de l'ACF at Dieppe, offered to supply him with one of the first lightweight air-cooled six-litre V8s that the Billancourt firm was developing. As the first of these did not appear until six months later, however, there was only one viable option: the Antoinette.

Designed five years earlier by Léon Levavasseur and Eugène Welfëringer specifically for aeronautical applications, the original 13.8-litre prototype Antoinette had powered the former's ill-fated *Aéroplane de Villotran* in 1903, and smaller versions subsequently met with great success in hydroplanes and racing powerboats. They were even fitted to cars. The 1906 50HP version was a compact 7.3-litre 90° V8 weighing only two kilos per horsepower – "the highest power-to-weight ratio yet produced," trilled *Scientific American* in 1906. A square configuration with a bore and stroke of 105mm, it was engineered to exceptionally small tolerances for the time and was one of the first engines in the world for which every component was designed to bear its calculated load and no more.

A tricky unit, nonetheless. For lightness, Levavasseur did away with carburetters altogether on the aviation versions, substituting a primitive direct injection system whereby the automatic inlet valves were fed fuel under variable pressure via short, minutely perforated tubes – the notorious '*mouches*'. The result was a fettler's nightmare. The tiny jets blocked easily, and balancing all eight to deliver an equal volume of fuel was a virtual impossibility. Ignition was via tiny batteries and a trembler coil, with a fiendishly sensitive advance/retard control. And of course, the dozens of taut steel wires securing the 100-kilo V8 in its slender wooden cradle had to be scrupulously retensioned after every run.

Development during late August and early September therefore concentrated on getting the engine to run satisfactorily. Initially, it yielded only a fraction of the advertised 50 horses, and recalcitrant nags they were, too. Despite the combined mechanical talents of the Voisins and Colliex, Farman and his chief engineer Maurice Herbster *(appendix III)*, his motor racing mechanic Charles Kneffer, advice from the magneto manufacturer Edouard Nieuport and the ministrations of the gruff, red-bearded Levavasseur himself, whole days sometimes passed without the V8 firing evenly. And when it did so for long enough to attempt a flight, equally frustrating hours were spent pacing along wheel tracks in the dew, dust or mud to find any interruption that might signify a momentary ascent.

Henry Farman's pristine Voisin being manhandled out of its shed over the perimeter wall of the *champ de manœuvres* for its initial trials in August 1907. Soon after Farman erected his hangar, Ferber applied for permission to do the same; a few days later, Archdeacon and Delagrange, frustrated by yet more fruitless waterborne trials at Lac d'Enghien, rented a plot of land on a market garden nearby on which to build their own.

Day after day, Farman arrived with Herbster in his buttercup yellow Panhard coupé, dressed in tweed Norfolk jacket and plus fours, and set to work. Curious crowds started gathering from the early hours each morning, and Captain Ferber later described his young apostle Voisin restlessly bestriding the drill ground during these tests "with the whiskers of a cat and the teeth of a wolf," having "captured the hearts of every young woman present."

Writing to Chanute on September 7th after witnessing these unproductive trials, Wilbur Wright, having sacrificed lightness for reliability in a new version of their far simpler four-cylinder power unit, concluded "the French aeroplanists are busy, but we see no indication of a practical machine in the near future." Despite his loyalty to the Wrights, Chanute demurred. "Are you not too cocksure that yours is the only secret worth knowing, and that others may not hit upon a solution?" he wrote to Orville. "I suspect you realize Esnault-Pelterie, Ferber, Blériot & Voisin, Barlatier & Blanc, Vuia, Cornu, Cody and a German syndicate are all experimenting with dynamic flying machines. Some of them may develop into something…"

The activities of the French had indeed preoccupied the Wrights ever since Santos-Dumont's hop in 1906, but not because they feared being overtaken – after all, the Flyer III had already flown 24 miles in 38 minutes at Huffman Prairie (observed not officially, but by the beekeeper Amos Root) a month before Santos's freakish ascent. "Imagine a locomotive that has left the track, and is climbing up in the air right towards you, a locomotive without any wheels, but with white wings instead," wrote Root. "Well, now, imagine this white locomotive, with wings that spread twenty feet each way, coming right towards you with a tremendous flap of its propellers and you will have something like what I saw." In France, though, notwithstanding such colourful testimony, the Wrights were still considered more aloof than aloft. Along with many other French titles, *La France Automobile* dismissed Root's account and the Wrights' other claims as "an impudent bluff".

Although adamant that there was "not one chance in a hundred that anyone would produce a machine of the least usefulness", the Dayton brothers were nevertheless canny enough to realise that any departure from terra firma, however fluky, would diminish the perceived value of their technological advantage by making controlled flight seem easier to achieve than it actually was, thereby

Above, Farman in front of his Voisin, newly equipped with the single plane elevator, while Charles Voisin holds the lower main plane.

Left, the top of the thin radiator tubes can be seen above Farman's lap. Note the steep inclination of the elevator as he prepares to taxi yet again across the Issy parade ground.

weakening their negotiating position. As an editorial in *Automotor Journal* pointed out, "The Wrights must see the danger of being supplanted if they delay in substantiating their claims any longer. If their 'secret' is so unassailable as their confidence in it suggests, it is not too unreasonable to suppose that flying by their method may be too difficult an art to be worth acquiring at any price."

Pragmatists both, Voisin and Farman knew from the start that a considerable period of learning by trial and error would be required before their machine could achieve the purpose for which it had been designed. Indeed, writing in *La Revue de l'Aviation* in August, Voisin echoed Lilienthal's famous mantra extolling the imperative of practical experiment via his mentor Ferber: "Designing a flying machine is nothing; building one is easy; testing is everything."

They were on a learning curve, so protracted development was to be expected. While Blériot was experimenting with yet another design altogether (the Langley-inspired *Libellule*, which managed several hops of almost 150 metres before coming to grief on September 17th), Farman and Voisin's first major modification was to replace the cumbersome biplane front elevator with a two-part single plane carried high on the nose by two upwardly curving wooden supports. At first, it was operated by a horizontal bar connected to two substantial but primitive wooden struts passing above the nacelle on either side of the tanks. At the same time, the ignition advance/retard quadrant was moved from its previous position halfway up the wing strut to a more handy location on the side of the cockpit.

The vertical tail panels were abbreviated and the rudder moved back to the extreme rear of the cell to provide more purchase on the air; the nacelle was also clad in fabric, like the wings. Methodical as ever, Farman persevered with his experiments. Although frustrated, the team knew they were on the right track – so much so that on the last day of September, Gabriel Voisin, Farman and Delagrange signed the papers to found the Aviation Club de France, along with Paul Roger, Marquis de Puybaudet and Count de Fayolle.

Fortuitously, it was on this same day, after minor modifications to the angle of the tail cell, that Farman's machine finally left the ground on two successive attempts, for 30 and 80 metres respectively. Although these hops did much to raise the morale of the tired and dispirited team, they weren't the

Chanute's list of the other main French contenders for the Deutsch-Archdeacon Grand Prix: *Clockwise from top left:* Esnault-Pelterie's sleek, light and sophisticated REP 1, Paul Cornu's ungainly helicopter, Ferber's promising N°IX, Blériot's strikingly prescient Type VII, Traian Vuia's optimistic second aeroplane and the heavy Barlatier & Blanc monoplane.

breakthrough everyone was hoping for. There was no obvious reason for the machine to have risen; like Santos-Dumont's 220-metre hop in 14$^{\text{-bis}}$ ten months earlier, it could have been a fluke, or caused by freak gusts. In any case, the phenomenon was not immediately repeatable.

Pressure from the competition was hotting up, too. Apart from Delagrange, Traian Vuia and Robert Esnault-Pelterie were making progress – the latter slowed down by developing his own engine as well as his metal airframe – as were Ferber, the Austrian Alfred von Pischof and Santos-Dumont, this time with his diminutive Type 19 *Demoiselle* microlight. Louis Blériot was regularly careering across the parade ground in his pretty white Type VII at speeds approaching 90km/h, continually having to shut down its Antoinette to prevent take-off before he had fully mastered the controls of his sleek new machine – the archetype of all monoplanes for decades thereafter. As so often before with its predecessors, however, the undercart eventually gave way with predictably disastrous results.

Farman's first real break finally came on October 7th. Since taking delivery in August, Farman and Voisin had carried out between four and ten trials a day whenever weather conditions permitted – more than 250 in all. Progress was so laborious that in sheer pique at yet another land-bound run, the normally undemonstrative Farman abandoned the elevator control he had been so carefully nursing and, in an uncharacteristic fit of pique, gave the suspension upright a resounding clout with his fist. As he did so, he saw with amazement the coil spring lengthen to its full extent as he felt himself take to the air. Not for long – only 30 metres or so – but nonetheless aloft.

The short duration of this and previous bounds was mainly down to the pilot's technique. As usual, though, the press got it wrong. "Articles were published saying that I had made my aeroplane fly by jumping out of my seat while piloting it," Farman protested. "An assertion no more sensible than it would be to affirm that a boat could be stopped by pulling a rope attached to its bow."

In fact, Farman had been intuitively wrenching the big front elevator skywards every time he had built up enough speed to attempt to leave the ground, so it acted as a huge air brake at the very moment when any loss of impetus would slow the machine to below the required take-off velocity. Once aloft, the constant fear of a nose-dive led to similarly counterproductive corrections.

Above, the angle of incidence of the single front elevator that replaced the cumbersome biplane arrangement was initially controlled by means of large wooden spars connected to a horizontal bar in front of the pilot. Note also the shortened tail panels and the mounting step crudely cut out of the canvas of the nacelle by the cockpit.

Inset top right, Gabriel Voisin does the lion's share of the pushing (behind the main plane) while Farman draws on an autumnal cigarette behind the large tail cell. Backlit by the low afternoon sun, the sewn-in panels bearing the owner's and manufacturer's names are just visible.

However, the fact that the machine had finally taken off while the elevator was at the mercy of the airstream set Farman thinking anew about the pitch of the planes as the machine sliced through the air. The angle of the propeller axis in relation to the fuselage and wings had been calculated on the basis that the latter, together with the front elevator, required an angle of at least seven or eight degrees to generate enough lift; but in abandoning the elevator, he had allowed the fuselage to take its natural horizontal position in the air. This was what Farman later claimed as his crucial insight: "the secret of the small angle".

Others attribute this observation to Voisin. During yet another attempt mid-afternoon on October 15th, Farman took off into windier conditions than usual in less than ten metres and described an undulating trajectory over some 285 metres, inadvertently touching down once, but flying without the pitching described at the time as "the usual rolling motion of an aeroplane".

Gabriel Voisin, following on foot closely enough to see for himself how Farman was setting the angle of the elevator too steeply, and fearful of the effect of sudden crosswinds on the machine's low altitude and unpredictable attitude, frantically signalled the pilot to land and return to the hangar in order to debrief him accordingly.

Whichever is true – and, given the two egos involved, the truth is probably a combination of both – a week of considerable modification ensued to achieve the small angle of incidence required. Over the next two days, the undercarriage geometry was reconfigured by introducing spacers to raise the front of the airframe and incline the suspension uprights backwards, thereby bringing the axis of the front wheels further towards the nose.

Lighter and stronger U-shaped forks replaced the fabricated square-shouldered originals, lower bump stops were fitted and bungee cords wound around the top of each upright as shock absorbers. Since these changes had the effect of increasing the machine's angle of incidence by 2°, the angle of the tail cell was modified by the same amount. The side panes were also shortened. On October 19th, the day that Esnault-Pelterie also made his first brief flight at Buc, near Versailles, Farman flew the revised machine for 100 metres after four fruitless initial attempts.

Above, as if to exemplify the sheer laboriousness of the hundreds of flight trials conducted during the autumn of 1907, Farman's longsuffering Voisin is pushed into position yet again across the sodden surface of the windswept parade ground at Issy-les-Moulineaux.

106

They had cracked it – almost. Apart from the question of power, the ideal relationship between the craft's centre of gravity and its centre of pressure was still unresolved. "It is difficult to define where the centre of gravity is when one is in the air, without any connection with the ground," Farman recalled three months later, characteristically taking all the credit himself. "I soon discovered that the centre of gravity ought not to be below the apparatus, but at a point between the principal planes, very near, but not quite, in the centre of the rear of the apparatus. I also found that the centre of gravity and the centre of pressure of the propeller were not the same, so that I had to create a compensating balance between the two gravities."

In the ensuing four days, the Antoinette was mounted closer to the pilot to bring the centre of gravity forward, and a larger propeller substituted. These modifications entailed making a cut-out in the middle of the trailing edge of the upper wing to clear the airscrew. A new front elevator mounting was also fitted, slightly further forward and adjustable to four different positions. As a result, Farman flew some 170 metres on October 23rd, although the new propeller was damaged by a heavy landing and its blades had to be replaced overnight (at a time when the factory was already working flat out completing the Antoinette stand for the Salon de l'Automobile). Nevertheless, in the presence of Archduke Leopold of Austria and Don Jaime de Bourbon, Archdeacon, Kapférer and other Aéro Club officials, fellow aeronauts including Orville Wright, Delagrange, Ferber, Blériot, Victor Tatin and a large crowd of journalists and spectators, Farman made five attempts the following afternoon. The first, at three o'clock, was a success, covering an officially observed 185 metres in 15.4 seconds, and thereby winning the first of the Aéro Club 150-metre prizes (an enamelled silver plaque and a cheque for 200 francs). On his second sortie, Farman was forced to land early because of spectators wandering across his flight path, and was not officially recorded; the remaining three were even shorter, mainly because Farman was trying out steeper elevator settings. The day after saw several more flights of up to 190 metres.

But it was on Saturday 26th October that Farman definitively mastered the Voisin. This time, security guards were stationed around the drill ground to keep the spectators behind the perimeter wall and to make sure the field was clear of cars, dogs and other potential hazards. The first few attempts in the

Above, the leading lights of the Parisian aeronautical community saw Farman's confidence with the machine grow with every attempt: Captain Ferber (left, in uniform), Henri Deutsch, Delagrange (in bowler), Farman, Blériot (with Aéro Club armband), Archdeacon (in flat hat) and a smiling Santos-Dumont (walking away).

Inset: the declaration signed by eyewitnesses to Farman's short flight on October 26th, including Delagrange, Louis Barthou, the journalist Baudry de Saunier, Colliex and his wife, the factory's chief carpenter Henri Métayer and the photographer from the Rol agency. Having successfully sustained flight, Farman's next challenge was to effect a turn.

morning were of similar duration to the previous day's. Gabriel Voisin was losing patience, as Farman had not bothered to explain to him the modification he had asked Herbster to make to the elevator overnight. In the final run of the morning, with the elevator in its fourth (and shallowest) position, the Voisin managed 363 metres. Adjourning for lunch at the nearby Café des Sports, during which Farman warmed up while his Antoinette cooled down, he asked his eminent spectators to sign a statement attesting to this new distance record. Refreshed, he resumed his tests with a 403-metre flight. With all the Aéro Club officials present, he made what Archdeacon timed as a 27-second flight two hours later, which Gabriel Voisin and the journalist François Peyrey measured as 350 metres.

Then Farman went for it. Deciding on the spur of the moment to fly diagonally across the parade ground rather than parallel to the perimeter wall, he gave the Antoinette its head. With a Renault full of Aero Club bigwigs in hot pursuit, the big Voisin rose majestically six metres into the chill air – and stayed there for nearly 53 seconds, covering 771 metres at some 34mph before landing safely just 10 metres short of the far wall. To the elated cheers of his exhausted team, this new official world record for duration and distance snatched the Archdeacon Cup (held for a year and three days by Santos) from Esnault-Pelterie, who made a less successful attempt the next day. As well as also winning Farman 1500 francs for the AéCF prizes for the first officially observed flights of 300 and 500 metres, the feat was particularly relished by Archdeacon and Santos-Dumont, both of whom had in July laid 5000-franc wagers against 500 metres being flown by the end of 1907.

"Farman's performance today confounds once and for all those critics who claim that the aeroplane is only capable of climbing and diving, but not steady horizontal flight," declared *L'Aérophile*. Congratulations were cabled from the International Aeronautical Congress in New York.

"I had discovered the long-sought 'knack', for so I must call it," Farman told reporters. "Instead of making a mere jump, I was able to keep up a soaring movement and remain in the air some six feet above the ground. I could easily have risen to a height of 50 or 60 feet or more, had I so desired, but that would have been extremely dangerous and foolhardy, for I had lost my equilibrium the machine would have probably turned right over, and I should in all likelihood have been killed. In all my flights, therefore, I have carefully aimed at remaining within a safe distance from the earth."

Under the snappy headline 'In an Odd-Looking Structure Bearing a Curious Resemblance to an Automobile Farman Wins Great Triumph in Aeronautics', the *New York Times* devoted a complete half-page to praising this sensational event: "An unprecedented feat accomplished with the skill, ease and confidence of a scientist giving a familiar demonstration. Indeed, Mr Farman impresses one as more of a scientist than as an intrepid automobilist and aeronaut. Just after he had completed his record flight, and while the spectators were still literally delirious with enthusiasm, he turned aside compliments with questions about horsepower and talk of a new propeller."

The reporter's staccato account captures the breathless excitement of witnessing such a phenomenon for the very first time, not to mention the struggle to find a suitable vocabulary for doing so: "It looked anything but birdlike. It looked bizarre, almost absurd, even as a walking swan. The whole apparatus strikes the observer as being awkward and far from strong. It is not poetic. Farman, calm and workmanlike, bareheaded and dressed like a chauffeur from the repair shop, takes his seat and a moment later the motor – a marvel of concentrated energy – is rapping out its sharp tattoo. The commission from the Aéro Club, in two automobiles, fall in behind the canvas monster.

"Here there should be a blare of trumpets, but there is not. Farman barks a few quick orders to his assistants. They stand back. Everyone but Farman holds his breath. The hammering racket of the motor seems suddenly deafening. Then – zip! The propeller disappears into a blur of speed, our canvas monster glides forward gladly, faster, faster still. Then, before you have drawn another breath, you see a marvellous thing. The wheels leave the ground. Instead of bumping down again as wheels have always done before, they go higher and higher. You look again at the machine. A moment before so awkward and helpless, it now seems instinct with life – a kite, an automobile and a man made one. It gives an impression of infinite power and nobility. Tense with speed and purpose, it takes to the air as to its natural element. It is as remote and different from all things you have ever seen before.

"The high-powered automobiles skurrying (*sic*) along in its wake look strangely incompetent and old-fashioned. You see not one flying machine, but a swarm of them skimming over a frightened army. What a difference from the lubberly steerable balloon! What speed! The crowd in the distance began to cheer the moment the flight began. Before the sound reaches you, all records have been broken, and still the swan sails swiftly on. You half expect it to disappear into the sky, where it belongs. For the first time since he began his experiments, Farman shows his power and self-possession by undulating. Down and up the great bird rushes ahead – twice, thrice. But the limits of the cage are almost reached. Directly ahead are the stone bulwarks of the fortifications of Paris. The swan again lowers its head slightly and a moment later has taken to the ground without a jar. The propeller slackens and stops. The life goes out of the bird like the light from an extinguished candle.

"Again it stands helpless, ready to be pushed back into its stable or aviary by plodding workmen. Mr Archdeacon followed the flight in a swift automobile and is the first to congratulate Farman, loading him with hearty praise. Farman smiles and turns his eyes towards his machine. He is modest and a man of few words. 'I'm satisfied,' says Farman simply. 'I can fly at will in a straight line. Now I must learn to turn around. It will take practice.' "

This vivid eyewitness reportage is made all the more striking by the prescient military image suddenly darkening the innocent tale of a mechanical ugly duckling metamorphosing into a deadly caged swan...

Even allowing for the fact that English was his second language, Farman's own somewhat stilted attempt to describe flight to the reporter from *Fly* magazine similarly betrays the lack of an appropriate lexicon: "Flying is like walking. I dash up diagonally into the air with all my present motor force, but the slightest slowing of the motor, or at an untoward shifting of my body, the down dip begins and I go tobogganing down upon the air. Before I get too low, I must put my advance spur on the motor, raise the lifting rudder and turn the down dip into an upcurving dash."

"A decisive step in the history of aviation," proclaimed the ever-partisan Archdeacon at the subsequent Aéro Club dinner. After giving due credit to the robustness and quality of Voisin's creation, he went on to hail Farman's achievement in terms both patriotic and idealistic, with a withering attack on the Ohioans: "The famous Wright brothers can claim what they like. If it is true (which I increasingly doubt) that they were the first to fly, the glory shall not be theirs. For the recognition of history, instead of indulging in their incomprehensible secrecy, they should have carried out their trials in the full glare of the sun and before official observers and thousands of witnesses, as Santos and Farman have done."

Warming to his theme, Archdeacon went on to attack the very idea of the secrets of controlled flight being the intellectual property of any individual: "The first experiments in self-propelled flight took place in France, and will continue to do so. The Wrights' much-vaunted 50 kilometres will I am sure soon be overtaken well before they decide to reveal the chimeric machine they have been hawking – without success, to my knowledge – to the governments of the world. Farman's recent successes definitively prove that true pioneer aviators employ solely established methods and cannot therefore claim exclusivity through patent protection. Any government that pays the Wrights a million for their so-called invention, however well it works, might just as well throw it out of the window, because nothing can prevent the engineers of tomorrow from copying from A to Z existing designs that work even better. This is as it should be, since we desire above all that aerial navigation be spread throughout the world to make its immense contribution to universal wellbeing and the progress of humanity."

Wilbur was neither offended nor impressed, laconically dismissing the flight as being shorter than that which they had achieved in 1903. Farman made several other sorties over similar distances over the following days; in the process, he also set a new official speed record. These successes caused a sensation in the press – and, more importantly for the Voisin brothers, they were enough to fulfil the terms of the original contract, so Farman handed over the much-needed cheque for the final tranche of the agreed purchase price.

Turning posed the next big challenge. Although the wing warping-cum-rudder technology that lay at the heart of the Wrights' invention had allowed the Flyer to complete a circle back in September 1904, turning remained a contentious issue in France. Some commentators still questioned the need for aeroplanes to turn at all, since they travelled as the crow flies; others, including such influential figures as the respected Panhard engineer Arthur Krebs, deemed turning to be impossible on the basis that, unlike a car or a boat, an aeroplane had nothing against which to exert pressure in order to effect a change of direction. Even the eminent mathematician Jean-Gaston Darboux, dean of the science faculty at the university of Paris and secretary of the Académie des Sciences, insisted to Commandant Renard that in all probability powered flight would only ever be possible in a straight line.

Farman had learnt enough to know that this was not the case – indeed, at the very moment that he was securing the distance record, Esnault-Pelterie was being filmed by Gaumont newsreel cameras making S-shaped flights at Buc. But because of the inherent stability of the Voisin design, turning by rudder alone was no easy matter. There was the dreaded side-slip to consider, for a start – if the outside wing picked up too much airspeed it would rise, and if the turn was persisted in, the lower wing would be in danger of slipping groundwards at the low altitudes involved. It was even said the difficulties were caused by the parade ground being full of 'air holes'.

"It was all very well to be able to rise in the air and to come down again without danger, but I could only fly in a straight line; I had yet to learn to turn, and to maintain my equilibrium in the air," Farman admitted. "I could scarcely get any sleep for thinking of how I could solve these difficulties. I was always up and off to my shed before daybreak, trying all sorts of experiments with the rudder and with the propellers."

The combination of his cycling background and his gliding experience led Farman to the erroneous conclusion that shifting his body weight would help to effect the desired change in direction: "I soon began to find that by turning the rudder suddenly to the left and swinging over my body to that side, the aeroplane veered to the left, and I began to place myself very much in the position of the expert cyclist who can pedal very fast with his hands in his pocket and who without touching the handlebars can veer to the left or to the right by throwing the weight of his body on either side."

Writing as late as 1909, Farman declared that "since winds are stronger a few feet up than at ground level, turning at low altitude risks capsizing the machine altogether." The problem was that turning slowed the machine, losing height in the process; without the margin of power to compensate for this deceleration, Farman intuitively climbed before attempting to change direction. In any case, skidding round on rudder alone required a lot of space even at low speeds, as any modern pilot will confirm - but the parade ground was only about 900 metres across at its widest point.

Despite this lack of roll control, Delagrange had nevertheless succeeded in coaxing his Voisin into an apparently stable 300-metre turn early in November. Inspired with renewed confidence by this example, Farman recalled: "I succeeded in making a half circle and then a complete circle. I'd solved the difficulty of turning left or right as desired, but it took me a long time to discover the exact proportion of effort, the precise turn to give the helm.

"The question is very complicated," he explained, "because in the air there are four essential kinds of equilibrium to be mastered. The man on a bicycle has only two forms of equilibrium to study - that of the right and left. But the man in a flying machine has not only to consider the left and the right, but also a plunging movement forward and a tilting movement to the rear. Nor is this all, for besides these four cardinal points, the machine may take a plunge or suddenly move up at any angle, and it is a most intricate calculation to have to bear all this in mind while flying and handling one's motor and helm. For this reason I have come to the conclusion quite recently, as a result of the many difficulties I have had to encounter, that in the present state of knowledge only a small number of persons will be able to make flights in a heavier-than-air machine. Indeed, the question as to whether a man will or will not be able to fly depends nearly all the time upon some insignificant detail which, in 90 cases out of 100, will escape his attention." During the next two days, the emphasis was therefore on making the machine easier and more intuitive to control. The sliding bar actuating the elevator was replaced by what soon became the characteristic Voisin steering wheel, whose column slid back and forth in a fixed sleeve to actuate the elevator via a diagonal tubular steel linkage above the nacelle, with a fixed pulley around which passed the rudder control cable – an altogether more ergonomic arrangement than the sliding bar. (Some reports mistakenly described it as rigged so that the wheel turned in the opposite way to the intended direction.)

Farman had a spectacular opportunity to try out these new controls on November 5th, when the hapless Delagrange bellyflopped his Voisin on the far side of the drill ground. As someone who, having enjoyed nearly ten years of public adulation for his prowess in gruelling and dangerous sports, must have felt himself to be every inch the hero down to toes of his gartered tartan stockings, Farman leapt into the cockpit of his own machine and flew across the parade ground to rescue his fellow Voisiniste from the sorry mess of fabric, wire and shards of spruce. Because that's what heroes do.

On November 7th, the weather was propitious, with a light breeze. As the evening light faded, the Voisin flew 600 metres - low, at around three metres - in a wide arc that a US reporter described as "the most wonderful flight ever made in such a contrivance," when a strut failed. But for the press as well as the Voisin team, Farman had the Archdeacon prize in the bag.

Two days later, Archdeacon watched at dusk as the Voisin described an undulating trajectory towards and around the listless flag barely visible through the mist at the far side of the drill ground, covering 1,036 metres in a circle in the process - the first kilometre flight in Europe. Immediately afterwards, he flew from end to the other in a huge 'S' to prove to himself and others that he could return the Voisin to the horizontal at will. On the 14th, Wright saw Farman make two semicircular flights until the propeller failed yet again. On Monday November 18th – the day that the second Wright patent was lodged in France – the Aéro Club officials were summoned to a repeat performance of the circular flight to claim the prize. Farman's father and brothers came, along with Ferber, Blériot, Santos-Dumont, Esnault-Pelterie, Orville and the Wrights' agent Hart Berg, accompanied by the poet Walter Savage Landor. The news spread fast – a crowd of more than 1,000 journalists, sportsmen, inventors, young men about town and their elegant escorts gathered to witness the feat. At noon, the *Ville de Paris* dirigible thrummed into view. Kapférer and his mechanician Louis Paulhan set the giant dirigible down on the parade ground, having flown Deutsch and Surcouf from Sartrouville to see Farman in action.

He made no fewer than seven attempts between 2:30 and four o'clock. On the first, the big Voisin failed to make the turn at all; on the second, it touched down momentarily mid-turn; a misfire marred the third. On the fourth and fifth attempts, the machine had not risen by the time it reached the start line. The sixth run was aborted after a wheel grazed the ground at the start of the turn, and Antoinette gremlins prevented take-off on the seventh. It was only on the last attempt, just before dusk, that Farman almost succeeded in completing the circle, but landed 50 metres outside the marker poles. Orville was nevertheless generous in his praise, opining to *The Herald* that in Europe, "Mr Farman takes the lead over everyone else as far as flying is concerned. I consider him to be an ideal aeronaut, who will probably help to develop the art of flying to a very great degree."

Above, from November onwards, the team's flight trials were conducted in the public spotlight, often attracting crowds of more than 1000 inventors, young men about town, schoolboys and elegant *demoiselles* in addition to the journalists and the agency photographers lugging their Kodaks across the flood plain.

Writing to Stanley Beach three months later, Wright gave a more technical assessment: "Only when working perfectly did the motor furnish the power required for flight on a level course. Many trials were unsuccessful on this account. In the longer flights there was evidence of difficulty in keeping off the ground, due to a slight falling off in power of the engine. We believe that all light motors show a greater power for the first minute or so. Then in the flights when the machine was not allowed to rise more than a few feet, it showed a tendency to come to the ground immediately upon a curve being attempted. This was no doubt due to the additional power required to describe a circle. We understood the weight of the machine had been reduced by 40 or 50lb just before this successful flight."

Having overcome the challenge of getting into the air and at least in part, that of turning, Farman and Voisin turned their attention once again to what Wright had correctly perceived as the main factor limiting more sustained flight: the Antoinette itself. For three months, they had worked ceaselessly with Colliex and Herbster to cajole 50 dependable horses from the V8 for more than a few minutes at a time. Aéro Club observers attended further attempts on the 20th, 21st and 23rd November, when the propeller disintegrated while taxiing, bending the crankshaft and throwing a connecting rod through the crankcase in the process. The team's disappointment was compounded by reports of a *Berliner Zeitung* article a few days earlier recounting that Wright had flown 39 km (albeit in a machine as yet incapable of taking off unaided under its own power).

More modifications ensued. Between November 24th and 28th, a new 2.3-metre propeller was fabricated to replace the failed 2.1-metre screw, with a pitch of 1.4 metres rather than 1.1. The consequent improved thrust was attenuated by the replacement Antoinette revving 200rpm more slowly, effectively reducing its output to around 35HP. The fuel tank on the nacelle in front of the pilot was moved to the top of the upper wing, offset to the right to avoid vapour lock, feeding the engine-driven variable rate pump. The pump itself proved prone to sudden seizure through lack of lubrication; adding oil to the fuel was not an option since this would block the tiny injector jets. As it was, the ultra-fine particle filter Levavasseur had fitted upstream of the pump clogged with monotonous regularity, occasioning lengthy sessions filtering fuel through a chamois leather membrane. In addition to endless experiments with the jets of the *mouches*, Farman had by the end installed no fewer than

120

three filters in the fuel line for this purpose. The camshaft-driven distributor behind the pilot having proved bothersomely vulnerable on wet days, a Nieuport magneto was fitted beside the fuel pump under the seat in place of the trembler coil to try and ensure more reliable running in damp conditions.

Most obviously, the unwieldy six-metre tail cell was replaced on December 4th by a 2.7-metre version. Voisin had originally opted for such a large cell to maximise the machine's stability, despite the extra drag involved; but by this time, Farman's piloting skills had turned this characteristic into a handicap rather than an advantage. The compact new tail weighed some 35kg less than the cell it replaced and saved the equivalent of five horsepower in drag, as well as making the machine more manoeuvrable and reducing the considerable force required to operate the elevator. At the same time, the thin-tube radiator was removed entirely and replaced by a sizeable condenser tank (unlike the fuel tank, conical only at the rear) suspended above the engine, fed by a large diameter tract rising from each cylinder. The undercarriage geometry was adjusted once again to maintain the correct centre of gravity to compensate for moving the fuel and water tanks aft.

On December 6th, the Voisin sustained damaged after "toppling over" as a result of the lighter new tail cell. This was bad news, as Blériot made two impressively rapid 500-metre flights on the same day in his sleek Type VII, prompting the military aviation pioneer Patrick Alexander to write to the Royal Aeronautical Society's Baden Baden-Powell that in his view "Blériot with his new machine is now leading the way." True to form, however, the machine in question had turned turtle and destroyed itself within a fortnight. On the 7th, von Pischof's inelegant Anzani-powered biplane, with its much more efficient Chauvière laminated wooden propeller, also briefly left the ground for the first time.

December 20th saw Farman make a 500m flight with a second new magneto and yet another airscrew, and he reported that the new tail cell had indeed made turning easier. The next day, he is reported to have coaxed an extra 50rpm from the Antoinette "by warming the fuel in the jacket of the motor."

After Christmas – probably on New Year's Day – the seaplane pioneer Henri Fabre came to inspect Farman's Voisin, having travelled from his native Marseilles for an Aéro Club dinner. He pointed out to Gabriel Voisin that the exposed main spars on the upper surface of each wing must be

generating considerable unnecessary drag. By Fabre's own account, Voisin dismissed this observation on the grounds that the air acted on the lower surface of the wing rather than the upper – unlikely, since it would imply a fundamental ignorance of the principles of aerodynamic lift. Farman merely stroked his beard (although he later claimed credit for the improvement himself). The remark clearly made an impression, however, for by the end of the first week of January, both the main planes had been recovered to smooth the airflow over the exposed spars. If indeed this saved the equivalent of 10HP, as one report suggested, no wonder Farman admitted after achieving the closed circuit kilometre that this modification had "helped me in no small measure toward my success today."

This was the configuration for the kilometre attempt. Confidence was running high: on December 30th, after flying a complete circle in front of a large crowd, Farman said that he expected aeroplanes to be able to stay aloft for up to 12 miles within the year, but, in an aside, confessed to the dexterity and skill required of the pilot: "I don't believe that flying will ever become a sport of the masses – it will always be too difficult for most people to learn." If this was true of a Voisin, it was even more so of a Wright, but Wilbur said nothing. On New Year's Day 1908, he had written to Chanute: "I still hold to my prediction that an independent solution to the flying problem will require at least another five years."

For the Grand Prix at least, the technology gap was closing more quickly. Farman was ready, and everyone knew it. So much so that on January 8th, Delagrange approached Gabriel with an offer of 50,000 francs, the value of the prize itself, to allow him to make an official attempt before Farman. After reflecting for some 20 minutes on this tempting proposition – a large sum for a fast expanding but cash-strapped little firm that by now had the wages of 19 workers to pay – Voisin refused. By then, Farman's tenacity and skill as a test pilot had firmly established him as the favoured customer; for all his undoubted charm and amiability, the less single-minded Delagrange had always been more preoccupied by worldly distractions, as well as lacking Farman's mechanical abilities.

Uncomfortably aware of the progress being made by Blériot and Santos (who had registered with the Aéro Club every week since mid-December for an official attempt on the kilometre with his agile *Demoiselle*), the Voisin brothers could not risk any delays that might be occasioned by the sculptor's inferior piloting abilities. They had to move fast. Farman made two perfect kilometre flights in the

Top left, Archdeacon accompanies Charles Voisin as he measures the kilometre course by the turns of his bicycle wheel, with Delagrange and Blériot in conversation behind.
Top right and above, before and during the momentous flight that finally secured for Henry Farman the Deutsch-Archdeacon Grand Prix on January 13th, 1908.

modified machine on January 4th, landing heavily after a short ascent on the 6th. On Sunday 12th, he made two final 1800-metre runs. This time, they were confident that the Aero Club observers had not been summoned in vain. Gabriel Voisin confided to the reporter from *Fulmicoton*: "Tomorrow, my dear sir, weather permitting, you should return here to witness the dawn of a new era in the history of humanity."

It broke on a crisp Monday 13th in weak January sunshine. Against a skyline dominated by the vast Astra and Clément Bayard airship hangars, the plumes from the tall chimneys of the nearby factories rose almost vertically in the lightest of westerly breezes, the frozen ground dusted with powdery snow. Since the Antoinette ran with only thermosyphon cooling, the 7° temperature was an advantage. Herbster diligently began the final checks as the sun rose.

According to *L'Eclair*, the shiplap boarding of the hangar walls visibly shook when a resounding backfire from the Antoinette within echoed across the parade ground. Farman retarded the ignition. At the second attempt the V8 burst into life, the big propeller swirling dust and detritus around the still-gloomy enclosure.

As usual, Colliex oversaw the removal of the large hangar doors from their hinges to be laid across the perimeter wall. After checking the fuel tank and ignition setting one last time, Farman settled himself in the cockpit and ordered the Voisin to be manhandled across its precarious ramp so that it could be pushed into position, 200 metres behind the start line.

By nine o'clock, Aéro Club officials arrived, along with the usual posse of hacks. There were fewer spectators than usual, as nothing much usually happened before about 11 o'clock. Charles Voisin accompanied Archdeacon to erect three posts flying the blue and gold pennants of the Aéro Club to define the course. Two marked the start/finish line; the 500 metres to the third, where Blériot remained, were measured by counting the turns of Charles's bicycle wheel. To follow the flight, de la Vaulx and Kapférer then climbed aboard Santos's Mercédès (an ex-Jenatzy Grand Prix car) and Archdeacon and other officials piled into Count de Mortimer's Renault. Deutsch arrived with his daughter minutes before Gabriel Voisin himself swung the prop at 10.12.

Farman in 1^{-bis} on the big day, with the articulated sliding steering column which controlled both the rudder and the elevator angle visible on the left, above the patched and oil-stained fabric of the nacelle.

Farman (centre) listens to Herbster on the frozen parade ground before the kilometre flight; in the foreground, jugs of lubricant and coolant for the Antoinette stand beside the folding wooden steps for climbing up into the cockpit.

The Antoinette obeyed. To the impatient roar of its deafening exhaust stubs, Colliex and Herbster held the trembling machine in place until Farman bade them release it with a curt 'Lachez tout!' The big Voisin began trundling over the frozen ground, gathering pace quickly enough to rise four metres into the air some 100 metres before the start line, climbing steadily to eight metres to make the turn around the far pylon.

What happened next depends on the prejudices of the reporter. Wrightists described the turn as an "ungainly manoeuvre", with the machine "skidding around precariously in a wide yaw to avoid side-slip and stalling." By contrast, the account in *The Engineer* was far more positive: "He glided round very easily at a much sharper curve than would have been deemed possible, with only a slight inclination of the planes, and then continuing with a flat curve behind the post for about 50 yards or so, he turned again somewhat sharply and steered almost straight home and brought the machine to the ground as gracefully as a bird, without any shock."

The evidence points to the latter account being nearer the mark; grainy and flickering as it is, the Gaumont footage of the flight shows a smooth, confident turn, banking slightly before resuming an even keel for the home straight (though hardly at the "vertiginous speed" of *The Times*'s excited report). Farman's own description verged on the banal: "I soon felt the earth moving away from me. I regulated the elevating plane, and rose higher still. I had to use some caution when crossing the starting line, for a yard outside this would have meant another trial. I headed for the flagstaff on the other side of the field, which I had to fly around. My machine was working beautifully and I had absolute confidence in success. My confidence in the aeroplane was not misplaced, for on coming around the flagstaff, when half of the journey was accomplished, the machine was flying better than ever. It was only a matter of a few seconds until I was up again in front of the starting line. I waved to my friends and they gave a cheer, for I had won the much-coveted prize."

Farman completed the circuit in one minute 28 seconds, and touched down where he had started to a chorus of hat-throwing hurrahs - understandably so, for as well as winning the purse of 50,000 gold francs, his achievement marked the moment when the third element had officially been conquered. Europe's first practical aeroplane had arrived.

Le Petit Parisien was one of dozens of popular publications around the world to run hat-doffing illustrations based on the famous snap of Farman crossing the finishing line of the closed circuit kilometre.

130

The crowd rushed over to greet Farman as he descended the steps from his cockpit, from where Charles and Gabriel Voisin bore him shoulder-high to the Aéro Club commissaires; the only emotion he allowed himself to show was when his younger brother Maurice emerged from the throng to embrace him. Archdeacon, his public pronouncements on the superiority of French aviation in the face of American claims finally vindicated for all to see, intoned solemnly over the noise of the elated onlookers that the terms of the Grand Prix had been satisfied in every respect and that the result would be homologated that very afternoon. Gabriel Voisin, described as "a slight, thin, wiry young man with an exceedingly intelligent face", stood close by, his face "by turns livid with emotion and white as a sheet with excitement".

"I thought I'd faint with joy," he recalled, adding that Blériot was sulking at having been pipped to the post. Despite visibly trembling hands, the phlegmatic Farman was not the sort to bathe in the limelight. Within minutes he had remounted his machine, bidden Herbster to restart the engine and, according to the reporter, "swung round the flag post in a long graceful curve and landed almost in front of the front door of his shed."

More than a century later, it's easy to underestimate the resonance of those 88 seconds aloft. By 1908, Modernism was in full swing – especially in Paris, the undisputed cultural capital of Europe. In science, fine art, literature, politics, architecture and the performing arts, barriers were falling right, left and centre. The special theory of relativity was only two years old. In architecture, Gropius was already working with Behrens, and Le Corbusier was exploring new design vocabularies with reinforced concrete. Schoenberg was composing atonally. Jung had met Freud. Braque had met Picasso, who had just exhibited *Les Demoiselles d'Avignon* – and both were among the crowds flocking to Issy-les-Moulineaux during 1908, along with Robert and Sonia Delaunay and other poets and artists in the van of the greatest cultural revolution the world had ever seen. For its revolutionaries, human flight had a potent symbolic value: for everyone else, it was soaring affirmation of the optimistic belief that whatever men can imagine, they can realise. After centuries of dreaming here was proof that the remaining element had at last surrendered to human ingenuity and endeavour. Aerial navigation opened up the prospect of hitherto undreamed of freedoms and perils. National frontiers were suddenly weaker; on that cold January day by the Seine, the whole planet shrank.

Above, the Voisin brothers carry Farman shoulder-high after the kilometre flight.

Left, Henry Kapférer looks on as Henri Deutsch de la Meurthe embraces Farman immediately after his epic Grand Prix flight, beside Santos-Dumont's ex-Jenatzy GP Mercédès; behind, a grinning Herbster holds the mounting steps. Note the newly-applied fabric over the main wing spars.

Within hours, the news had sped worldwide. They had, in HG Wells's words, "domesticated the impossible". Farman (and less so, Voisin) shot to instant global fame, his achievement trumpeted on the front page of broadsheets on every continent.

The Anglophone press of course appropriated Farman as one of their own. Jingoistic headlines abounded throughout the English-speaking world: 'Conquest Of The Air. A Successful Aeroplane. A British Invention' trumpeted the *Sydney Morning Herald*, noting that "So far this is the most solid machine of its type ever constructed, as is proved by the fact that in spite of scores of flights accomplished in every direction within the last six weeks, it is still in as good condition as on the first day, and all its parts are intact." If only they knew...

In the same vein, the *Brisbane Courier* shrilled: 'French Prize Won By A British Inventor'. Another scribe hurrahed, "What George Stephenson did for the locomotive, Farman has done for the aeroplane!" And under the headline 'Success of an Englishman', *The Times* hailed "an epoch-making day, that of the victory before official witnesses of human intelligence in its efforts to solve the problem which brought Icarus to grief, and which tormented the brain of Leonardo da Vinci."

(Farman himself had no doubt of his national allegiance. In a letter to the *London Gazette*, he wrote: "You would esteem me less should I deny the origins of my family, but having been brought up in France and studied there, my heart is truly French. If I have succeeded in drawing a little of the world's attention upon myself, it is in France that my efforts have been crowned with success - I consider myself a Frenchman in every acceptation of the word." Tellingly, he added: "Moreover, at the time of the international Gordon Bennett cup contest, England refused to be represented by me on the grounds that I was more French than English.")

The pilot's nationality, though, was irrelevant. The point is that from January 1908 onwards, the boxy outline of Voisin's cellular biplane became totemic, and entered the cultural discourse in everything from the covers of popular song sheets, children's pencil boxes, romantic postcards and other ephemera to the writings of Kafka and the painter Robert Delaunay's revolutionary experiments with colour.

Above left and centre, as co-sponsor of the Grand Prix, Ernest Archdeacon (in Astrakhan hat) congratulates Farman as Kapférer (in bowler) confirms his time. Next to the pilot, an excited Gabriel Voisin, already sensing that he will be written out of the history books, wonders what will happen next.

Immediately after the kilometre, the ever-phlegmatic Farman's reaction was typically understated: "I must admit I did feel a little excited, but at no time in the flight did I feel nervous in the least."

Top right, to the delight of the spectators outside the perimeter wall of the *champ de manœuvres,* the normally reticent Farman celebrates by treating himself to a toy dirigible.

Right, the Voisinistes celebrating after the Grand Prix victory, with Charles and Gabriel Voisin behind their two pilots, Farman and Delagrange.

Overnight, aviation had become serious - which is why, before the week of the kilometre victory was out, Gabriel Voisin had joined Blériot, Breguet, Esnault-Pelterie and a few others to found the first French aviation industry body, the Chambre Syndicale des Industries Aéronautiques, with the aim of projecting an industrial and commercial image for an activity hitherto considered a sporting pastime for wealthy dilettante.

The Aero Manual was in no doubt as to the true significance of Farman's kilometre flight: "It was an epoch-making day, for those sceptics who had previously maintained that aeroplanes were huge jumping machines, capable of making wild leaps in the air, but were incapable of a real flight, were silenced for ever. That circular flight of roughly one mile had proved to the world that the aeroplane was a practical machine."

The Wrights were dismissive. "The Farman machine uses nothing but dihedral angle for lateral control," *Scientific American* was told on January 16th. "Farman is reported to have said that some other method would probably be necessary. He is now face to face with new problems which others have only solved with new inventions which are of a patentable nature. Mr Farman has not yet found any solutions of these problems, much less one free from infringement."

Back home though, even the Wrights' domestic audience was beginning to lose faith in the face of the brothers' continuing refusal to demonstrate their machine's capabilities in public. As the *American Magazine of Aeronautics* opined: "Henry Farman has perhaps done more, through publicity, to brush away the cobwebs of doubt and ridicule than have the Wrights. [..] Even here, we doubt that the Wrights ever flew, while we read of the flights of Farman with less astonishment than at the cultivation of a seedless apple or the invention of a headacheless booze." James Means, US publisher of the *Aeronautical Annuals*, agreed: "We have to face the fact today that, owing to the public exhibitions of flights with motor-aeroplanes in France, the Frenchmen are in a fair way to get years ahead of us in aviation, as they did in the development of the automobile. However well we may have accomplished the task of catching up in automobile design and construction, we should be far from content with having such a task saddled upon us in the case of the motor-aeroplane."

Paradoxically, Farman's kilometre flight partially validated the Wrights' claims in France, insofar as he had proved that the feats they had described were indeed possible to achieve.

Buoyed by the Grand Prix success, Farman himself predicted the rapid development of aviation: "I'm certain that in a year's time, there will be aeroplanes able to travel 100 miles at an insignificant cost compared to the automobile for the same distance."

As to the methodical Farman himself, his initial reaction predictably focussed on the job in hand: "The only thing that worries me is the insecurity of the propeller," he pondered. "[The blades] turn at the tremendous rate of 1410 revolutions a minute. The other day one of my blades, six feet long, snapped while at full speed. Happily it happened to snap off downwards, so no harm was done, the blade burying itself three feet deep in the ground, thus showing the tremendous force of its projection. Supposing, however, it had broken off in an upward direction? What would have happened? One of my wings would have been smashed to pieces, and I should have come heavily to the ground. If one broke off horizontally instead of vertically, it would travel like a cannon shot for a short distance, and inevitably kill any living being on its trajectory. Every morning I have my propeller blades carefully polished, for after use they are pitted like a person with smallpox. The dust and the grains of sand and earth which the whizzing of the propeller raises up become embedded in the metal like so many small shot in wood. But we shall get over this difficulty – the new propellers in view are stronger than any we have yet tried."

These must have been variants on the inefficient rivetted aluminium Voisin device, because for the remaining 15 months of its active life, the aeroplane never sported one of Chauvière's new *Intégrale* laminated wood propellers being adopted by many others.

In a syndicated article entitled *The Art Of Flying – How I Learned It* (tellingly subtitled *An Inventor's Story*), Farman speculated a few days later that the desire to fly may be rooted in an ancestral evolutionary memory: "Since I have found out the way to rise and fly about in the air, the idea has impressed itself upon me very strongly that there exists in every human being a 'flying instinct'. It may be some special form of atavism. Perhaps in the prehistoric ages primitive man had wings. I do not pretend to know, but it is to my mind curious that man's idea of a supernatural being is an angel with wings."

He was certainly far more bullish about the prospects of heavier-then-air flight than his downcast prognosis of just a fortnight earlier: "Although I think aeroplanes are still in their infancy, and must for some time to come remain purely a sporting occupation, I can foresee the day when aeroplane omnibuses will travel from Paris to London in five hours," he remarked. "I myself cherish the hope of travelling in an aeroplane from Paris to Rouen in 60 minutes within the next two years."

Though taken months earlier, this syndicated photograph of Farman was reproduced on the front cover of *The Illustrated London News* and many other leading publications worldwide after the closed circuit kilometre.

"If, instead of the drill ground at Issy, I was able to fly over the plains of the Beauce, a flat treeless plain near Chartres, I think that even with my own primitive machine I could fly over 20 or 30 miles without difficulty. It is necessary, however, not to be hampered by houses or other obstacles, for if one of the wings or any other portion of the apparatus were to come into collision, however slightly, with a roof or a branch, the aeroplane would in all probability immediately overturn."

On January 16th, a banquet was held in the library of the Aéro-Club, with Farman at the high table beside the president, Louis Cailletet, Prince Roland Bonaparte and Baron de Zuylen, president of the Automobile Club. Esnault-Pelterie took a characteristically broad view. He described pioneer aviators as footsoldiers fighting under the same colours to subdue a common foe: the atmosphere itself. And Farman's feat, he declared, marked the surrender of the enemy's main defences.

After presenting the cheque and gold medal to Farman, Deutsch was understandably ebullient: "In a single bound, your feat has brought aeronautical theory into the world of living reality, transforming our timid and hesitant faith into absolute and invincible certainty.

"I pay tribute to your energy and tenacity, thanks to which aviation is no longer a vain aspiration: by unravelling its secrets, you have succeeded in paving the way for the incalculably fruitful consequences of the conquest of the air for the greater good of humanity. Not so long ago, I had the pleasure of congratulating the first ever world champion of dirigible ballooning (a reference to Santos-Dumont, who had in October 1901 won Deutsch's 100,000-franc prize for the first to fly over Paris), and today we celebrate the triumphant arrival of the aeroplane. Our victory is complete: we own the realms of both lighter- and heavier-than-air. We own the air, we are masters of space itself!

"Like me, gentlemen, do you not marvel at the astonishing pace of progress in the aeronautical sciences these last few years? One after the other, we have seen machines constructed more audacious than any that Jules Verne would have dared to imagine. I envy the young amongst you who will help to realise the vast and brilliant potential of aerial locomotion. Let your inspiration be Farman, who, far from resting on his laurels, went out the next day after his victory to better his superb performance of the day before!"

140

Farman had indeed made a 1.5km flight in the Voisin the next morning (presumably somewhat the worse for wear, judging from the snap of the elated Voisin quartet taken on the Monday evening), and after a day's rest, resumed testing on the day of the great banquet.

His immediate preoccupation was to determine the margin of weight the available power would allow. With 30 kilos of ballast, he could not take off at all; 20 kilos exhausted the Antoinette after a hop of only 200 metres, and Farman declared that the aeroplane 'possessed no life'. With 15 kilos, although the Voisin flew well enough in a straight line, it was caught by a light wind and proved only just controllable enough to make a sudden turn before it was blown towards the old city wall fortifications that marked the northern limit of the parade ground. When the ballast was removed altogether, take-off was easily accomplished in only 50 metres, and two kilometres flown in three minutes, with a perfect landing right in front of its hangar.

These tests confirmed what Farman already knew: his aeroplane was operating at the limit of its capabilities, and, until the advent of a lightweight engine reliably capable of delivering more power, it was difficult to see how this condition could be remedied other than by making small incremental improvements wherever possible. Revealingly though, in a paper entitled 'Systematic trials of a cellular aeroplane' which Farman penned soon after the kilometre for presentation to l'Académie des Sciences on January 20th, he declared weight to be a less important factor than air resistance, in that a heavier streamlined object was generally preferable to a lighter, unstreamlined one.

By now oil-stained and tatty after four and a half months of almost continual experimentation, the hardworking Voisin was dismantled and towed back over the river to Billancourt for a comprehensive refit in preparation for the eventful second chapter of its remarkable career. There were plans to ship it to England with Gabriel and Charles Voisin to compete for the *Daily Graphic* prize for the first one-mile flight, but its destiny lay elsewhere...

❖

1~bis

The large air-cooled Renault V8 briefly fitted to I⁻ᵇⁱˢ in March 1908, with geared rather than direct propeller drive. Note fan-assisted ducted cooling arrangements, aluminium mudguards, drilled pilot's seat and suspended fuel tank.

How much of the airframe of the kilometre machine was replaced is unknown. To reduce drag and improve lift, it was reclad in rubberized Continental fabric of the type Surcouf sold for dirigibles, smoother and stiffer than the uncoated material and impervious to atmospheric humidity. The inscription that Gabriel Voisin painted on the side panels of the tail now made it clear - more prominently this time, and below the client's name - that the machine had been 'designed and constructed by les Frères Voisin'. Aluminium bicycle mudguards with vestigial mud flaps were fitted to the main landing wheels, and even the pilot's bench was drilled to save weight. In this form the machine was renamed 'Henri [in lower case] FARMAN 1 -bis'.

While his Voisin was being refitted, Farman went to London on January 20th, scouting around the burgeoning aviation village at Brooklands in search of a suitable base from which to make an attempt on the £10,000 *Daily Mail* prize for the first to fly from London to Manchester in 24 hours.

The biggest change was to replace the Antoinette by a prototype of Renault's new 40HP V8. With twin fans forcing air into ducting around its finned cylinders, dry sump lubrication, magneto ignition and an automatic Renault carburettor, it was bulky – and some 50 per cent heavier than the Antoinette. Driving the prop at two thirds of crank speed, it also carried the extra weight of the reduction gear.

Manufacturers of engines and other components competed ferociously to climb aboard Farman's now world famous flying bandwagon. The *Chicago Record Herald* captured the frenetic atmosphere: "Everyone knows that the rivalries of motor manufacturers have caused the present deadlock. Why cannot the Count de la Vaulx get a sufficiently powerful A or B motor? How came Vuia to offer his money in vain to the only three companies claiming to make aeroplane motors? Now he is getting one of the latest C models, like De la Vaulx – after the C people gave up hoping to interest Farman. Why, they had agreed to pay a friend of Farman's 20,000 francs if he could persuade Farman to make a deal with them!

"'Why could not de la Vaulx get an A or B motor?' I asked. 'Because Farman would not allow it. He won the Archdeacon prize with the A motor – in spite of the royal offers from the Bs and Cs. Having honestly fulfilled his engagement with the As, he was free to accept a B motor. Now he has both, he keeps them fighting over him like Lucifer and Michael over the body of Moses."

Above, the few flights Farman made in 1 -bis with the Renault V8 at Issy were witnessed by the eminent Russian balloonist and founder of Petrograd's Central Aviation School for Officers, General Aleksandr Matveevich Kovanko, who was so impressed that he entered into negotiations with Voisin Frères to build several machines.

On observing the same flights, CS Rolls presciently remarked: "Great credit is due to Monsieur Voisin as the designer, but the chief difficulty of this type is that it will not stand side gusts. Its principal use in a few years will be military."

"Naturally, the As hope to retain the splendid advertisement. Naturally, Bs hope to wrest it from them, but they have not a really practical aeroplane motor yet, although they may have shortly. There's been lots of temptation to kill time. There are automobile motors and marine engines – even dirigible balloon engines. They all differ, according to the requirement. From the Parisian point of view, the true aeroplane engine is still being evolved, and jockeying and rivalry retard its evolution. They all want Farman. If they can't get Farman, they'll take Delagrange.'

"When Farman took delivery, the A engine was the only aeroplane-adapted one on the market in Paris. Moreover, Blériot of the Voisin firm, a rich young man, owned the bulk of the A stock. In strength and lightness, tested on land, the famous marque showed magnificently. Weighing less than three pounds per horsepower, it had neither flywheel nor carburetter, for the sake of lightness. Its carburation was delicate; and at vital steering moments Farman had to turn around to admit more or less air. In a flimsy aeroplane frame, the vibrating motor would twist a tube or pinch a joint, compromising the cooling; or a fuel tube would vibrate and impair the flow, bringing Farman promptly down to earth. Thus the engine that gave 50 horsepower in a test rig yielded, say, but 30 horsepower in the air, some days more, some less, and Farman struggled with that engine, while the A strove to improve it. Having committed to winning the Archdeacon prize with it, he finally succeeded on a very cold day, which prevented its habitual overheating. Meanwhile, the two other world-famed engine firms announced that their aeroplane units were almost ready. That is, orders for them could be taken. But the first order they wanted was Henri Farman's."

At any rate, the underdeveloped Renault unit proved a retrograde step. Although Gabriel Voisin transported 1^{-bis} across the Seine to its hangar on February 26th, two weeks passed before the new engine was ready for its first flight tests. Five ascents of no more than 600 metres were made on March 14th, including a partial turn; when the reduction gearing was dispensed with two days later, it blew apart.

Testing resumed with the rebuilt Antoinette unit, and the mudguards were discarded. With a new water tank, smaller in diameter and with an expansion chamber above, mounted above and parallel to the engine, Farman made several flights, including an impromptu race around the drill ground

Issy-les-Moulineaux, March 21ˢᵗ, 1908: Farman joins Delagrange in the cockpit of the latter's Voisin for a short flight across the parade ground. Note the wing-mounted fuel tank and the tall collector added to the condenser tank above the engine.

148

against a horse ridden by the music hall proprietor Gustave Zittel as a publicity stunt. Commendably unflappable as the impresario's nag must have been, the Voisin won.

Delagrange's discomfiture at seeing his rival win the Archdeacon prize stoked the rivalry between the two as they flew gradually increasing distances around the drill ground. The dapper sculptor had grown in both confidence and competence since January, and on March 17th, he challenged Farman to a contest – in effect, the world's first air race. Four days later, both Voisins were wheeled out in front of the Aéro Club posse..

"Another history-making day!" cried *The American Magazine of Aeronautics*. "Decidedly, aviation advances. In the dense fog the frail appearing aeroplanes looked like spectres. Lining the fortifications was a horde of Paris *gamins*. The weather was uninviting, but expectation was in the atmosphere. Everyone wanted to see Farman beat his record of the 13th January, and they wanted to see Delagrange win. After the two flags of the AéCF had been planted the 500 meters apart, the flyers emerged from the garages like two immense birds. After some preliminary flights in the fog, which prevented seeing the distant points, Farman started on his long flight. After rolling 50 meters, he left the ground at a height between 3 and 7 meters. At one of the poles were the officials of the club. Farman made two complete circuits of the course in 3 minutes 31 seconds for a distance calculated to be 2004.8 meters. Taking into account the turn, the real course must have been nearly 4 kilometers in that short space of time. Farman had thus tripled his own record. As soon as Farman's machine was put away, Delagrange started and made several creditable flights. At noon he described a superb loop, which measured 1500 meters, in two minutes. Delagrange had beaten his own record."

Then an extraordinary thing happened. Having been beaten by the maestro, Delagrange promptly invited Farman to insinuate himself into the space between his seat and the hot Antoinette, and the two flew some 50 metres (albeit at head height), to the delight of the crowds. Unless Delagrange's engine had more power, that he did so at all seems to gainsay Farman's assessment two months earlier of the Voisin's maximum payload. For whatever reason, Delagrange had by now mastered his machine to such an extent that he was beginning to fly further and faster than his bearded rival.

The horse and cart era meets the age of the aeroplane: in rue de la Ferme in May 1908, two curious neighbours look on as Gabriel Voisin (*centre, looking away*) and Maurice Colliex (*with hands on hips*) oversee Delagrange's machine being crated for its voyage to Italy.

On March 24th, with a newly enlarged rudder, Farman flew three kilometres, followed by a one-kilometre turn at 12m altitude the next day. On the 27th, however, his luck ran out. After an initial 45-second sortie, the lower left wing tip touched the ground as Farman attempted a turn in gusty conditions on his second flight, sending the nose groundwards and ejecting him three or four metres in front of the machine. Unconscious for almost two hours and sustaining minor injuries to his hands and face, Farman driven home for a few days' rest while 1⁻ᵇⁱˢ was towed back across the river to the cramped rue de la Ferme workshop for repairs. His recovery was certainly rapid, because on the following afternoon Gabriel and Charles Voisin took him to see a revival of Alfred Jarry's scandalously scatological avant garde farce, *Ubu Roi*.

A new 60HP Antoinette with a larger 110mm bore was fitted at the same time as the nose and wing repairs, which Farman tested at Issy on March 30th, including a brief hop with Gabriel Voisin aboard.

In April, Delagrange pushed even harder. He beat Farman's distance record with five circuits of the drill ground on the 11th - almost 10km, although only 3.9 kilometres was officially homologated, because of a momentary touchdown. Farman tried a new type of radiator on the 22nd, with which he expected to manage 20-minute flights, but it proved ineffective and was abandoned. The tail cell of 1⁻ᵇⁱˢ was further modified on the 30th, in preparation for both men's attempt on the 10,000-franc Armengaud prize for first in France to fly for more than 15 minutes.

A triangular course was marked out on the *champ de manoeuvres* under the auspices of Louis Armengaud himself, accompanied by an adjudication panel including Archdeacon, Chauvière and Captain Ferber. However, the changeable weather of Paris in the spring proved less biddable than the *commissaires*. Strong gusts precluded any flights at all before six, when engine problems forced Delagrange to abort his first attempt; within 45 minutes, Farman had done the same, frustrated as much by the thousands of spectators milling around as by the exacerbated the drill ground's inability to accommodate his machine's necessarily wide turning circle in any but perfect climatic conditions. Sensibly so as it turned out, because soon after seven, Delagrange's next attempt came to grief when his misfiring machine, subject to the same spatial constraints as Farman, clipped the roof of a fleeing taxi while trying desperately to find a space free of gawkers on which to make a forced

The much larger new Voisin works at 34, Quai du Point du Jour, Boulogne-Billancourt. Consisting of ten buildings around a spacious courtyard, the former sawmill was comprehensively equipped with a carpentry shop, a foundry, a forge, a fully equipped machine shop, a sewing department and a rudimentary wind tunnel. Gabriel and Charles Voisin occupied the house on the left, which also housed the drawing office.

152

landing. Voisin Delagrange No.II was reduced to matchwood; Delagrange was thrown out, but escaped with bruises. Both pilots concluded that the Issy site was simply too small.

Neverthess, Farman's optimism was by now boundless – enough to challenge the Wrights publicly to a $5000 contest of speed and duration. Disdainful as ever of anything that reeked of what he termed 'vaudeville', Orville denied receiving any such challenge, adding that in any case Farman was then only at the stage they had reached several years before, and that he would therefore have had "not the slightest fear in entering a race with him".

Remarking on the recent successes of Santos's little *Demoiselle*, Farman observed in March: "It can only be a few years before these small machines will be as numerous as motor cars. I know for a fact there are 20 on similar lines already in Paris. It will be possible to build simple flying machines for £100 each." Together with the enormous publicity surrounding the events of January 13th, such comments caught the popular imagination in a big way, and there was a huge international demand to witness the miracle of flight, like a novel circus act. Refreshment vendors, coconut shies and hawkers of toy aeroplanes did a roaring trade. Flying was the spectacle of the moment, although it was still so poorly understood that Farman received an offer from a London impresario to fly around inside one of his theatres! Farman, however, was more interested in crossing the Channel to consolidate his position as Europe's leading aviator. Reuters reported in March that he had been engaged to fly around the then new Brooklands track and compete for the £1000 prize offered by *The Graphic* to the first to fly one mile with a passenger.

Also in March, the Turin banker and amateur racing driver Dr Aldo Weill-Schott had approached Delagrange on behalf of the Italian aviation committee with an offer of 50,000 francs to make exhibition flights in Rome, Milan and Turin, and he set off in mid-May. But Delagrange was not the only one on the move. As the orders came flooding in to Les Frères Voisin, the company left the tiny rue de la Ferme workshop it had outgrown (by now, complete with rudimentary wind tunnel) and moved on May 11th to much larger premises nearby – a 3500m² former sawmill on the opposite bank of the Seine to the Issy parade ground, at 34, Quai du Point du Jour, Billancourt.

Despite the feverish atmosphere, the Voisins made no effort to conceal their activities. Quite the reverse; as *Aeronautics* commented about a visit to the new works, "In pleasant contrast to the impenetrable air of mystery which surrounds even the most trivial aeronautical project in this country, the whole works were thrown open for my inspection. I was allowed to see everything with the utmost readiness; every question was answered without reserve; every point explained with goodwill. Secrets there were none – nor do any exist in aeronautics – save clever and thorough workmanship and a rare degree of unselfish enthusiasm. This, surely, is the best way to success."

Gabriel Voisin was of course the first in the world to earn his living from aeroplanes, as the same reporter observed: "While America first showed the practicability of dynamic flight, it remained for France to make the flying machine a thing of commerce [...] one concern, Messrs Voisin Brothers, has a complete factory exclusively devoted to manufacturing aeronautical models, aeroplanes, airship frames, propellers, etc. During 1907 a dozen or more full-sized machines were made and sold."

While the move to the new premises was taking place, August de Breyne, a noted Belgian balloonist and ambitious president of the Aéro Club des Flandres, learned at a reception in Paris to honour France's most feted bird man that Farman also wished to move on. Issy was too small, and hardcore enthusiasts apart, the local appetite for seeing the novelty attraction had begun to diminish through familiarity. Farman had inspected a site in rural Vichy, which proved unsuitable, as had Brooklands. Time was of the essence. He knew that his advantage over competitors was slight, and that he should cash in on the big remaining prizes while he could.

For de Breyne, this admission presented an opportunity not to be missed. He told Farman that his own city of Ghent (Gent or Gand), the capital of Flanders, was ideal for hosting public exhibitions to a new and aviation-inclined audience. After all, had not the great Jean-Pierre Blanchard made his country's first manned balloon flights from there 125 years earlier? Furthermore, de Breyne promised to put the members of the Aéro Club at Farman's disposal for the duration.

After his disappointing negotiations in the UK, Farman demurred. The fee he demanded was hefty, as were the expenses, and his assent depended on personally verifying any proposed site. On May 11th, he was met at Gent-Sint-Pieters station by Albert Feyerick, a local industrialist and patron of fencing and golf as well as vice-president of the Aéro Club, and driven to the military training area at Plaine St Denis. Farman instantly rejected this location for its insufficient size and because the soft terrain would prevent the Voisin from reaching take-off velocity. Unfazed, Feyerick drove on to a second, far larger site – an area of some 150 hectares of reclaimed marshland in the Muide, a working class neighbourhood in the port area which was being prepared for an ambitious expansion of the city's docks. Bordered by the *canal périphérique*, the site of the *nouvelles installations maritimes* boasted a levelled two-kilometre stretch nearly 700m wide. With a little more levelling here and there and the removal of a few gas lamps and rail tracks, Farman pronounced it to be a suitable venue - closer to the town, and easily accessible by tram.

At the end of the week, Farman phoned de Breyne to accept his invitation. Financially, it was a good deal. There were 12,000 shiny gold francs to be won on a single bet, for a start. A few weeks earlier, at an ACF dinner on March 9th, a postprandially grandiloquent Fernand Charron had bet Farman, Archdeacon and Santos-Dumont this not inconsiderable sum that no passenger weighing 60 kilos or more would be taken aloft for at least a kilometre in the ensuing 12 months. (Farman knew Charron well, having successfully competed against him since their cycle racing days in the 1890s. Their rivalry had subsequently transferred to four wheels: although the industrialist had won the first Gordon Bennett race in 1900 on a Panhard, Farman had soundly trounced the Panhards of all three CGV founders in his little Darracq on the 1901 Paris-Berlin event.)

Farman knew the wager was winnable. Apart from his impromptu hop with Delagrange, he had, with 30 litres of water and 10 litres of fuel aboard two vertical panes on either side of nacelle, taken his father, Thomas, aloft for 200 metres at Issy on May 9th, as well as Gabriel Voisin in April. But he also knew that, given the Antoinette's fluctuating output and the possibility of bad weather, there was no guarantee of being able to take off from the bumpy terrain with the extra weight of a passenger. He nevertheless telegraphed an invitation to Archdeacon in Paris, by way of thanks for his unstinting support. And despite the limitations of 1[-bis], he announced his intention to go for the two 10,000-franc prizes: the Armengaud and the Coupe Michelin for the first 20-kilometre flight.

Above, one of the faltering initial flights made during a break in the atrocious weather that marred the first days of the event; *below,* soon after his arrival in Ghent, Farman inspected the newly reassembled I -bis in its spacious new hangar.

The event was a good deal for the burghers of Ghent, too. The Aéro Club had pulled off a great coup, and the city fathers seized the opportunity to aggrandise their town before a world audience. Farman's visit allowed them to create a whole new identity for the place. Formerly publicised as the *Ville des Fleurs,* Ghent was rebranded the *Ville des Sports* on the thousands of four-colour posters and tens of thousands of flyers hastily printed for distribution throughout Belgium and the frontier towns of neighbouring countries. A dedicated electric tram service was allocated to the site and special *Rapides pour l'Aéroplane* trains laid on, offering one-franc fares from anywhere in Belgium for the occasion. Similar services drew visitors from the big towns of northern France, where local tourist clubs organised group excursions to see man fly. A gold medal was struck to honour the heroic visitor at a grand welcome banquet. This was a big deal, as well as a good one.

"Witnessing the continent's first flight outside Paris is sure to fascinate the scientific world and all those remotely interested in progress in our century, and will attract many foreign visitors to our town," the mayor enthused. And at the behest of no less a personage than King Leopold himself, the great and the good put their hands in their pockets to finance the wholesale clean-up required to beautify the town for its proud municipal showcase event.

Farman made a second visit to finalise arrangements on Sunday May 17th, when the Flemish Aéro Club had organised a hot air balloon rally in the former zoological gardens. The following week, while the enormous crates containing the nacelle, main and tail cells of 1-bis were being hoisted onto three freight cars at the Gare de la Chapelle in Paris, work began on removing rails from the site. Preparations were in full swing. A stout fence was erected around the flying field and cartloads of soil imported to fill troughs and holes. A large, sturdy hangar was hastily erected to house the Voisin – measuring 23m x 8m and 7m high, it was far more spacious than its equivalent at Issy, to allow for paying visitors to inspect the machine. The hangar was guarded with dogs by night, and there was a strong police presence throughout. The Grand Garage Gantois even built a secure parking area for visiting *sportsmen*'s automobiles.

A seaside atmosphere began to emerge, with merry-go-rounds, waffle houses, coffee bars, a bodega, buffet restaurants and funfair amusements. A race was even planned between Farman's Voisin and

Under the watchful eye of the military, Farman puts a protective hand on the lower plane of I-bis as it emerges from its temporary hangar for the first time at Ghent in May. Note the extra expansion tank suspended above the engine.

a 50HP motor car. In the town centre, a large projector and screen were borrowed from the local circus proprietor to show a programme of short films of aviation experiments, with explanatory comments provided live by de Breyne himself, to educate the public about the new science. Hundreds attended the screenings every evening.

Via the press, the Aéro Club tried to manage public expectations as to the weather-dependency of flight and, aware the limited control at the pilot's disposal, issued stern injunctions as to the dangers of obstructing the flightpath in any way. In the interests of promoting awareness of aviation, the club also insisted on affordable ticket prices. They were nevertheless not cheap: at 5 Belgian francs, entry to *aérodrome* for the week would have cost the average craftsman a week's pay. Access to the hangar was one franc more. The elaborately printed passes required the punter to supply a signed passport photograph for incorporation into the ticket, for which purpose a booth was provided in the Excelsior Wine Club, where both the Automobile and Aéro Clubs des Flandres shared a clubhouse.

On May 23rd, the train bearing 1-bis, Herbster and two mechanics drew into Ghent Zuidstation, where it was unloaded into the bonded warehouse of the shipping agents financing the new dock. From there, they were transported to the newly levelled terrain to be unpacked. Farman boarded the express from Paris the next day to find the city plastered with posters announcing his arrival. After an obligatory welcome luncheon, he was driven to the hangar to oversee the final stages of the assembly of his Voisin (which the local press was already referring to as a Farman).

The event did not start auspiciously. So dreadful was the weather on Monday that the Aéro Club decided to postpone the opening ceremony by a day; instead, de Breyne explained the machine to local dignitaries in the hangar, while Farman demonstrated the controls. Conditions hardly improved on the Tuesday, Farman's 34th birthday. Nearly 2000 people trooped through the entrance gates from early morning onwards, but four hours passed before the Antoinette could be coaxed into running satisfactorily. Whenever it did eventually fire, not all cylinders obliged, even under full throttle with the ignition set at full advance.

Top left, the Ghent site was hardly obstacle-free. *Top right*, Farman surveys the 'aerial buoys' for the altitude attempt. *Above left*, the vast hangar, *right*, Farman applied to contest the Armengaud and Montefiore prizes on June 28th.

Torrential rain prevented any sorties until later in the afternoon, when Farman made a couple of taxi runs from the short stretch of planking laid over the sodden ground before managing one ascent of some 350 metres, despite the unpredictable wind. On the final attempt, the Voisin remained airborne for some 30 metres before being dashed groundwards, to be abruptly brought to a halt by the landing wheels sinking axle-deep into the soft terrain. Much panting and swearing ensued from helpers conscripted to help manhandle the machine back into its hangar. Fearful of any damage to their charge, Herbster and the crew returned thaat night to their hotel in low spirits.

In the interim, mindful of Farman's intention to carry the world's first aerial passenger but, unaware of his arrangement with Archdeacon, de Breyne publicly called for a lady to volunteer for the purpose, diplomatically specifying that she should be "light and not overly bulky."

Despite the relentless rain, the crowd on the Wednesday was even bigger, and included a delegation of Flemish politicians and municipal bigwigs. Farman made three short hops when the downpours momentarily abated during the morning; in the windswept afternoon, not even that. Despite the motley fairground attractions, a kite flying contest and the best efforts of the Aéro Club, the lack of spectacle was testing public patience; an ill-timed trip to the *pissoir* risked missing all the day had to offer in terms of aeroplaning. The press nickname 'Farceman' was in danger of sticking. To appease the malcontents, Farman made another attempt at 5 o'clock (by which time the entrance fee had been slashed to one franc). When the Antoinette barked reluctantly into life, the assistants holding back the big Voisin let go on Farman's order, and the machine left the ground after some 50 metres and rose three metres into the air before being forced down by high winds 250 metres later. Mollified rather than satisfied, most spectators had left by 7 o'clock. The few diehards who remained were rewarded an hour later, when calmer conditions prompted Farman to try again. This time, he flew the entire length of the site (1,650 metres) at an average 58 km/h. The Voisin was swiftly manhandled around, and Farman flew back - now, at a height of some 10 metres.

"Seen from the other side of the manoeuvre ground, it had the appearance of a huge crow, plunging forward on wings rigid and outstretched, skimming along above the ground before landing," the local newspaper reported. "Its speed did not seem very great, but appearances very deceptive, for the accompanying motorcar bearing the prize committee, though powerful, proved unable to keep pace."

162

Apart from the weather, cooling remained an intractable limiting factor. Wright was right. Gabriel Voisin reckoned that overheating robbed the V8 of as much as 40 per cent of its power after a few minutes. The coolant reached boiling point in less than five minutes from cold, and was consumed at the rate of half a litre every minute thereafter; at the end of 10 minutes, the unit risked imminent seizure. In a note to Alexander Graham Bell later that month, the distinguished Canadian engineer WR Turnbull wrote: "Farman told me that he did not use any radiator with his Antoinette, but simply carried a small quantity of water in the water-jackets and allowed this to boil away, thus his runs were necessarily short. He is not finishing his *Flying Fish (see page 239)* at present, simply because there is no really satisfactory engine on the French market; apparently all the French motors, particularly the air-cooled ones, give their rated horsepower only for about ten minutes, after which the horsepower rapidly falls off as the engine overheats."

At Ghent, Farman tried packing the expansion tank with ice just before take-off. "The conditions were most unfavourable," he complained later. "I had no oil tank and was forced to put an extra quantity into my motor; I was thus hampered, and then, too, it was not sparking well." Nevertheless, he managed two sorties across the flying field when the wind eventually abated in the evening of Thursday 28th.

The trouble was that the sudden violent gusts were interfering with the delicate fuel injection system. To shield the *mouches* from these squalls, Farman instructed Herbster to add vertical panes between the main planes on either side of the engine, with central cut-outs on the leading edge to allow some lateral visibility. (Antoinette engineers later sought to remedy this vulnerability to high winds by installing longer induction pipes, terminating in intake trumpets which curved towards the airstream, rather than vertical stacks.)

Archdeacon arrived from Paris the next morning; coincidentally, Wilbur Wright, still bearing the scars of his recent crash, landed in France the same day. Work on the Voisin began early with a thorough inspection of the engine, and continued all morning. Again and again, the magnetos were tested and the injectors meticulously cleaned. New batteries were installed, and the Moto Naptha petrol was laboriously filtered through leather once again to remove the tiniest impurity.

In these posed shots, Archdeacon (*below*) does his best to ignore what must have been the considerable discomfort of shoehorning himself into the cockpit beside Farman at Ghent. Neither wore jackets for the flight itself.

For the purposes of winning Charon's wager, the Antoinette's recalcitrance made the weight issue more crucial than ever. On the brief passenger flights three weeks earlier, Farman had carried "eight gallons of water for cooling the motor and 2.6 gallons of alcohol for fuel" according to an eyewitness report filed for *The Aerial Experiment Association Bulletin*. But at Ghent, Gabriel Voisin later calculated that the V8 was yielding less than 40 horsepower at 1100rpm; with the addition of Archdeacon increasing the total mass to 645 kilos, the power/weight margin was so slim that Farman replaced the 30-litre fuel tank with a tiny copper reservoir just big enough to power the brief flight. At the last moment, he also removed the radiator.

When the wind fell soon after 7 o'clock, Farman made a solo 500-metre test flight, followed by one of double the distance. A third followed with a sandbag beside the pilot, sustained over the 1,800m length of the aerodrome, with a wide turn assayed at the end. Two 130-metre trials with Archdeacon aboard were accomplished before dusk fell. Pressed by the *Journal de Gand* for his impressions, the ever-bullish Archdeacon replied: "The movement is so soft that one notices neither leaving the ground nor returning to it. One would search in vain for a more complete mode of transport."

They were as ready as they could be for the official attempt. Summoned by de Breyne, the official observers of the Aéro Club duly took up their stations to mark the flightpath with white pennants on the 30th, while the Voisin was positioned at the extremity of its makeshift runway. Nothing was left to chance. Before climbing up into the cockpit, Farman removed his jacket and waistcoat to save a few more precious grams and handed his wallet and cigarette case to Herbster; Archdeacon did the same before squeezing in beside him on the narrow spruce perch.

At Herbster's third swing of the uncomfortably thin-bladed Voisin propeller, the V8 stuttered into life, emitting puffs of white smoke until all eight cylinders were firing evenly. Advancing the ignition with one hand and opening the throttle with the other, Farman barked the order to let go and the Voisin began bumping along the uneven planks, its tail cell swinging perilously from side to side. The two occupants, cramped between the suspension uprights, were reported as looking tense until finally, just before the end of the impromptu boardwalk, the big biplane heaved itself to the air and remained aloft for exactly 1,241 metres, at an altitude of nearly seven metres.

Charron's wager was won, with the benefactor of European aviation becoming the third passenger to fly in a heavier-than-air machine, and the first officially observed. As Farman and Archdeacon dismounted, the crowd burst into wild cheers. But with the Antoinette running sweetly at long last, the elated Farman decided to attempt the official altitude record while he was at it, if only to reward the longsuffering spectators. He had arranged for a row of ten balloons on 10-metre tethers to be placed across the aerodrome earlier in the morning – the first time 'aerial buoys' had been deployed for the purpose. Flying solo, Farman cleared the bobbing gasbags by a comfortable two metres before gliding back to terra firma, although the Antoinette failed to deliver enough power to execute the turn for his planned return flight to the start point.

His altitude record was duly homologated (despite the vastly superior but unaccredited capabilities of the Wright), but when Farman wrote six weeks later to request official homologation of his 'first passenger' flight, the ACF replied that as no such category existed, he would have to be satisfied with a certificate attesting to his achievement. Nevertheless, the journalists present rushed to file their copy by telegraph; in the morning editions, 'the City of Sport' would make itself known on both sides of Atlantic.

The next day saw the arrival of more than 20,000 Sunday spectators, including many from France. Yet again, the unseasonal weather prevented any flights before early evening, when Farman made three kilometre-long sorties. More noteworthy was what followed – the world's first flight with a female passenger (an honour often mistakenly accorded to Delagrange, who flew with his partner Thérèse Peltier five weeks later). Of the volunteers who had responded to de Breyne's appeal for a suitable candidate, the Aéro Club chose Pauline, the waif-like 28 year-old daughter of the local parish mayor, Louis van Pottelsberghe de la Potterie.

Farman was obliged under the terms of his contract to fly on the final two days of the meeting, but he did so with little conviction. Exhausted, Herbster and the mechanics lolled around on the grass waiting for the proceedings to end, and the spectators knew they'd seen all there was to see. On the last evening, a coolant pipe burst, bringing the trials to a premature close; the Voisin was lugged back into its hangar for disassembly and reshipment to Paris.

For *L'Aérophile*, Farman's Ghent exploits represented the first step towards a viable 'aerial automobile', and the constructors of his mount were praised accordingly. Given that in Rome, while Farman was ferrying Archdeacon, Delagrange had flown 12 kilometres in a near-identical machine before the King and Queen of Italy (and 100,000 spectators), the journal concluded that it was no accident that only Voisin machines had so far captured aviation records. They were "the product of the science of flight, laboriously acquired and rigorously applied. There's no mystery or magic involved - just a relentless programme of improvement and tenacious fine-tuning. This is what has allowed [Voisin] to make the first safe, easily mastered aeroplane accessible to all *sportsmen*."

Quite apart from relieving Charron of a fat cheque, Ghent had proved profitable for Farman (although despite 20,000 paying spectators, the Aéro-Club des Flandres somehow contrived to make a loss). And the Aéro Club members had been so enthusiastic and helpful that he looked favourably on an offer from a group of Flemish entrepreneurs to undertake a public cross-country flight – another world first. He was driven on June 3rd to conclude arrangements for using a suitable stretch of beach from which to begin the 12-mile journey along the coast from Blankenberghe to Ostend. Officialdom soon intervened, however. Too dangerous by far.

Still searching for a suitable location, Farman went to Spa two days later, but the site was both too small and on a marked incline. Tired, he returned to France for a few days' rest. After ten solid months of 90-hour weeks (his wife said that her husband habitually left home at 10 and returned at 10, often later), it was well deserved. He did, however, make time to meet Wilbur on June 16th. Having written to request a meeting before the American returned to New York, Farman lunched with him in Paris at the *Bœuf à la Mode*. Unsurprisingly, they got on famously. By the following Saturday, Farman had taken the sleeper to Milan to see Léon Delagrange make his second round of exhibition flights in Italy before treating himself to a short break in Venice.

On his return to Paris in late June, Farman made attempts on the Montefiore prize for the first five-minute flight in Europe and the Armengaud, both of which he abandoned because the tail cell had been badly refitted after Ghent. Mindful of Delagrange's near miss with the taxi at Issy three months earlier and the near-riot in Rome, his Belgian escapade confirmed the need for a larger airfield than

Above, as in New York a month later, boards were hastily laid at Ghent to compensate for the soft, uneven ground. *Below,* a beaming de Breyne stands between Farman and Archdeacon after their triumphant flight on May 30th 1908.

the increasingly crowded drill ground at Issy. In any case, Prefect of Police Lepine had announced the temporary suspension of aviation activities on the *champ de manœuvres* from July 25th on the grounds that, with the number of flights now taking place, it was no longer possible to assure public safety.

Farman's new base was on a site that Herbster had found at Mourmelon le Grand near Châlons-sur-Marne, on the vast empty plain around the old 10,000-hectare Second Empire military base of Camp de Châlons, near Reims. Permission for the aeronauts to use the site was granted by the Minister of War, General Picquart, and Farman had a workshop and hangar built on private land at nearby Bouy in September. In *Collier's*, the historic site was described thus: "The delicate etched beauty of the French landscape gives way to something more savage, more arid and more rude: a wide, rolling, hard and bare plain which gives the nostalgia of the Texas prairies. Here, King Merovius and his Franks once hammered during the whole day the heads of the Huns to send them flying out of the Europe they had been ravaging, unwittingly preserving the idea now flying fully-fledged above the ground, where, beneath white wings, now and then grinning skulls are still found."

There was also the small matter of driving a works Panhard in the Grand Prix de l'ACF at Dieppe on July 7th to prepare for. A 25-kilometre road course was improvised for practice purposes around Mourmelon, on which Farman's Panhard proved much slower than Henri Cissac's identical car. All to no avail, as it turned out - Farman crossed the finishing line in last place, having taken more than two and a half hours longer than Lautenschlager's winning Mercédès to cover the 478 miles of the race. He never drove competitively again; by now, his ambition lay skywards. Indeed, back at Issy-les-Moulineaux the day before the Grand Prix, he packed the radiator of 1-bis with ice, as he had at Ghent, and in the presence of Armengaud, flew eleven consecutive circuits of the drill ground, stopping after 20 minutes at the insistence of Gabriel Voisin, who feared that the Antoinette must be in danger of seizing. No matter; Farman had wrested the distance and endurance records from Delagrange with a flight of 19.7 kilometres, thereby winning Armengaud's 10,000 francs.

His confidence newly bolstered, he then accepted an irresistible offer from the New World, in the form of an invitation from a consortium of US businessmen from St. Louis. The terms negotiated

July 26th 1908: looking uncannily like a tall Wilbur Wright, Holland Forbes (*left*) and fellow balloonist Augustus Post (*right*), a founding member of the Aero Club of America, accompany Farman aboard the tugboat *Morane*, which the US aeronauts had chartered to ferry him to the pier after the transatlantic crossing. Other members of the welcoming party included the telephone and automobile pioneer Charles Glidden and the eminent naval architect Simon Lake.

in Paris by Frank Lahm seemed attractive: for touring America for 90 days with 1^{-bis}, starting with demonstrations in New York in the first two weeks of August, Farman would get a $24,600 lump sum, with $800 to cover shipping and $200 for each flight, plus expenses. The contract was drawn up by Tom McMechan, editor of *The American Aeronaut*, who formed a syndicate, The Aeroplane Company of New York, to manage the tour. As was the case at Ghent, much was expected: "These public demonstrations ought to bring about a great popular realization of the practicability of dynamic flight and bring capital into the industry," enthused *Aeronautics*.

Knowing that Glen Curtiss had flown his *June Bug* 1.5 miles to win the $25,000 *Scientific American* Cup for the first public demonstration of powered flight in America on the 4th of July (the Wrights having refused the invitation), Farman gave instructions for 1^{-bis}, still in its final Ghent iteration, to be prepared for shipment to New York on the SS *Kroonland* from Antwerp. (The second machine mentioned in some reports was almost certainly the part-built Henri Farman N°2, for spares.) At 14 metres, the largest of the three heavily padded crates was too big for the hold, so permission was urgently sought from JP Morgan, who owned the Red Star Line, to carry it on deck. The precious cargo was duly loaded on trailers and towed to the Gare du Nord for shipping to Antwerp by rail. Herbster, who oversaw its loading, sailed with Alphonse Ploquin and three other mechanics (plus two carpenters, according to some), reaching New York on July 27th - the day after Farman himself, who arrived from Le Havre, with $400 in his wallet to cover immediate expenses, aboard the *Touraine* (coincidentally, the vessel which had brought Wilbur over to France two months earlier).

The Americans greeted their guest with characteristically generous razzmatazz. Headed by the newly victorious Curtiss, the welcoming committee of the Aero Club of America sailed out to meet the liner on a tug chartered for the occasion and escorted Farman and his wife back to the French Line pier, where a brass band provided a suitably rousing welcome and a convoy of a dozen automobiles waited to whisk the distinguished visitor to the new Hotel Astor on Times Square.

Farman's arrival had generated much excitement. Senior US Army and Navy officers were reported to be greatly interested in witnessing his demonstration flights, and with US government tests of the Wright and Herring machines due at Fort Myer in a few weeks, an international aerial contest

The nacelle and tail cell of Farman's Voisin in its makeshift hangar beside the Brighton Beach track, with three of the 25 hands hired to work under Herbster to help unpack and assemble the machine. The ambitious itinerary initially reported for Farman's tour included Philadelphia, Cincinnati, St Louis, Kansas City, Denver, Salt Lake City and San Francisco, and thence to Japan, but it was not to be. In his public pronouncements, Farman gave little credit to Voisin. "My machine is a combination of the ideas of other inventors, including Langley and Delagrange," he declared, conceding only that "It was modelled under my supervision by the Voisin brothers."

seemed on the cards. While still in mid-Atlantic, Farman had cabled a wireless message repeating his challenge to the Wrights to enter a public flying contest for a $10,000 purse; he received a curt cable by return declining the challenge. Orville Wright and Augustus Herring had made no secret of their objections to Farman bringing a flying machine inferior to their own to the US. When asked for his reaction, the Frenchman's reply was judicious: "I have met William [*sic*] Wright, and I think the Wright brothers know a great deal about the subject on which they are so successfully working. [..] Maybe my machine *is* inferior to theirs. This is just what I want to find out. If they consider their machines superior, why don't they accept my challenge? I'm sure I could gain much valuable data from a contest with the Wrights and Herring, and surely my machine, with its long list of record flights, has at least some points of information for my brother aviators."

Curtiss and other members of Alexander Graham Bell's Aeronautical Experiment Association had also wanted to take part with their *June Bug* until Bell vetoed the idea on the grounds that engaging in commercial rather than scientific activity would make them vulnerable to the litigious brothers from Dayton, so no such contest transpired. When challenged by a reporter that his wager would contravene New York's gambling regulations, Farman simply replied: "like a quarrel, it takes two to make a bet, and as yet no one has accepted my challenge."

The chosen venue was the horse racing track at Brighton Beach on Coney Island - a modish resort peninsula at the southern tip of Brooklyn before the days of mass transit. A parallelogram-shaped site, complete with large grandstands, the track had the previous year been converted into a motor racing circuit for the first of the gruelling 24-hour endurance races known as 'Grinds'. Farman arranged to have eight 20-metre sections of the infield fence removed to accommodate changes in the direction of the prevailing wind for take-off purposes.

Transporting 1^{-bis} to the venue was far from straightforward, as the *Brooklyn Daily Eagle* noted. "In theory, it should be the easiest job to take a flying machine from a steamship dock to Coney Island. If airships can fly, then why can't they fly when badly needed, instead of requiring derricks and longshoremen to budge them? Practically, the job of moving an aeroplane down to Brighton Beach is almost as difficult as moving a small house."

It took hours. At high tide, the upper deck of the *Kroonland* was too close to the roof of the dock for the main two-tonne crate to be hoisted into the pier house by the enormous derrick specially erected for the purpose, so they had to wait for the tide to fall before unloading could begin. Eventually, the big crates were driven to the track on the morning of July 29th on articulated trucks normally used for transporting theatrical scenery, and unloaded in the old betting ring, where it was hidden from view by a wall of heavy canvas. The delay caused further problems, because in the absence of a Customs officer to cut the seals and examine the contents (even though it had been imported free of duty, as a scientific instrument for educational purposes), the gang of stevedores hired to unload the machine had to be turned away. When the revenue men did eventually arrive, Farman and Herbster had to recruit a motley crew of unskilled locals on the spot. "We are being hampered by official officialdom!" protested McMechan. The crates were unloaded for inspection by means of a primitive arrangement of improvised skids and rollers.

After removing the Antoinette from its crate, the appraiser declared it to be the finest piece of machinery he had ever seen. According to press reports, "All who examined the machine were greatly impressed with its workmanship, which is exquisite, from the stitching of the canvas planes to the finish of the metal parts." The rudder, however, was damaged when the third crate was unceremoniously dropped off the truck, where it remained until the next day. This was spent repairing the damage, supervising reassembly and installing the V8.

The cream of US aeronautics attended a banquet at the Astor to welcome Farman the following evening: "The ballroom was full of balloonites, with here and there a submarine fiend, an auto crank or a common scientist wedged in among the number," joked one report. Samuel Langley's former engineer and test pilot Charles Manly congratulated France on the *esprit de corps* of her experimenters and described Farman as having "the energy of an Englishman, the equilibrium of a Scotchman and the speed and daring of a Frenchman - a man destined to do great good for aeronautics and create enthusiasm among millions of people." Farman's reply was at first equally diplomatic: "We foreigners owe credit to Octave Chanute for the basic principles of our apparatus," he reassured them, adding: "We also owe much to the Wright brothers, pioneers after Mr Chanute."

The guests were then treated by the chef of the Astor to a lavish but hilariously inaccurate scale model of 1^{-bis} confected entirely from spun sugar. Less sweet was the speech that followed. In a barely veiled dig at the Wrights' secrecy, Farman went on to proclaim: "I carry on my experiments in public because that seems advantageous to me. The work is difficult enough anyway, and it is better for others to see what you are doing and for you to see what they are doing, each improving by the mistakes of the other, and each reasoning out other plans on which to experiment."

Even on their home turf, Farman was by no means alone in resenting the covert nature of the Wrights' researches. "We are disgusted with the conduct of some American inventors who have been hard at work chasing the almighty dollar instead of solving the problems of heavier-than-air flight," railed McMechan. By impeding the free exchange of ideas, he argued, their secrecy was a disservice to progress in general and to American interests in particular, and that they should therefore forfeit the right to be remembered for making the world's first flight. Consequently, he added: "We think that after Mr Farman's flight, not only will inventors get to work on the problem but there will be no difficulty raising capital to finance the cost of building aeroplanes and conducting experiments."

First, though, the flights had to be made. The ground was no more suitable than it had been at Ghent, being traversed by innumerable ruts and small ditches, so a similar stretch of planking was laid. At only 840 yards from end to end, the site was also too small. More ominously, the syndicate members were less than forthcoming when it came to handing over the first $6000 payment to Farman. At the last minute, the track's owner William Engeman was induced to part with a fat roll of Benjamins so the show could go on.

Apart from these financial wobbles and the inadequate size of the track, cooling remained Farman's main preoccupation. Although fitting the Antoinette with larger cylinders put five more horses at his disposal than at Ghent, there was still not enough power to overcome the weight penalty of a radiator. "If we could carry sufficient water to keep the engine cool," he said, "We could stay in the air 30 hours as easily as 30 minutes." (Apart, presumably, from the small matter of fuel.) Wind was his second concern: "After the machine itself, the greatest difficulty to overcome is the question of air gusts. To make good flights, a steady, strong wind is what you want – but if the wind becomes too strong, great care is needed in manipulating the machine. Another difficulty is the presence of trees, houses and other obstacles which divert the wind from its course. At Ghent, the wind is steady and little interfered with by obstacles, while at Issy there are hills and houses to bother one. I generally fly 15 feet above the ground, so these things interfere. I can fly higher, but have never made a flight as high as your skyscrapers, as you call them, although I hope to some day."

Such comments reveal Farman's characteristic reliance on calculated risk-taking tempered by great caution. While his Voisin was being rebuilt as 1^{-bis} back in February, he had confided to the *Daily Tribune*: "I am a *casse-cou* if you like, but at bottom I am the soul of prudence. When I risk my neck, which of course every man who mounts an aeroplane is bound to do, I at least have the certainty that I have left nothing undone to make my apparatus as perfect as possible. I take no unnecessary risks in the way of height – I could, if I wanted, soar off into the air to any height I please if my motor would work long enough. I could clear the Eiffel Tower, but at the present stage it would be folly to ascend a yard higher than is necessary, for the aeroplane is at present a very delicate machine and something may snap at any moment. You remember how Blériot's aeroplane simply doubled up when in full flight? The aeroplane is not like a parachute. If anything happened to disturb its equilibrium, it would shoot to the ground like a flash."

Besides, at an event for paying spectators, Farman preferred not to fly high enough to be visible from outside the track. He managed public expectations accordingly: "I want to emphasise to the people of this country that an aeroplane does not fly over the rooftops like a balloon; I hope they will not be disappointed to find that they can view airships without craning their necks."

It was with this measured attitude that late in the afternoon of July 31ˢᵗ, before the first scheduled public show, Farman gave a private demonstration for members of the Aero Club. According to the *New York Times*, "Several hundred persons were near the curtained-off part of the betting ring in which the machine is kept when it was pushed out on the brick pavement and turned around. Then those who watched got some idea of the driving power of the propeller. A mechanician turned the motor over by twisting about the propeller blades, then while five men held the aeroplane, Mr Farman advanced the spark and opened the throttle. The whirling propeller blades shook the shrubbery 60 feet

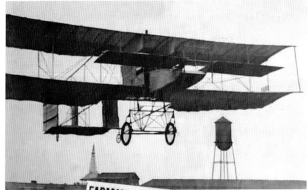

away as in a windstorm, while dust clouds were blown up 75 feet away. The crowd was kept back as the aeroplane was rolled out at the western end of the oval. While Mr Farman and his mechanicians were preparing their machine, Charles K Hamilton arrived in his dirigible to witness Farman's flight.

(Hamilton was then a more famous aeronaut than the Wrights, let alone Farman. With Israel Ludlow, he had since 1905 conducted experiments towing manned kites and gliders behind powerful automobiles, and suffered severe injuries in the process. Notwithstanding, the idea of powered flight had generally attracted more ridicule than anticipation in the US ever since the Board of Ordnance and Fortification had watched its $50,000 investment in Samuel Langley's machine sink into the Potomac in 1903. Beyond a small coterie of cranks, automobilists and teenage boys, nobody much cared any more.)

"No sooner had Hamilton landed than the propeller of Farman's machine began to revolve swiftly, and the machine moved across the turf for 200 yards when a shout came from the crowd," continued the *New York Times*. "The machine left the ground, mounted ten or twelve feet in the air and moved along swiftly, with an easy, bird-like glide. Two-thirds of the way to the eastern extremity of the oval, a group of men with a wagonload of boards were busy covering a ditch. A small calf ran about and the crowd infringed. As he bore down on these obstructions, Mr Farman stopped his propeller for a moment, while the guiding planes were inclined downward. As the aeroplane neared the turf, Mr Farman let his propeller shoot around for a moment. This made the landing as gentle as that of any creature of the air. It was a delicate piece of airmanship, and the crowd cheered."

The press found Farman to be no more loquacious than the Wrights, however. Elbowing his way to meet the 'human bird' in the ensuing throng, the *Brooklyn Daily Eagle* correspondent found a less imposing character than expected: "Farman was the most insignificant man in the room – a modest, retiring fellow of not more than five feet six, slender as a reed, with the most pleasing twinkle in his steel gray eyes. He looks something like the Czar of all the Russias, his face covered by a yellowish brown Van Dyck beard. It was mighty hard work to get the Frenchman to say anything."

Farman's subsequent public flights were less successful. A northwest breeze gusting up to 22mph prevented the ascent planned for the next day, as official stopwatches timed the little blue weather

Above, the popular Irish-born racer Joe Tracy towing 1-bis onto the infield at Brighton Beach at the wheel of his Peerless. His bid to buy Farman's Voisin was not the first time he had been instrumental in importing the latest European technology to America; a talented self-taught steam engineer, he joined Locomobile in 1906, in which capacity he had the previous year prepared a confidential report on the innovations at the Paris Salon for the US Automobile Manufacturers' Association.

Left, the inadequate size of the Brighton Beach track for the purposes of Farman's flight demonstrations is evident from this 1910 shot, by which time the oval was used for automobile racing rather than equestrian events.

180

balloons zigzagging their way across the leaden sky, followed by red and blue ones. The Voisin was wheeled out and paraded in front of the grandstands, to an accompanying explanation of its workings. After being repeatedly warned to hold onto their hats, the crowd watched as Farman mounted and started the engine, with six men holding it back. When the Antoinette fired, "there was a terrific blast of air straight backwards towards the hundreds of persons behind. Instantly a cloud of straw hats went hurtling into the air, high into the roof of the grandstand. The blast cleared a path as clean as that of a cyclone. Fifty people were blown off their feet."

Amusing as this may have been, it was not what the 8,000-strong Saturday crowd had paid to see, and they dispersed ill-temperedly at seven o'clock when Farman announced the postponement by megaphone in his thick French accent from the centre of the ring. Commenting on "the spanking sea breezes that met the conservative foreigner", the next day's *New York Times* acidly described Farman as "walking through the clover at the Brighton Beach infield to see if the wind was strong enough to justify his determination not to fly."

Events then took a turn for the worse; for Farman, the day of rest turned out to be no such thing. No preparations had been made for a Sunday demonstration, so no police or other officials were on hand - only Israel Ludlow (paralysed from his crash at Ormond Beach two years earlier) came with Frank Lahm in the morning to inspect the Voisin from his wheelchair. But despite the Manhattan weather bureau's forecast of continuing gusts, conditions were perfect: sunny and calm. While Farman was in his makeshift hangar fettling 1[-bis], several hundred of the previous day's disappointed visitors made their way to the main gates to the track. McMechan went out to try and pacify the sullen throng by assuring them that the Saturday tickets would be valid for future flights, but to no avail – his words were soon drowned by a chorus of yelled threats as the crowd started pressing against the gates. Worse still, the notorious Coney Island mosquitoes were out in force.

When news of the disturbance reached the hapless Farman, he realised that something had to be done to prevent the situation from becoming even uglier. "These people are right – I don't blame them," he said. "They paid their money to see me fly - many of them probably working people who cannot get here any other day. Tell McMechan I'll fly! Tell him to let them in. Hurry!"

Herbster (*left*) oversees the nacelle of Farman's Voisin being hastily crated up behind its hangar at Brighton Beach, ready to be rushed away to the docks before it could be impounded at the ignominious end of its ill-fated sortie to the New World.

To an objection that there were no police to control the crowd, he replied "I don't care – I don't want the police. I have seen enough of the American people to satisfy me they don't need police if you give them a fair show." Minutes later, the crowd surged as one through the gates, raced across the infield and surrounded the temporary hangar so tightly that it became impossible to roll out the Voisin. According the *Herald*, "Farman, with his new-found confidence in American intelligence and fairness, took matters into his own hands. Ordering the canvas doors to be drawn back, he climbed on the machine and shouted at the crowd to stand back. They cheered in a half-hearted skeptical way, but fell back and quietly followed the aeroplane as it was rolled out onto the meadow."

Veteran announcer Johnny Lunn mounted the fence and bade everybody be patient. A few hooted, but most obeyed. The wind that had swept over the field on Saturday had died down and the merest breeze floated in from the west, with scarcely enough energy to lift the flags on the housetops. The free show was about to begin.

"Finally there came a clattering sound from the aeroplane, and a cloud of dust could be seen leaping into the air," wrote the *Herald*'s excited correspondent. "The propeller flashed faster and faster, then the great machine was seen to dart forward, rolling rapidly over the ground. 200 feet from the start point, it leaped into the air, rose to a height of some 25 feet and came whirring over the field with the speed of an express train. At the end the flight the motor was stopped, the slant downward begun, the motor started again for a few revolutions to lessen the shock of landing, the machine rolled along the ground for about 100 feet. (This was Farman's standard landing technique: 'I have found that in order to effect a satisfactory landing it is better to cut off the ignition when in the air and glide down instead of coming to ground with the propeller revolving at full speed.') "For a second or two the crowd was silent before the throng in the grandstand stood and cheered," the *Herald* continued. "But it was all over in less than a minute. Before slow wits had time to take in what was really happening, the aeroplane had sped across the field from end to end and was again gracefully rolling across the greensward. Then it was that the crowd dashed across the field to tell Farman that he was not a fake after all, but that he was the real thing. Farman took it all very coolly and begged the men not to hurt the machine."

Unlike the Paris crowds, the New Yorkers who packed the stands to see Farman had little idea of what to expect from such a spectacle, and nothing against which to compare it. As Mme Farman (above) complained to the New York *Sun*: "The people are not ready for such an advanced idea. They would rather witness a race between two donkeys than see Farman fly. The machine is too technical for them to grasp its meaning and Farman flew so easily that they thought it didn't mean much. He would have drawn more crowds if he had made several ineffectual attempts to sail and broken the machine a little – just enough to give an idea that it was dangerous. In France it is different. Over there, flights have been public and no one has to pay, I have seen as many as 30,000 present at a flight. We are compelled to ask newspapers not to mention the flights in order to keep away the crowds." The editor agreed: "Farman's work seems almost too businesslike. At least he might make the machine wobble a little and dip dangerously to remind us that he really is flying and not running an automobile on some invisible aerial road."

"'I'll fly every day when the weather and winds are right,' he told them. 'And I won't fly if they are not. Aeroplanes are babies yet – in the creeping stage – and you must be patient with them.' The singular part of yesterday's demonstration was that many of the men who were yelling themselves into a state of perspiration over Farman's achievement were only five minutes before denouncing him equally vociferously as a fraud and endeavouring to excite the more unruly elements of the assembled company to demand their money back or 'have fun' with his machine…"

Described as looking like "a pair of lemonade booths that had taken to the air", and complete with four small Stars and Stripes fluttering from the tail and main planes, the Voisin had nevertheless flown. But the trip seemed doomed. Farman told a reporter that in the event of his leaving the country early, he would be willing to sell the Voisin for $6,000 plus duty – he even suggested that the US government might be willing to take it off his hands to take part in the forthcoming Fort Myer trials. The Vanderbilt Cup-winning racing motorist Joseph Tracy made an offer, which Farman turned down.

Matters didn't improve. Curtiss wrote on August 5th: "Farman's attempts were very disappointing indeed. The first day he flew 140 yards at an elevation of three feet in 11 seconds, at a velocity of about 20mph. He made two such flights and then wheeled the machine back to the tent. Next day there were about 3,000 persons attending and as it was too windy he did not attempt to fly at all. They were given 'wind checks' and told to come again the next day." On Thursday and Friday, rainstorms precluded any further flights, and only three were made on the Saturday and Sunday; attendance was down to fewer than 500 people. By then, the punters were showing more interest in the amateur motorcycle races thrown in at the last minute as an added attraction.

If nothing else, the disappointing Long Island escapade showed that making money from flying was no easier than flight itself. The combination of inadequate spectacle, misleading advertising, poor organisation and critical press coverage brought the Aeroplane Company of New York to its knees. No sooner had it collapsed than Joe Kowski, the contractor who had erected the temporary hangar, attached the machine for a debt of $120. Farman promptly sent him $50, and acting on a tip that other creditors would soon follow suit, bade McMechan hire a fast car, some trucks and a local gang. By the early hours of Friday morning, 1-bis had been clandestinely dismantled, repacked into its crate and hustled off to the Manhattan Custom House ready for when it opened, and then loaded safely aboard the Cherbourg-bound freighter *Hudson* on West 22nd St pier.

With the Voisin out of harm's way, Farman accepted an invitation from Thomas Edison to visit the 'play shop' at the great man's New Jersey laboratory. There, "after discussing many scientific curiosities", the lights were dimmed and 1-bis flickered jerkily onto the screen, in its hangar and then aloft (a film advertised for public screening in that month's *Variety* magazine). Movie stardom notwithstanding, Farman had still only received $7500 of his promised remuneration, and nothing for his expenses. His wife, "on the verge of nervous prostration", was not best pleased: "I didn't suppose that a country existed with so much trickery, selfishness and cowardliness as we have found here. The treatment accorded to my husband has been outrageous," she said. "Mr Farman did not ask to come, but yielded to the solicitations of men who promised him a lucrative engagement. In every respect, he kept his word, but as soon as hard luck came, those to whom he had a right to look for assistance deserted him."

Hinting that Farman's obstinate self-sufficiency verged on arrogance, the *New York Times* riposted: "Mr Farman failed to use letters of introduction he had to men who certainly would not have tried to exploit him, and that some of the men who knew he had these letters repeatedly made proffers of courtesies, only to have them ignored. The indications are that Mr Farman is a bit 'difficult' and a bit overconfident of his ability to steer his way unaided among strangers." Commenting on what it described as 'a bad business', the editorial of August 17th concluded that it was a case of *caveat aviator*. "Mr Farman's course seems to have been correct in every particular except one: he did not exercise wise caution in the selection of his managers, nor did he adequately safeguard his own interests. Inventors are notoriously incompetent in business matters, and it is not only in the United States that their bright hopes of fortune fail to materialize. [..] He should not judge us too harshly."

Aeronautics took a different view: "If the grounds had been large enough to allow long circular flights, and the first flight had been successful, people would no doubt have been anxious to see the flights," intoned the editorial, "But with a straight flight of only a few hundred feet possible, people thought they had not seen enough for their money. We realize that a flight of any length is yet wonderful but the general public wants to see a spectacle, which a short straight flight is not. [..] Mr Farman certainly fulfilled his side of the agreement as far as the limits of the ground permitted and must be of the opinion that interest in aeronautics on this side of the pond is really less than he anticipated."

Farman was equally pragmatic. "I said to myself before I came to America that I was not sure that the people were ready for such an exhibition of mechanical flight in the restricted area that seems a necessary adjunct to the charging of an admission," he told the *New York Times,* adding: "If for no other reason than that the newspapers here have treated me with such marked kindness, I am glad the trip was made."

Later, after a meeting with his lawyer, he was more realistic – but at what must have been a difficult time, his optimism remained: "I shouldn't have made the journey now. There are most important things abroad which I left unfinished to come here. I'm working on my new aeroplane, which will be only about a half the size of my present machine, but which I believe will fly at least 50% faster."

Disillusioned, the Farmans headed back to France aboard the *New York* on August 15th, with the Voisin following on the freighter *Hudson.* (Farman's Long Beach flights with 1-bis were commemorated thirty years later by the social realist painter Alois Fabry with a huge egg tempera diptych called *Brooklyn Past and Present* in the central rotunda of Brooklyn Borough Hall. Perhaps appropriately, the mural was destroyed in the McCarthy era for being un-American.)

The ill-fated New York adventure prevented Farman from witnessing the triumphant vindication of the Wright Type A at Les Hunaudières hippodrome, five miles south of Le Mans, on August 10th. It was Léon Bollée who suggested Le Mans for the demonstrations because of its ease of access by rail from Paris. Permission to use the military encampment at Auvours was initially denied on the grounds that it was being used for troop manoeuvres, so the horse racing track provided an obvious, if more public, substitute. Having approved the site before Farman's departure on June 18th, Wilbur had the crates containing the Model A (badly damaged in transit) sent from Le Havre to the Bollée works, along with one of engines built in Neuilly to their spec by precision instrument manufacturers Barriquand & Marre over the winter.

Above, the Wright shows its graceful paces at Auvours. Its astonishing eagerness to turn ("heeling over as suddenly as a bicycle on a banked track") was in stark contrast to the French machines, and prompted collective gasps from the crowd. There was talk of a turning radius of no more than 40 metres.

Right, Wilbur listens to the banker Lazare Weiller, for whom his aeroplane "presaged the ruin of the world's navies." Under the terms of the contract they had signed with Weiller five months earlier, on 27th March, the brothers stood to earn 500,000 francs from the flights at Le Mans.

After seven weeks of remedial work (hampered by a bad scald occasioned by a ruptured radiator tube early in July), Wilbur took the Model A to the racetrack for final preparations on August 4th. Its first flight six days later came like a bombshell to all who witnessed it. As the counterweight fell on the launch derrick, instead of describing a low, gradual trajectory over the long grass as expected, the machine leapt into the air, banked steeply to effect a 90-degree turn and headed promptly for the grandstand at the far end of the track and executing a couple of tight, graceful laps with effortless aplomb before setting the machine down to land again beside the pylon.

Even for the Wright partisans, it was an astonishing display; for the brothers' detractors, the effect was damascene. Eyes filled with tears of incredulity and awe. The spectacle that left Blériot, Kapférer and Delagrange speechless, and triggered what can only be described as a bout of Wrightmania in European aviation circles; in the public prints, it was hailed as "one of the most exciting spectacles in the history of applied science."

The next day's *New York Times* subhead summed up the difference: 'Under Perfect Control. Wilbur veritably jumped into the air rather than bouncing along, grasping for it like the French machines.' The London *Times* agreed: "At the first bound, obedient to the handling of its pilot, the aeroplane rose, stable, harmonious, and superb, and rising to some 80 or 40 feet twice without a hitch, glided round the Hippodrome, finally alighting gently with the ease and grace of a wood pigeon some 50 feet from the point of its departure. The enthusiasm was indescribable. Those present received Mr Wright, who had just won for his brother and himself the title of the real creators of aeroplanes, with the most extraordinary enthusiasm."

Surprisingly, even the Wright's lack of landing gear was described as an advantage: "It is incontestable that the skis on which the Wright aeroplane is mounted enable it to descend on rough ground which would wreck the wheels and framework of a French machine," but conceding that: "If the French aeroplane found moderately smooth ground to alight on, it could take flight unaided, whereas to reascend into the air the Wright machine would require the rail, the little car and the catapult, which would have to be brought to it, or to which it would have to be conveyed."

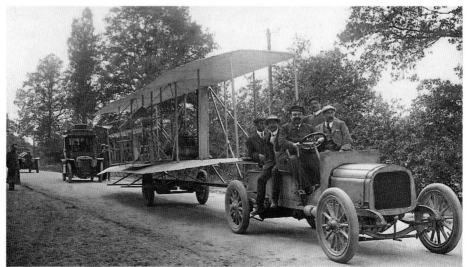

Above, the Wright's main planes newly assembled in the Bollée factory in August 1908, and (*right*) being towed to Auvours behind a beaming Léon Bollée at the wheel of one of his latest models. As Wilbur's first and most trusted French friend, Bollée had made a balloon ascent with him in July 1907, and admired the American's diligence, manual skills and modest self-sufficiency.

Surcouf (by now building a staggered wing monoplane for Kapférer) declared the Wright to be "a long way ahead of the French machines." Esnault Pelterie disagreed, avowing that he had not altered his long-held opinion that the Wrights were but wonderful acrobats. He shared Voisin's view that the inferiority of the American machine to French aeroplanes was self-evident not only in its construction but in its conception and stability: "The man who will best succeed is not the acrobat, but he who will build an easily managed flying machine which can be put into the hands of the public. It was a deplorable error to invite the Wrights to France. We were just about to overtake them when they arrived; without the approbation we have given them, they would have remained unknowns from Dayton. And how do they repay us? They want to cut us off from America, just as they have done for the automobile. [..] In 1903, the Wrights patented a system whereby the rudder is activated at the same time as the wings are twisted. But such a patent only has value in the absence of precedent, and in this respect the Wrights were preceded by Ader, Mouillard *et al.*"

This was indisputable. Chanute had indeed patented a wing-warping glider on Mouillard's behalf in 1892; at Yale, Edson Gallaudet built his large biplane *Hydrokite* with warping wings controlled by gears and rods in 1897. But for all these protestations, there was only one aspect in which the French could feel truly confident of their technology leadership over the transatlantic interlopers: the engine. "They are well aware the motors they have at their disposal are far from perfect," said *The Motor* in October 1908. "But they are the result of long study by celebrated engineers, who have for years enjoyed the highest reputation; and they refuse to admit that a motor designed by the brothers Wright, who were simple bicycle makers, or, rather, menders and vendors, can possibly be a really reliable machine. They are convinced that in any case Wilbur Wright will not have less difficulty in keeping his motor running for an hour than they will have to keep theirs going."

This was not quite true. With its aluminium crankcase, automatic inlet valves, gravity feed and crude fuel injection, even the original 3.3-litre horizontal four-cylinder Wright engine weighed only 80kg, exceeding by 50 per cent the 8HP minimum the brothers calculated was necessary to power their machine. The later 3.7-litre version built in France with much argument under Orville's supervision by Barriquand & Marre was better engineered and more powerful, and proved easily adequate.

Behind the large front elevator of his machine, Wilbur converses with the Italian royal delegation at Le Mans in 1908. The long, slender skids, set wide apart, allowed landings on terrain far rougher than could be contemplated with any wheeled undercarriage, and with relatively light landing loads spread throughout the airframe, mishaps were rare. On witnessing the flights at Le Mans, an excited Delagrange declared that his sceptical fellow countrymen had made the biggest mistake of the century, and that the doubters should now make honourable amends to the Wrights, although his later reflections were more nuanced. Surcouf hailed Wright as "a titanic genius"; even the jingoistic Archdeacon said that he wanted to be among the first to apologise for the "flagrant injustice" of having regarded their claims as a bluff.

The verdict of Delagrange, who is often misquoted as admitting "we are beaten", is illuminating. He pondered the inscrutability of the Wrights, and the difference between their impassive austerity and the more expansive French character. As one commentator remarked, "[Wright] comes to France enveloped in a cloud of rumour, leisurely selects a suitable spot and thereafter settles himself down on it with such quiet serenity as to be a perpetual irritation to the French temperament." But Delagrange also told *L'Illustration* that his Voisin was both better constructed and more complicated – too complicated, he now thought, compared to the simplicity of the Wright. "My machine is like a large, safe ocean liner that requires lots of room for manoeuvre," he declared, "whereas the Wright is like a light racing yacht, capable of heeling over and righting itself in the blink of an eye."

This was the crux of the matter. Without a tail or the encumbrance of 70kg of undercarriage, the new Wright was indeed much lighter than the Voisin – sans pilot, it tipped the scales at only 364kg. But the dissimilar flight characteristics of the two aeroplanes were the result of their being conceived according to two entirely different schools of thought. Achieving stable flight had been the main goal of French experimenters since Alphonse Pénaud's rubber band-powered models of the 1870s, with their long tails and dihedral wings. The task was simply to get sustainably airborne, achieving stability by balancing the forces of lift, weight, thrust and drag so that the centre of pressure corresponded with the centre of gravity.

The Wrights, though, had always focused on achieving three-axis control. In their first public address on aeronautics, Wilbur had in 1901 told the Western Society of Engineers: "When control has been worked out, the age of flying machines will have arrived, for all other difficulties are of minor importance." And if control rather than flight is the priority, it is easier to persuade an inherently unstable machine to change direction than one predisposed to follow a stable course through the air. This is why they had opted for *canard* configuration – not because it behaves more gently in a stall than the headlong dive a wing-first design tends to adopt, but because having the wing's aerodynamic centre and centre of gravity behind the neutral point makes the craft unstable. Ever since George Cayley in the early 19th century, it had been known that the tail of a flying machine promotes longitudinal stability by creating a restoring moment around the centre of gravity when

Although most French pundits decried the Wrights' reliance on skids rather than wheeled undercarriage as a weakness, their supporters read it as a sign that Wilbur, unlike his French counterparts, was confident of returning to his starting point on every flight (which as it turned out, he did not)..

194

the pitch is disturbed, thereby tending always to maintain its equilibrium. Knowing this, the Wrights gave the Flyer no tail precisely because they saw instability as a precondition of responsive control.

The concomitant conceptual leap that set the Wrights apart was the wing warping system. Esnault-Pelterie was right; their patent covered the flight control system of their 1902 glider, not a powered flying machine, on the basis of their belief that no one would be able to fly controllably in anything without applying ideas the patent contained. Wilbur had first demonstrated the principle in 1899 by twisting an old inner tube carton; on the Flyer, similar distortion was achieved by removing the fore and aft diagonal trusses from a Chanute-type biplane cell and attaching cables to the tips of each plane. Combined with its large forward elevators and no counterbalancing fuselage or tail to confer longitudinal stability, a Wright would climb, dive or turn very quickly indeed, unless corrective controls were continuously being operated with vigilance and precision.

"One of our machines, due to its having no tail, rises and dips almost instantaneously. The addition of a tail to an aeroplane causes an increase of resistance," Wilbur explained. "A dragging effect which increases in proportion to the size of the tail. The sluggish action of a Voisin in flight is very noticeable, while the darting motion of a Wright forms a strong contrast. The increase in resistance due to a tail decreases the speed and largely explains why a Voisin uses twice the power of a Wright and, though approximately the same size and weight, is slower. The Wright is the 'true bird'."

Its agility certainly astounded all who saw it. "The weights fell, and with whirling propellers the fairylike machine tore along the rail by the turn of one lever and soared into the air, turning and wheeling up and down as graceful as an albatross," said the *New York Herald*. "It had an undulating movement of its own. Activated by these wonderful levers, the aeroplane glided down to the ground, skimmed over it, then went up forty meters, down again, and so on. As it turned the movement of the wings drowned out the sound of the motor, and an 'Oh!' was heard from the crowd, but there was no pause as the aviator, wheeling on a frightfully acute angle, again circled."

It was this instant manoeuvrability that astounded the journalists fortunate enough to be taken aloft by Wilbur at Le Mans: "Seated as I was by the side of the engine, the noise was deafening.

"The sharp crackling of the open exhaust reminded me of a racing automobile gathering speed. As soon as the motor was fairly humming, Mr Wright climbed into the seat by my side, and with his left hand gripped the lever controlling the elevator. His right hand held the rope controlling the weights. He gave me the prearranged nudge and I pressed down the catch on the magneto. The motor responded instantly and roared still louder. 'Now!' said Mr Wright, and let the weights drop.

"Good God, what a rush! I never before felt any sensation like it, except once when dashing down a water chute. The sensation lasted about a second, until we had cleared the rail, then all sensation ceased. We glided in the air. There was no shock of any kind, no vibration. All impression of high speed disappeared as the machine progressed. Although we were rushing through the air at more than sixty kilometres an hour, all objects were so far away they appeared to pass by slowly. Mr Wright sat calm and cool. Except in taking the turnings, he never used the levers to twist the wings. His left hand, however, was constantly at work with the elevator. It was like a man playing billiards. To each of his movements the machine responded instantly. [..] It was all so definite and so absolutely complete that the conviction formed in my mind that this man is not making experiments but real demonstrations of the art of flying. As we got nearer the ground, the speed appeared to increase - when travelling a couple of feet above the ground the whole apparatus seemed transformed into an automobile, minus the vibration. The ground fairly ripped by. Suddenly Mr Wright struck the cord which passed close to my chest and instantly the motor stopped, while the machine planed gently to the ground and glided a score of yards. There was no shock, and it was not easy to tell when we first touched earth. But Mr Wright had made a mistake. Dazzled by the setting sun, we had landed two hundred yards from the desired place…"

This would not have been a problem in a Voisin, of course. *Le Figaro*'s Franz Reichel was even more eloquent, with good reason. Setting off at dusk, his aerial excursion lasted some 55 minutes, demolishing all previous records for ascents with a passenger in the process as well as fulfilling one of the two 50-kilometre flights stipulated in Wright's contract with Weiller. So dark was it by the time they landed that oil lamps had to be suspended from the starting pylon to guide Wilbur down.

Reichel described it as the most marvellous experience of his life: "I have today known a magnificent intoxication. I have learned how it feels to be a bird. I am still astonished, still deeply moved. When we started, it was like a plunge into space, which gave me a *coup a l'estomac*. Then suddenly it was all very smooth, cradled amid the thunder of the motor. It was strange and exquisite. The air flowed upon me caressingly. I could keep my eyes wide open: the air bathed me, but did not whip me. And then came the first turn. Oh, that turn, those turns! If flying straight in an aeroplane is a delicious sensation, turning is pure intoxication. My heart swelled. Tears came to my eyes. At first I dared not move. Gradually I grew bolder and waved to those below. It is dusk. Night falls and the moon shines. But we fly on, chasing our shadow, which the moon casts in front of us. At last, we glide to earth. Ravished, fascinated, stirred beyond words, I throw myself on Wright's neck and clic-clac, I give him a kiss!" Wilbur apparently "submitted with goodwill to the ordeal."

Although its intrinsic pitch instability made the Flyer far trickier to fly than the Voisin, it was this speed of response that so amazed the French spectators at Le Mans. To an inordinate degree, it has to be said; even when it crash landed on the Thursday, Kapférer opined that the accident itself was "as fine a demonstration of the practicality of flying as any of the actual flights."

"Must we admit defeat?" Delagrange continued, "Emphatically not – on the contrary. In many ways, we are greatly in advance. It is not, furthermore, in the French character to let ourselves be beaten."

But although the Voisin brothers were by then too *parti pris* to admit it, France was won over. Ever generous, Ferber gave the Wrights their due, citing his feelings after he first shook Wilbur by the hand in June. He told a reporter: "Without this man, I would be nothing, because I would never have dared, in 1902, to entrust myself to wings of if I had not seen the possibility of doing so from his photographs and writings. Without him, my experiments would never have taken place, I would never have had Voisin as my pupil, the financiers like Archdeacon and Deutsch de la Meurthe would in 1904 never have endowed their famous prize, the press would never have been so uniformly supportive – and your newspaper would not have quadrupled its circulation!"

In fact, Gabriel Voisin never denied the Wright's claim of achieving powered flight in 1903 any more than he pretended to be the first in the world to do so himself. He simply believed

Contrary to popular belief in France, then as now, the Wrights' initial ascents from December 1903 to September 1904 were made without the catapult. Although some 40 flights were made from the launch rail alone, a strong headwind was required to compensate for the feeble output of the engine, even with the 16HP of the larger bore 1904 unit.

Top: the launch rail is clearly apparent in what is claimed to be the photographic evidence of Wilbur's historic fourth flight, of 260 metres, on December 17, 1903.

Left, on the 9-degree slope at the foot of Big Kill Devil Hill, the wheeled launch dolly which supported the lower plane of the Flyer is seen to the left of the launch rail.

that his own design to be theoretically and practically superior, and more influential on the later development of aviation. His critique remained consistent for half a century. In August 1908, *Le Matin* quoted him as saying "[Aviation] is there to be used by the world. You must not doubt my admiration for the Wright brothers, but their machine, which in its way is the pinnacle of perfection, is not, and never will be, practical. A sporting machine perhaps - a commercial product, never!"

Whether as a reference to his rivals' background or not (and it would be odd if the Wrights' belief in control being predicated on instability had not been influenced by their experience of bicycle dynamics), Voisin chose cycling as his analogy. "Allow me to make a comparison. In cycling, there are three degrees. The tricycle, which anyone can control in half an hour. The bicycle, which one can learn in a few hours; and finally, the unicycle. To ride a unicycle, a long apprenticeship is required, together with the skills of an acrobat. Well, the Wright is the unicycle of aviation. It will never be an amateur's machine or an enthusiast's. It's too big, to start with. It would be impossible to keep on course with such wings and to turn with ease. And then, so much depends on the pilot. A wrong move and disaster! – the bird is dashed to the ground. We hope to manufacture aeroplanes barely larger than a big automobile, which anyone who knows the elements of driving a motorcar can learn to pilot in a few hours."

The Dayton bicyclists drew different lessons from the same the analogy to illustrate the intuitive nature of the balancing skills involved: "After gaining the level at which we wish to sail, our concentration for the next five minutes is fixed on the management of the levers to see that everything is all right. After that, the management of the flyer becomes almost automatic, with no more thought required than a bicycle rider gives to his machine. The whole thing is worked on a reflex action, for there is no time while you are in the air to give conscious thought to what has to be done in an emergency. Action becomes, and must be, instinctive. The sensation is so keenly delightful as to be almost beyond description – one of perfect peace mingled with an excitement that strains every nerve to the utmost." More excitement than peace, one suspects.

Voisin became less charitable towards the Wrights as time passed. In *Flying is a French Science*, he pointed out in 1953 that the four Kitty Hawk flights of 1903 had depended to a considerable extent

Although it required considerable muscle to raise the 600kg weight to the apex of the Wright's launch derrick, the force with which it catapulted the light machine along the greased launch rails resulted in swooping take-offs whose alacrity was more spectacular than the slow-revving props would suggest.

on wind speed, adding that Wilbur had been able to run alongside the aircraft pushing until it had lifted off. Having launched many of his own gliders in this way, Voisin questioned whether the Flyer had taken off from the level or landed at a point as high as that from which it had started.

Writing to the British pilot Harald Penrose in the early 1960s, he further contended that the Wrights were only able to make their epochal first flight because a chance gale was blowing, and they had complete competence in controlling almost identical engineless planes in just such conditions; theoretically as well as practically, neither Flyer I nor even II could have taken off from the available rail length without assistance from the catapult or a high wind, from which he concluded that the Wright flights of 1903 must have been flukes.

This is not as harsh a judgment as it may seem; the inability to duplicate the Wrights' 1903 feat in recent tests of a replica the first Flyer by the American Institute of Aeronautics and Astronautics suggests that the historic flight depended on a freak combination of temperature, altitude, humidity and wind speed on the day in question.

The original Flyer had indeed relied on headwind to get aloft in their first experiments. Indeed, the Wrights had opted for the dunes of Kitty Hawk and the Outer Banks of North Carolina precisely for their strong prevailing winds, in the knowledge that this would lower the relative ground speed for lift-off and landings. Without them, neither the 1903 or 1904 Flyers took easily to the air, and neither were their feats as reliably repeatable as science demands. The launch rail was progressively lengthened to provide more time to accelerate the machine, which made its repositioning even more arduous every time the wind direction changed. "When the wind averages much below 10 feet per second (6.8 mph), it is very difficult to maintain flight because the variations of the wind are such as to reduce the relative speed so low at times that the resistance becomes greater than the thrust of the screws," Wilbur wrote to Chanute of the Huffman Prairie experiments in late August 1904.

First used a week later, on September 7th, the launch catapult was therefore devised to eliminate this reliance on headwinds. Wilbur told Chanute that the new starting apparatus would allow them to "start in calms and practice circling" on the relatively small area of Huffman Prairie. For all its encumbrance, the system did allow takeoffs in as little as 23 metres.

The Wright Model A's flight controls consisted of a left-hand lever operating the front elevator and its pair to the pilot's right, whose longitudinal motion actuated the rudders, while lateral excursions warped the main planes. Although more pilot-friendly than the prone position of the 1903 Flyer (*inset*), the fact that the ergonomics were less than intuitive compounded the difficulty of flying a highly unstable machine. Note the lengthy chain drive.

However, despite the universal misconception in France (then as now) that all the Wright flights had been catapult-assisted, some 40 ascents were made before the derrick was built, from December 1903 to the 436-metre flight on August 22nd 1904. Even thereafter, it was sometimes dispensed with when the headwind was deemed sufficient. Nevertheless, Wilbur and Orville continued to use the catapult and rail long after they needed to, in the belief that it offered an advantage over wheeled undercarriage: wheeled craft needed a lengthier take-off run, and took longer to attain the speed at which their flight controls became effective.

The launch catapult the Wrights brought to France involved erecting a pylon six metres high, laying 30 metres of wooden rail and manoeuvring the aeroplane manually into place on cumbersome two-wheeled dollies strapped to the underside of the wings. Once over the rail, the dollies were removed and the machine dropped onto a launch trolley with two rollers in tandem. A 600-800kg weight was then hoisted to the top by means of an automobile or a tug-of-war team of strong volunteers, and a rope attached which passed around a pulley at the foot of the pylon to the far end of the rail, round another pulley and back to the aircraft. With the engine at maximum thrust, the weight was released and the aircraft was hurled into the air, leaving the launch trolley behind. A Voisin, by contrast, just gathered speed and took off. But the use of downhill slopes, headwinds and launch catapults did not negate Gabriel Voisin's acceptance that the Flyer was the world's first successful flying machine; his contention was that for all its aerial agility, these aids made the Wright a powered glider rather than a usable aeroplane.

The Wright's secrecy made matters worse, of course - indeed, some have concluded from his letters that Wilbur became psychologically unable to separate from his precious juju. Though this is probably an exaggeration, misinformation certainly abounded from the very first press report of the Kitty Hawk flights; the astonishingly inaccurate account published in the Christmas Day 1903 edition of *New York Times* described the machine as "a box kite with one propeller working on a perpendicular shaft to raise or lower the craft and another on a horizontal shaft to move it forward."

Even five years after the event, not a single photograph had yet appeared – only sketches so crude and incomplete as to be misleading. All the tests were deliberately conducted in unpopulated areas.

Above, en route to the race track at Les Hunaudières.

Right, three generously upholstered *mancelles* inspect the crippled Model A on August 13ᵗʰ 1908. The crash did nothing to abate the Wrightmania that swept France – in Le Mans, there was even a vogue for Wilbur Wright caps.

Then, when they finally demonstrated Flyer III at Huffman Prairie before credible witnesses in early October 1905, the brothers promptly dismantled the aircraft and hid it away for two and a half years until May 1908 in order to protect their intellectual property.

Unlike Voisin, they admittedly had a lot of intellectual property to protect. Whereas most of the Europeans (except Esnault-Pelterie) proceeded on the basis of dogged empiricism, the Wrights had always adopted a rigorous scientific method. After their initial gliding experiments at Kitty Hawk in 1901, they tested more than 200 types of wing in the wind tunnel they built in the little Dayton workshop. They were the first to produce useful balances to measure the minute forces playing across the miniature planes tested in the airstream. Made of hacksaw blades and bicycle spokes, the two tiny balances - one to measure lift, the other resistance - provided mechanical confirmation of the equations they were using to calculate performance. Discovering that the published data (mainly Lilienthal's) were incorrect, they compiled accurate tables based on their own observations, which determined the wing design of their 1902 glider. Knowing the value of this aerodynamic information, which could not be patent protected, they decided that it should be kept secret and made available only to whoever bought the patent rights.

This was real knowledge, and it underpinned their scathing assessment of Europe's trial-and-error gropings: "A machine which in expert hands does not fly the first time as well as on any subsequent occasion is either incorrectly designed or badly built," wrote Wilbur in 1909. Glossing over the fact that the original Flyer had been transformed through three iterations by 1908, he continued: "For four years the main principles of our machine have not been changed. We did not arrive at our conclusions by repeated trials alone, but by calculations, which in all the tests to which we have subjected them, do not err. [..] It is the complexity of the flying problem that makes it so difficult. It is not to be solved by stumbling upon a secret, but by the patient accumulation of information upon a hundred different points, some of which an investigator would naturally think it unnecessary to go into deeply…"

The relative merits of the Voisin and the Wright designs became the subject of a long and animated controversy. Much was made of the Wright pilot's need to make constant fine adjustments to the

controls. These criticisms gained ground when, not long before Orville's accident which killed Lt Thomas Selfridge at Fort Myer on September 17th, Wilbur suffered a less serious aerial mishap himself in France by "pulling the wrong lever."

This was easily done. Although their 1905 machine had been reconfigured in May 1908 with upright seating for a pilot and passenger and a new upright control system, the ergonomics of the Wright were less intuitive than on the Voisin. Perched on the lower wing to counterbalance the engine alongside, feet hanging over the leading edge, the pilot of a Wright had two levers to operate simultaneously in different planes in order to remain aloft. As anyone who has tried to pat their head while rubbing their tummy can attest, this takes practice. Apart from a release for the catapult mechanism at take off and a decompression tap to stop the engine, there were no other controls; the engine ran at a constant full throttle. But the coordination of the two main levers required considerable skill, a delicate touch and, in continually unstable flight, the utmost concentration.

Wilbur described the controls thus: "Moving this lever forward, you warp the right wing downward into a greater angle of incidence and lessen the angle of the opposite wing. That throws a greater resistance on the right side. It tends to turn the machine, but when I move this lever forward, the rear vertical rudder moves to the left and counters any turning effect. The wings are warped with a fore and aft movement, and with the same hand the top of this lever can be bent to the right or left and the rear rudder turned to steer in a corresponding direction. When desired, by bending over this lever to the right or left, the rudder can be worked independently of the wing warping."

With continuous pilot corrections requiring fore and aft movements with one hand and sideways movement of the other, this peculiar system of levers made the craft tricky to fly. Certainly, the US army later condemned the Wright controls as pilot killers. Stoically, Wilbur blamed himself for his accident, remarking that it proved the need for constant practice, to which Gabriel Voisin rejoined that however accustomed the Wrights were to their machine, they could never become so completely at one with it that instinctive movements would even approach "the delicacy and rapidity of the automatic relations between a bird's brain and its muscles and nerves." By contrast, the Voisins of Delagrange and Farman were comparatively simple machines for any amateur to master.

Above, when Farman established his base at Châlons, the inner vertical panels fitted to I-bis for Ghent and New York were moved out to the central strut on each wing, and a capacious rectangular radiator was fitted above the engine. Note the canvas windbreak installed ahead of the pilot, and the experimental intake trumpets sprouting from the V of the engine.

Right: watched by the owner of *Le Matin*, Philippe Bunau-Varilla, and two mechanicians, Maurice Herbster checks the business end of the Antoinette.

208

Arriving back in Paris from New York on August 25th, Farman was gracious. "The Wrights are superior to the French in their knowledge of the phenomena of wind in relation to aeroplanes," he conceded. "But you see, though I have made two thousand flights, I have only been flying for eight months, while Mr Wright, though he has not made nearly so many flights with a motor aeroplane, has done an enormous amount of work with gliders, and has practically lived with the wind for 10 years."

Pressed for more critical comment, Farman pointed to the unsuitability of landing skids as speeds increased. Citing an estimated 70km/h take-off speed for his *Flying Fish*, he also dismissed the principle of powering propellers by chain as being inherently 'unmechanical'.

So it was, of course – the Wrights' power-sapping chain drive from the engine to the propellers midway along each wing had only two merits: it was a simple way to minimise the gyroscopic effects of the two propellers by rotating them in opposite directions, and it allowed rapid changes of gearing by the simple expedient of replacing the drive sprockets. As we have seen, Wilbur dismissed objections to their lack of landing gear of on the practical grounds that taking off with wheeled undercarriage would require airfields with long runways.

More importantly (yet hardly remarked upon at the time), the two slow-revving wooden Wright propellers were far more efficient than the steel and rivetted aluminium Voisin equivalent - an even more critical factor in 'pusher' machines, where the props displace turbulent air. It was the Wrights' third great conceptual leap: the realisation that, rather than displacing a volume of fluid like a screw pulling itself through wood, an aeroplane propeller worked by generating aerodynamic forces like a vertical rotating wing, in which lift was vectored as thrust. They designed their profiles accordingly; having studied the physicist WJM Rankine, the Wrights applied a form of blade element theory to design their propellers, which had an efficiency approaching 80 per cent, right from the start. No other experimenters of the time came close ("No one there seems to understands their propellers, which look like a pair of paddles," observed Wilbur of the French), and it did much to compensate for the inferior horsepower on tap.

As time went on, I$^{\text{-bis}}$ proved the sturdiness of its construction in dozens of flights at Châlons. "The Voisin has undoubtedly shown itself to be the most easily driven and safest flying machine in existence," opined *The Aero*. "It presents the same workmanlike appearance that characterises Voisin productions. It is neither clumsily heavy nor flimsily light, but appears to have just a reasonable degree of rigidity which does the builders credit for their judgment in design."

Back at Châlons, further modifications to the Voisin continued apace. The main cell was re-rigged with no dihedral, and the inner vertical panels with cut-outs on the leading edge were moved to the middle of each wing, and outer ones added in a reversion to Hargrave's classic box-kite configuration. A larger fuel tank was now mounted transversely above the engine. 1^{-bis} was by now able to travel considerable distances, mainly because refinements to its latest Antoinette yielded enough reliable power to accommodate the extra weight of a large rectangular double matrix radiator which largely obviated the overheating problems. Thus equipped, after flights on September 26th, 27th and 28th in the presence of Archdeacon, Blériot and André Fournier, variously curtailed by failures of the rear landing gear and fuel pump, Farman flew his Voisin for 43 minutes at dusk on the 29th in a bid to beat Wright's 48-kilometre record of two days earlier, but the 36 kilometres he covered was insufficient.

As he had proved, however, Farman was a resourceful test pilot, and he continued experimenting with his modifications. On October 1st, tests were abandoned because of water pump problems, but he made a 42-kilometre flight the following day. A new engine was installed, and by the end of the month, large down-only flaps had been fitted to the trailing edge of the main planes, to which cut-outs in the long end panels of the main cell were added (first at the top and later at the base) to facilitate their arc of movement.

Farman is often wrongly credited with inventing the aileron, and the importance of those added to 1^{-bis} has been exaggerated. When Curtiss was in New York explaining the wing tips on the *June Bug*, Farman is said to have interjected "Ah, *ailerons!*" - the first time this French coinage (probably dating from 1904, when Esnault-Pelterie fitted flaps to his glider) had been heard in the USA.

But although he was perfectly aware of the American machine's 'tip rudders', Farman remained a staunch advocate of what he termed his 'big box rudder'. Nevertheless, when he hinted to his US Aero Club hosts that he had considered adopting a similar system, the news set alarm bells ringing in the Curtiss camp at Hammondsport, prompting Douglas McCurdy to telegram Alexander Bell on August 6th: "Farman contemplating using our tips. I hurry patent lawyers in securing applications?"

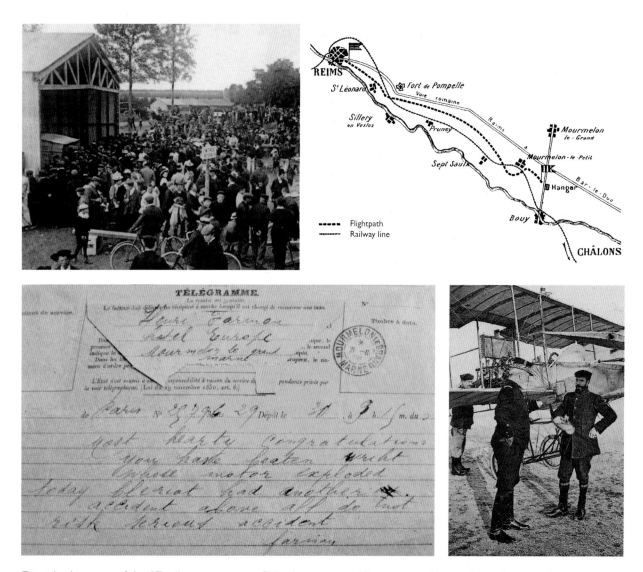

Top right, the route of the 17-mile cross-country flight that cemented Farman's position as France's pre-eminent aeronaut.
Top left, spectators came from Paris to see Farman's flights at Châlons, which rapidly become a centre of French aviation.
Above left, Dick Farman's telegram to his brother at Mourmelon reads: 'Most hearty congratulations. You have beaten Wright whose motor exploded. Today Blériot had another accident. Above all, do not risk serious accident.'
Above right, with Herbster in the background, Farman listens to General Felix Journée, the commandant at Châlons.

The 'Farman flaps' on 1-bis were of questionable utility. By Farman's own admission, they were never used for turning; their declared function was to improve lateral stability. The main benefit was probably psychological, insofar as they boosted his confidence in the machine. Certainly, he attached little importance to them – but then, his indomitable optimism in matters of aerial control sometimes led him to bizarre conclusions: "I believe the day is not too far distant when the aeroplane will respond not only to the slightest will of the operator, but that in time the automatic balance will be found. Then we shall see the aeroplane standing motionless in the air."

Notwithstanding such flawed predictions, Farman was now regularly flying considerable distances, often many times a day. In view of this, and the deteriorating autumn weather over the featureless plain, he had a crude canvas windbreak installed in front of the cockpit of 1-bis, and a new 75-litre fuel tank which gave a theoretical range of three hours. This was the configuration for the triumphant next step in the career of his trusty Voisin: flying between two places, rather than simply circling an aerodrome or enclosed circuit. Virtually a year to the day since the breakthrough of the 'small angle' at Issy, he found himself on the threshold of another landmark endeavour. At 9.30 on the morning of Wednesday October 28th, he flew for more than 40 kilometres over the newly ploughed winter fields. That afternoon, he made a two-kilometre flight with a distinguished passenger of Wilbur's a fortnight previously, the academician Paul Painlevé *(appendix XV)*.

Farman was on a roll - within the hour, he took the Voisin up once again, this time to an altitude of 40 metres, which he maintained for five kilometres before dropping a few metres to cut the ignition and glide back to land. His trials the next morning were curtailed by a broken fuel line, but all seemed set fair for the final proof of the aeroplane as a viable mode of transport: the world's first point-to-point aerial journey.

Except for one thing: Blériot. For Farman was of course not alone in his cross-country ambitions; 300 kilometres away, in the endless beet fields and big skies of La Beauce (which Farman had considered as a base before opting for Châlons), Louis Blériot had carefully reconnoitred just such a route for his sturdy new Type VIII monoplane. He had already made one attempt on October 21st

Above, Farman in the cockpit at Châlons, with the suspension bungees and advance/retard lever in the foreground. His epic cross-country flight elicited a sour response from Wilbur, who condemned the very idea as both useless and dangerous. "In spite of their skill and daring, the aviators will encounter a fatal puff of wind," he sternly opined, "which their machines are not sufficiently controlled to resist."

Right, In defiance of the taunts that he flew too low, and emboldened by the altitude he attained the day before, Farman soared over the 10-metre mast as he set a new world altitude record the day after the cross-country flight. It was a hollow and short-lived victory; since the regulations for the Aéro Club's second (25m) altitude prize specifically excluded craft launched by falling weights, Wilbur took off on extended track without the launch derrick on November 18th and flew far higher.

- a six-minute flight - but engine failure struck on the following day. Blériot's third try took place on the morning of Friday 30th, but luckily for Farman, negligent assembly of the elevator caused the Blériot to invert itself before it even left the ground – exactly the type of error that would surely have been revealed in the course of Farman's methodical litany of pre-flight checks.

So it was that at four that same afternoon, it was Farman and not Blériot who made the first cross-country flight in the world by flying along the 27 kilometres of the old Roman road from Bouy, near Châlons, to the cavalry ground at Reims. Pipped to the post once again, the hapless Blériot made a slightly longer cross-country flight the following day, although he was obliged to land twice en route. His aeroplane, however, only survived another four days before being reduced to a mass of splinters and crumpled fabric. Fortunately, the pilot was more robust than his aeroplanes.

Farman's account of his 20-minute voyage is evocative: "I was a bit emotional at first – the prospect of the journey scared me. What, I asked myself, am I going to do when I arrive at those large poplars at Mourmelon-le-Petit? All is well for now – the ground is flat and the countryside very agreeable. But as I was thinking this, the poplars were growing at an alarming rate. A squawking gathering of crows flew off in terror at my approach. Ah, those 100-foot poplars! Should I pass them on the right? On the left? My indecision doesn't last long, for they're scarcely 50 yards away. Oh well, here goes! A touch of elevator and the craft rises rapidly; it goes over, while I look anxiously down to see whether I am clearing the treetops. My tranquillity is, however, short-lived. Here's Mourmelon windmill and now Mourmelon itself. Bah! I thought, you only die once! The windmill, the village, the railway - I go over them all."

"And then, I'm suddenly not sure of my altitude. I'm told I was flying at 150 feet. Maybe so, because I went as high as I could to clear the poplars. I was giving my full attention to steering, to the noise of the engine, whose occasional misfiring worried me, and to the roar of the propeller. But I nevertheless experienced at that moment the greatest joy of my life: the charm of gliding above my fellow men while the scenery flew by in strips and where, from all sides, people were running towards me who seemed tiny, tiny. At that moment I found myself in pure air, caressed by a gentle breeze, and the sun lit the way, limpid and serene. It is my most cherished memory."

216

In a similar vein, the correspondent of *The Post* did his best to explain the emotional and aesthetic reasons for the popular enthusiasm which Farman's point-to-point journey aroused: "What is it that makes one's sensations, as one watches these flying men, so exciting and so ecstatic? Why is that, when the wheels of their machines leave the ground, when they rise with throbbing movement into the air, one feels so vivid a sense of triumph and joy, such an irresistible need of working off emotion by shouting and cheering the exploit on? You have seen a child's glee as a kite mounts up, and up. He gives delighted cries, and claps his hands and jumps about. That was just what I felt impelled to do when I first saw Farman during his record-breaking flight. Partly, these sensations are caused by the pride one feels at the conquest of the air, the age-old dream coming true. But mingled with this exultation is another: delight in the beauty of these great birds. For, whatever they may look like on the ground, they are beyond all question beautiful in the air.

"As they rise with steady swiftness into the blue dome, flouting the eye of the sun; as they swerve and swoop and circle; as they slide downwards in harmonious sweeps, and gently alight once more on solid ground; no one with any perception of the beautiful can help feeling that a new element has been added to the joy of life. They are indeed equally enthralling from the point of view of science and art."

Writing long after the event, however, Wrightists have sought to diminish Farman's feat. The historian Charles Gibbs-Smith was one such: "Creditable as indeed the flight was, it was obvious that [he] had chosen a route where, at any point, he could have landed with ease on the flat ground on either side of the road, or even on the road itself."

This ungenerous objection presupposes the existence of two adjacent towns unconnected by road, and that the endeavour would somehow have been more worthy if the chosen route had been more dangerous than it need have been. Having climbed high enough to clear the tall avenue of trees bordering the roads across the plain, Farman had already rebutted the taunt that he always flew low (he had been mocked as *Henri rase-mottes*), but he was determined to disprove the charge once and for all.

SCIENTIFIC AMERICAN

[Entered at the Post Office of New York, N. Y., as Second Class Matter. Copyright, 1908, by Munn & Co.]

Vol. XCIX.—No. 21.
[Established 1845]

NEW YORK, NOVEMBER 21, 1908.

[10 CENTS A COPY
$3.00 A YEAR.]

Henry Farman making the first cross-country flight that has ever been accomplished with an aeroplane. The 17 miles between the military camp at Châlons and the city of Rheims, France, were covered in about 20 minutes.

A NEW ERA IN AERIAL NAVIGATION.—[See pages 356 and 357.]

The most frequently reproduced image of I-bis on the world's first cross-country flight in fact shows no such thing. The church is St Martin's in Sartrouville, 200 kilometres west of Châlons, next to the house of another Voisin owner and former Surcouf dirigible engineer, Louis Paulhan. Since no such flight is recorded - and virtually every ascent was documented in contemporary periodicals - the image must be a photomontage.

218

With the darkness gathering, it was too late to fly back, so he arranged for trucks from the nearby Pommery Champagne house to collect 1^{-bis} for transport back to its starting point early the next morning. When it arrived, Farman joined Gabriel Voisin and Herbster in reassembling the machine. Within a few hours, in the presence of Aéro Club luminaries, he cleared the 25-metre marker to set a new world altitude record of 30 metres, wining the 2,500-franc prize.

Both these landmark escapades were ripostes to Wilbur's sensational demonstrations of the previous month. Having returned to France in July, Wright had left Le Mans for the closed military area of the Camp d'Auvours because of the thousands of onlookers who flocked to see his August flights. He was issued with a military pass to the camp in August 20th, and once installed, he began flying in earnest, demolishing the world records for time and distance on September 21st by remaining airborne for more than an hour and a half. He was only forced to land by the coolant boiling away. Several flights of over an hour followed – this time, with passengers.

Wright admitted that Farman's Voisin "arrived nearer to our aeroplane than any other," although he added that there was "still a good deal of ground to be covered" before it equalled the capabilities of the Ohio machine. But despite the Wrights' demonstrations and the long distances being covered by Farman and the unfortunate Blériot, even the serious prints still regarded aviation as a niche technology of limited practical application: "The aeroplane can never seriously be considered a means of transport on any extended scale," continued *Scientific American* that autumn. "The present indications are that a single machine can never hope to carry more than two or three passengers, and for the carriage of freight it is altogether out of the question."

The Wrights had always seen the potential for aviation as military rather than civilian. Interviewed at the Hotel du Dauphin in Le Mans by *The World* in August 1908, Wilbur insisted: "The aeroplane is the scout of the future. Capable of carrying two persons and rising to a height of a mile, of making a continuous flight of 100 miles and of alighting where the aviator wills, it should prove of infinite use in time of war." (These were no idle speculations. Radio pioneer Reginald Fessenden, for example, was already in talks with Orville about covering the Flyer's main planes in tin foil to allow the pilot/scout to communicate by radio with units on the ground.)

The Châlons-Reims flight proved a boon to the postcard industry, and in particular to the craft of photomontage. Shots of 1⁻ᵇⁱˢ were superimposed onto a variety of bucolic scenes to symbolise the aeroplane's ascendancy over every other form of transport, from the bicycle and horse-drawn cart to main roads, waterways and railways. Windmills often featured, as if echoing the machine's ability to harness the power of the air. In some of the cards, Farman's Voisin is even seen serenely making its way across the city itself (which of course it never did).

220

"The future of flying machines is with armies," Wilbur told *The Motor* six months later. "Every army will have hundreds of these machines, carrying three or four men and ammunition, and capable of keeping the enemy continually harassed. Naturally, these machines will take the place of cavalry, and will be much more effective than that branch of the service."

The Auvours flights led British military aviation pioneer Baden Baden-Powell (another of Wilbur's passengers) to the same conclusion: "That Wright is in possession of a power which controls the fate of nations is beyond dispute. It proves conclusively that the aeroplane will become a practical vehicle in the near future, and will be absolutely invaluable in war. May England wake up!"

In France, by contrast, discourse on the future of aviation was utopian. "The science of aeronautics is a pacific one," Voisin told *Le Matin* in November 1906. "The better aeroplanes become, the less we shall live in fear of war." A year later, the satirical magazine *Fulmicoton* agreed: "Given the difficulty of driving these machines, it's hard to imagine how pilots could possibly fire their weapons as casually as if they were quaffing absinthe in the hide of a local duck shoot. It's hard to imagine birds of death dropping bombs, shells, boiling oil or who knows what from on high. It's hard to imagine civilised nations tolerating such horrors, so unworthy of humanity even if they were possible. No, aviation will follow in the wake of doves of peace. As the spectre of war recedes with the progress of civilisation, man's finest conquest will never be enslaved to the forces of barbarism."

Six months later, Delagrange was more guarded. "The aeroplane will undoubtedly be used very extensively in the army," he said. "Every regiment will have a certain number for scouting and harassing the enemy." Unlike Wright, though, he foresaw an equally vigorous recreational market: "As a sport, flying will be unrivalled for touring, as it makes possible a journey, say, from Paris to Marseilles, or London to Monte Carlo, in an hour or so." Delagrange also predicted dramatic effects on the future of the motor industry: "As the result of the development of the aeroplane, long-distance motor car touring on high-speed machines, ruinous in upkeep, will fall off very considerably. Flying will be so much more economical, as well as more fascinating, that nobody will want to travel long distances by road. In my opinion, a single type of machine will not be developed, as has been done with the bicycle, for instance."

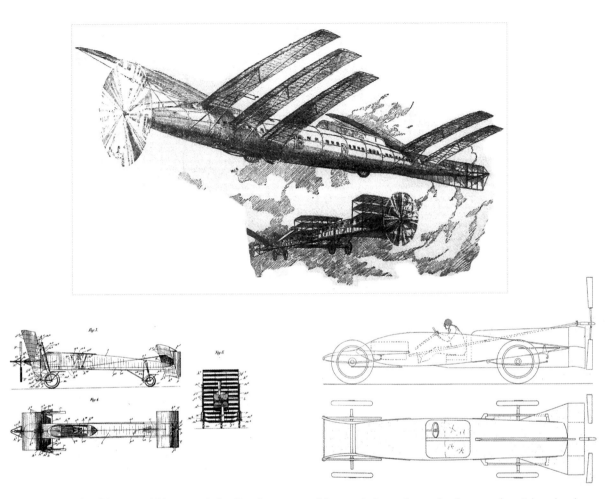

The breakthrough of January 13th opened the floodgates to wild speculations about the future of aerial technology. *Top*, Farman's somewhat fanciful sketches of the possible future of aviation (published in August 1908) suggest that he saw the staggered wing configuration of his *Flying Fish* as pointing the way forward to large airliners.

Above left, the multi-plane *Aéromobile* road/air vehicle with a variable/reversible pitch propeller patented by Charles Voisin in the same month; with the bulging order book the firm was by then struggling to fulfil, it seems an unlikely diversion.

Above right, in March 1908, Farman claimed this racer as his own ("with a little help from the Voisin brothers"). He argued that with the driven wheels of a fast car often spinning for reasons of poor traction, the 25 per cent mechanical losses of transmitting the power and friction between tyre and road, the 60-65 per cent efficiency of a propeller compared favourably. He estimated that at 400kg, a 50HP engine and a 1.8-metre screw would propel the bolide at 150km/h.

"There will doubtless be different types in two main categories – monoplane and multicellular. The types are so different that it is impossible to choose one over the other. The progress of the aeroplane will be ten times more rapid than that of the motor car, but it is likely to be arrested by accidents, which will inevitably happen to reckless *sportsmen*, who will take a pleasure in risking their lives by flying over towns – a thing that is absolutely useless in time of peace. In the very distant future it will be possible for an aeroplane to receive its motive power from electric stations on the earth. In five years' time, everyone will be flying."

Electric aircraft apart, Farman had a more realistic take on Delagrange's view that the advent of the aeroplane would harm the motor industry. Speaking before his flight from Bouy to Reims, he declared: "I believe that the aeroplane will be used very generally as a sport, and that journeys from point to point will very generally be undertaken during the next few years. And because of its development as a sport, the aeroplane is certain to have an adverse influence on the motor car. Though it will never drive out motoring, it will doubtless bring about a certain neglect of the high-powered car. During the next five years there will not be any attempt to cross mountain ranges or to fly over towns, but journeys along the seashore from one watering-place to another or from one holiday resort to another will be commonplace. Round trips of 100 miles, avoiding towns and attempted under favourable conditions, will be very common."

A keen Esperantist like Archdeacon, Farman's take on the military application of aviation was based on a humanitarian idealism very different from the Wrights' vision of securing decisive unilateral dominance. Farman saw the offensive capability of the aeroplane as such a powerful deterrent that it would eventually compel universal peace because of the prospect of mutually assured destruction.

"The lightning warfare of today cannot reach its ultimate purpose of peace unless it employs the swallow-like swiftness and hawk-like strike of the aeroplane," he reasoned in August 1908. "As the torpedo boat and submarine are diminishing the effectiveness of the battleship with its terrific armament, so the flying machine will spy out the enemy, make the greatest fortifications redundant and with marvellous celerity, hurl the bolt that will destroy the proudest aerial cruiser of the future. Battleships will carry aerial torpedo boats, stored in sections and assembled at an hour's notice, and

223

Farman's second Voisin takes shape in the spacious new works by the Seine at the Quai du Point du Jour, with the half-finished tractor triplane for Ambroise Goupy in the background. Since it is clearly not the 2-metre machine which Voisin michievously sold to Moore-Brabazon (*see page 36*), it may have been disassembled and shipped as spares for 1⁻ᵇⁱˢ to New York, although it was neither reassembled nor needed on site But as can be seen from the signwriter's guide tacked onto the side panel of the tail plane, Voisin obviously realised in the wake of Farman's success that his agreement with Blériot to name Voisin machines after his customers was already denying the firm the recognition it was due. Henceforth, he obviously intended the company's name to be written as prominently, if not more so, than his most important customer's.

able to travel at the speed of the fastest express train over a range of hundreds of miles, as a means of conducting offensive warfare. When the time comes that an aeroplane can leave the deck and fly several hundred miles away with its load of high explosives to attack a hostile fleet, nations will pause before hazarding their fleets against such terrible risks. And when every nation has its fleet of aerial destroyers, peace conferences will be compelled to declare an absolute edict against warfare."

Farman was equally sanguine about the development of civil aviation: "The way to fly is no longer a secret. We know how to sustain ourselves on the air and how to overcome its disturbances, which was the most difficult problem. Perfecting the motor is the thing upon which all experimentation is centred; it is only its unreliability and the inability to carry enough fuel that prevent almost unlimited flight. Within a year I expect to have a motor which will enable me to go as high as the amount of fuel allows. At a mile altitude, it is not necessary to have any fuel to return to earth; the motor could be shut off at that height and the machine be permitted to sail down on the air under the direction of the operator and land as gently as I did on my flights at Brighton Beach. Many people have wondered why I stop my motor before descending to the ground. If I came down with the motor running at full speed it would break the machine by reason of the tremendous impact with the earth. A bird sails down from a tree or fence and lands lightly, and my ability to imitate the landing of the bird emphasises the stability of the air."

Farman then elaborated his vision of the future of the personal aeroplane. "The flying machine of the next decade will only slightly resemble its forerunner. It will be a smaller vehicle. Everything will be spindle-shaped – that is, of a form so fashioned as to offer little resistance to the wind. All the parts except the wings will be hidden from the wind, with the passengers and pilots placed in a sort of car with glass windows. Its motor will have shrunk in weight and size, but its energy will have increased enormously in proportion to the losses in bulk. It will be able to navigate the treacherous air currents in the streets of modern cities. Where it is now relegated to unobstructed surfaces, it will then fly over and between and under roofs, walls and bridges.

"As an example of the terrific speed already accomplished by the aeroplane, I might mention the *Flying Fish*, my latest development and the embodiment of all my advanced knowledge, keyed to travel at 60 miles an hour. Mr Blériot, only the other day on the field at Issy in Paris, shot 150 feet into the air at a speed of 60mph in a monoplane, turning as swiftly as a bird and darting here and there with the rapidity and certainty of a swallow. Naturally the layman would ask how he, or any other aviator, can ride the air. This is easily understood when one asks what is air; no one, even the scientist, has been able to answer this question. The easiest definition is that air is a body with enough stability and enough resistance to support any amount of weight, if these weights are so arranged as to take advantage of this resistance.

"Man found that the gasoline engine would take the place of flapping wings; the bird's ability to remain suspended in the atmosphere on extended and motionless wings gave the experimenter the clew [*sic*] that mechanical flight was a question of merely sailing on the air with rigid wings, driven edgewise through the air by a motor, the velocity of whose propeller would be sufficient to enable the resistance of the air to support the machine. Unlike the dirigible or the water craft, the aeroplane must therefore have great speed. Stability can only be obtained by gaining air resistance, which in turn can only be gained by hitting the air hard, which is only a way of defining speed.

"For this reason, I doubt very much that the aeroplane will ever be used to carry great loads, and it is looking far into the future to picture it as having the facility to carry a dozen men with the facility exhibited by the dirigible balloon. There is no reason why the aeroplane cannot be used by the business man with just as much ease as the automobile runabout. The great speed will make it popular with the dweller in the suburbs who desires a quick run to and from his office. These flights will probably be made higher in the air so that if anything breaks down, the operator will have plenty of space and time in which to select his landing. It will be necessary to fit up landing places on all office buildings and on the roofs of many public buildings such as hotels and railway stations.

"It is not the scientist, but the daredevil devotees of speed who will force upon the public acceptance of wing flight," he presaged. "The spirit of rivalry aroused by furious locomotion will attract to the aeroplane the very men who lifted the automobile out of a mere pleasure vehicle by making of it a racing machine. As the automobile developed into the foremost type of distance-killing and time-conquering engine, so the flying machine will fill the popular mind as a vehicle possessing elements of commercial utility. With this irrepressible stimulus there will grow the desire to make use of its dominant speed and freedom of trackage [*sic*] as the method of communication so long the dream of the thinker."

As one might expect from a future founder of Air France, Farman was already thinking in terms of fleets that shrank time and distance. By contrast, Charles Voisin's reading of the future of aviation was both less ambitious and less feasible. He declared that it would develop in the direction of the *Aéromobile*, a hybrid car/stubby-winged multiplane that he and his brother had patented soon after Farman had returned from New York: "The flying machine of the future will not be more than six feet from tip to tip," Charles told *The Motor*. "Instead of merely two superimposed planes, it will have 20 or 30; it will run on wheels like a motor-car, but be driven by propeller. When used in towns or any crowded district, it will keep to the road and be used in exactly the same way as a motor car, with the difference that its four wheels will be free, drive being by propeller. When conditions are satisfactory for high speed, the elevation plane will be raised, the machine will rise from the ground and skim along at a very much increased speed a few inches from the surface of the road.

"For instance, on a journey from Paris to Marseilles, this flying motor car would follow the road as far as Fontainebleau, travelling like a motor-car. From Fontainebleau it would still follow the road, at times skimming over the surface, at times running on its four wheels. Further south, where absolutely flat, open country is reached, there would be no necessity to stick to the road, but the machine would never rise high into the air. Many an angle on the main road and many of the dips on our long straights would be avoided. In the Sarthe and elsewhere there are level straights and switchbacks stretching for miles which are so safe that every motorist wishes he could travel at 200 miles an hour. With this type of aeroplane it would be possible to leave the road, attain that speed, then come back again to run as an ordinary vehicle when passing through villages or over unsuitable country. It's true that Farman has just made a magnificent cross-country flight, but such trips will not become the norm. It's madness to attempt to fly over trees, houses, railways and other obstacles, for the whole time you are at the mercy of your engine. Wherever there's movement there's wear, and where there's wear there will sooner or later be breakage. Admittedly if your motor fails you won't come down like a stone, but nevertheless come down you must, and the place you have to descend on may be a roof, and roofs are not ideal landing places.

"Some years ago Panhard issued instructions to users of their cars that a speed of 35km/h could be attained in high gear, but they did not recommend its use owing to the danger of such a speed. In the same way, this type of aeroplane could travel high in the air; in fact, high in the air there would be fewer difficulties than near the ground, the atmosphere above the treetops being calm, or when there are currents, they are steady. Near the ground, on the other hand, there are eddies which make a flying machine difficult to handle. But because of the serious results which might ensue from a high flight we should not recommend the use of the machine for such purposes."

No doubt because of his brother's long experience with, and enthusiasm for, float planes, Charles's predictions extended to the personal seaplane. "The Channel will undoubtedly be crossed during the next six months. But with the aeroplane, as I see it, for practical purposes in the future there will be a hull, somewhat similar to that of a boat, with sustaining surfaces. The machine could either fly above the water or be sustained on its surface. Powerboats like the *Cobra* already have sufficient power to enable them to fly if their hulls were lightened and fitted with sustaining planes. Since all vessels of this class are bad sea boats, it would be an advantage to replace them by flying boats navigating on the water or above it. Doubtless aeroplanes of this type not more than 6ft wide, and having a maximum capacity of four people, will be sold for £600 each."

"Their maximum speed will be 200mph, but of course their average speed will be much lower, for frequently they will operate under the same conditions as a motor car. Undoubtedly such machines will be a direct rival to the present type of motor car, for their upkeep will be very much less, and their speed much higher. They will be invaluable for military purposes, for even on the road they will be exceedingly fast."

Or not, as it turned out. The point is that none of them knew in which direction the new technology was headed, except for the fact that the military would play a big part.

228

Back in the real world, 1^{-bis} looked pretty much of a dog's dinner by the end of the year, with its innumerable ad hoc modifications and slack, oil-stained and roughly patched fabric. Farman was by then awaiting the completion of his next aeroplane: Henri Farman II, the first of a series of 10-metre Voisins to emerge from the Quai du Point du Jour workshops with the main planes set two metres apart, as Farman had specified.

Having left Châlons for Paris on November 9th to inspect the Belgian-made aluminium Vivinus four-cylinder engine he intended to fit to this second machine, he had nothing to lose by pushing his experiments with 1^{-bis} further still. Back at Châlons a week later, having ordered the span of the main cell to be extended by 1.5m and the main struts lengthened to accommodate an additional seven-metre upper wing in a bid to increase lift, he began testing 1^{-bis} as a triplane. The upper plane of the tail cell was also extended, and the vertical end panes on each side lengthened. In this form, far less neat in appearance than the tractor triplane Voisin had completed the previous month for one of his main investors, Ambroise Goupy, Farman flew 1^{-bis} several times over distances of up to 10 kilometres on November 16th and 17th. By then, Farman had erected a second, larger hangar, an engineering workshop and living quarters on the site to receive 'Quinton's Tourists', an influential parliamentary commission of the great and good led by the eminent physiologist René Quinton (soon to become another Voisin shareholder).

A few days later, Farman had two metres removed from each end of the main planes to give what was in effect a stack of three short planes. Although this proved fast (up to 80km/h), the machine was significantly less stable, requiring constant correction. After modifying the pitch of the propeller, two further flights took place for the benefit of a military delegation on a gusty November 21st.

(It's worth noting that in Le Mans two days later, Wilbur used an extra-long launch rail that allowed him to take off without the catapult for an attempt on the altitude prize, thereby satisfying the Aéro Club's requirement for an unassisted take-off. To emphasise his contempt for a regulation deliberately calculated to exclude him, he cruised no higher than the balloons marking the 90-metre height of his own recent record.)

Heavily patched and looking well-worn, I^{-bis} lives out the closing days of its 18-month evolution on the plain of Châlons. In November, in addition to the ineffectual 'Farman flaps,' Farman experimented with a seven-metre upper wing, turning it temporarily into a fast but less stable triplane.

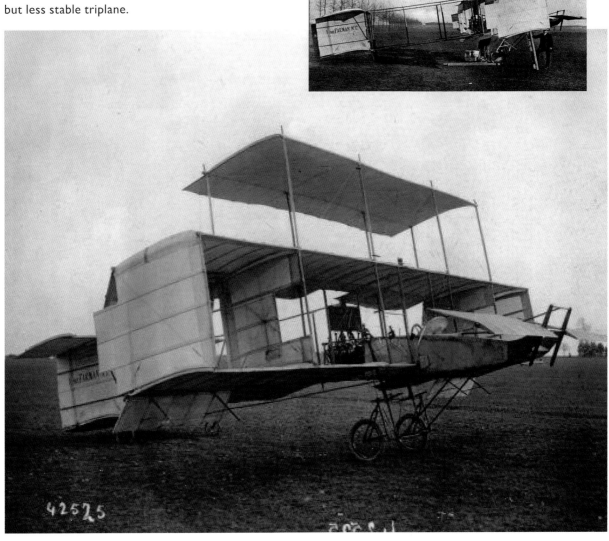

Since 1^{-bis} was by then virtually expendable, Farman determined to research the limits of its behaviour in turbulent atmospheric conditions. Three days later, with prevailing winds of around 35km/h, he succeeded in making several flights with turns. During one such, a particularly violent gust suddenly hoisted the Voisin some 20 metres into the air before dropping it back down to its original trajectory, and so the flight continued in a series of unpredictable undulations for several minutes. With a following wind, the triplane was approaching 90 km/h; into the wind, it made virtually no headway at all.

On November 26th, he completed a circular flight of nine kilometres in seven minutes. Given that only the Wrights had hitherto tried flying in anything more than a strong breeze, his conclusions seemed to vindicate the practical virtues of the Voisin's inherent stability: "There's no need for wing warping, nor rudders, nor elevators – to fly when it's windy, all you need is a stable machine," he defiantly declared.

What Farman really wanted to crown his (and the Voisin's) *annus mirabilis* was to beat the Wrights' 48-kilometre record to secure the 20,000-franc Michelin distance prize. Although 1^{-bis} was flying well and had almost twice the power of its rival, it was still not as fast. On November 28th, in a bid to increase his speed further still, Farman ordered the third plane to be removed and the span of the lower plane reduced to seven metres, but the penalty in terms of instability outweighed the advantages. The stack of three seven-metre planes duly reappeared on the 1st and 2nd December, but although he is also reported to have to given brief training fights in the overworked machine to members of the British Aeroplane Club (with a new 58HP Renault engine and 70-litre fuel tank fitted for evaluation) on December 13th, bad weather and sub-zero temperatures put paid to any serious long distance attempt before the New Year's Eve deadline.

Disheartened by losing the Michelin prize (Wilbur having flown 150 kilometres on December 28th) Farman decided that the time had come to part company with the old bus. So it was that on January 5th 1909, after a brief test flight at Mourmelon, the world's first truly usable aeroplane was sold (still in triplane form) for an undisclosed sum to the Wiener Syndikat zur Veranstaltung von Schauflügen, a Viennese consortium formed for the purpose of organising demonstration flights.

Above, Georges Legagneux about to embark on a demonstration flight in I-bis in triplane form outside Vienna in April 1909. *Below right*, the last surviving photograph of Farman's Voisin shows it on the floodplain of the Danube on the outskirts of Vienna on May 23rd 1909, by which time most of the accretions added at Châlons had been removed. Gone are the short upper plane and the four vertical panes between the main planes, both of which have a larger section cut out at the trailing edge, presumably to accommodate a larger propeller. The upper flaps have gone, along with the big radiator.

232

Georges Legagneux (1882-1914) was the last person to fly 1⁻ᵇⁱˢ (although he is here seen in one of the later 10-metre Voisins that he flew in Russia and Scandinavia as well as in France).

The fact that a leading syndicate member was Karl Wallner, director of the Theater an der Wien, says it all: it was show time for the old bird once again. By the end of March, 1^{-bis} was installed in the aero dock of the Military Balloon Corps, ready to be fettled for the last act. Even then, reports commented that this venerable machine had achieved more than enough to earn itself a restful museum retirement, but its final fling was yet to come. The syndicate was reported to have bought it because they were anxious to have an aeroplane at once, rather that wait for one to be built – and to be sure that it would fly for at least 20 kilometres.

The pilot and nominal head of the syndicate was Georges Legagneux, who had been recruited by Levavasseur as a mechanic in the early days of the Antoinette company in 1903, and was seconded three years later as mechanic to Captain Ferber, who taught him to fly in 1908.

On January 12th, almost a year after its greatest triumph, the old Voisin was transported by road back to Issy-les-Moulineaux, where long landing skids were fitted alongside the wheels. Since Farman had the week before announced the break with the Voisin company, this work was presumably carried out at the new factory Farman had acquired in Boulogne-Billancourt to make aeroplanes under his own name. By the end of the month, 1^{-bis} was back in Châlons to be demonstrated to the Austrians.

Having joined the Voisin flying school at Mourmelon as pilot instructor, Legagneux familarised himself with the machine on February 4th and spent Valentine's Day watching Farman make several flights in 1^{-bis} for his benefit, including one as a passenger. Legagneux then promptly performed a series of well-executed flights from two to five kilometres, and then ten kilometres a couple of days later, after which both Farman and Legagneux returned to Paris. Ten days later, Legagneux flew a kilometre to demonstrate the machine in triplane guise – its last flight in France before being crated for transporting by rail to Vienna.

Legagneux was unimpressed by the flying field provided on the flood plain next to the Danube: "What a godforsaken place! An enclosed one-kilometre track, surrounded by an impenetrable network of telephone wires and electricity cables, constructions obtruding at all angles and only the adjacent river as a possible escape route."

Legagneux' first demonstration - the first powered heavier-than-air flight in Austria - took place on 22nd April, when he flew only 200 metres. On his second attempt, he was caught out by a sidewind which send the machine to earth, damaging the right wing. Once repaired, he somehow managed a 4.8km on the 27th, much to the delight of the Austrian military, but on the following day a violent westerly once again brought 1-bis down – more dramatically this time, twisting the undercarriage, smashing the prop and wrenching the engine from its mountings as well as crumpling the lower main plane and injuring Legagneux himself. After three weeks of repairs, a few more successful public flights ensued on May 21st and 22nd. The machine's final ascent was on May 23rd 1909, when the Antoinette was spavined by electrical gremlins. Once again, the old bus attracted the opprobium of the spectators, and had to be escorted back to its temporary hangar by a platoon of hussars. "Legagneux has not yet succeeded in getting much out of the old Voisin," wrote one reporter. "He was to give an exhibition at Vienna, but was able to make only a few leaps of a hundred yards or so, and the big crowd was badly disappointed. But the grounds the syndicate behind him has provided are not particularly inviting. One is almost sure to get either into a ditch or the Danube. As a result of the failure to make attractive flights, the syndicate has been dissolved and the machine presented to the army."

The Voisin was duly packed off to the *Militär-Aeronautische Anstalt*, where a certain Oberleutnant Hirsch was charged make it airworthy again. The Antoinette was sent off to the Körting engineering works for testing, and the airframe was substantially lightened – by an improbable-sounding 100 kilos, according to some reports – but to no avail.

Finally, the old warhorse was moved to the Vienna Army Museum. Having escaped destruction for long enough to become an exhibit (despite no documentation of the transaction surviving at the museum), it seems hard to accept that only the propeller of this historic artefact, the archetype of the first series production aircraft in the world, has survived. Perhaps someone will one day spot the beak-like prow of a rickety nacelle through the motes of a reserve collection store room…

Back in France, Farman was now by far the most famous aeronaut in the world, a superstar with a massive margin of superiority over his domestic competitors. Having broken world record after

Moore-Brabazon innocently familarising himself with his new purchase by taxiing across the wintry *champ de manœuvres* on taking delivery of the first of his four Voisins, which may have been the machine originally destined for Henry Farman. Unlike those of the standard model, the main planes were set two metres apart.

record, instructed countless others and won a small fortune in prize money, he became a folk hero – the undisputed torchbearer of European aviation until the political symbolism of Blériot's cross-Channel flight six months later eclipsed his achievement in the popular imagination.

As Gabriel Voisin predicted, most press accounts referred to the machine as Farman's design, and if the Voisin brothers were mentioned at all, it was usually as the chippies who assembled it. Admittedly, the brothers' somewhat high-handed and abrasive attitude to the gentlemen of the fourth estate (especially those who solicited contributions for 'advertorial' coverage) did little to help matters, but the sense of injustice rankled deeply. Flushed with sudden success after years of professional ridicule, Gabriel and Charles Voisin came across as arrogant, vain and stand-offish. Together with the stresses of intense competition and the often intransigent egos involved on both sides, this exacerbated an already sour atmosphere as Farman and the Voisins' paths parted in the course of 1908.

Competition had bred conflict, as the co-founder of the Antoinette company, Robert Gastambide, observed: "For an endeavour that aspires one day to reuniting peoples and abolishing frontiers, aviation seems to be tearing apart the few who dare to take up the challenge. Voisin detests Levavasseur, who probably returns the compliment. Blériot and Voisin have been at daggers drawn since their joint enterprise was dissolved: if he could, the one would throw at the other all the wood he has smashed – and there's been a lot – together with all his many past, present and future monoplanes, only to receive in return all the biplanes of the other. Relations between Gabriel Voisin and Henri Farman are less than warm; Voisin thinks that Farman has stolen half the glory that is properly his, and believes he has nourished with his purest milk of aviation a snake that will one day plunge into the very heart of Les Frères Voisin the standard of a rival: Les Frères Farman. All these bird-men are cooped up in the same little rockpool at Issy-les-Moulineaux, like crabs trapped in too small a basket, seeking to devour each other."

As Farman did nothing to correct the misreporting, the resulting tensions may have been behind the Gabriel's decision in November to sell Farman's new Voisin to another well-heeled young amateur sportsman, John Moore-Brabazon *(appendix XVI)*, who, having declared his intention to cross the

Right and below, the fish that never flew – with only two of its three pairs of variable incidence main planes fitted, the substantial *Flying Fish* staggered wing tractor monoplane in its initial form at the rue de la Ferme. It would have been the first Voisin with a tractor propeller, and although it was never completed as such, its long, curved, fully enclosed fuselage may have been used as the basis for the tractor triplane later built for Ambroise Goupy at the Quai du Point du Jour factory.

238

Channel for the *Daily Mail* prize, had placed his order for "a machine like Farman's but with three planes" in September. Brabazon, who had built a hanger next to Farman's at Châlons, received a letter on the subject from his new neighbour a few weeks later: "I ordered an aeroplane from Voisin a few weeks ago giving the distance I wanted between the planes and the position of the front rudder and Mr Voisin agreed to build it but at my own risks as far as flying was concerned," Farman wrote. "The machine was paid for and ready at Voisin's. Dutheil was getting the motor ready for it and had taken all the principal proportions of the aeroplane to fit the motor."

That Farman had actually paid for his second machine puts the Voisin brothers' behaviour in a poor light, but this apparently inexplicable act of disloyalty may have been partly due to the delay in securing the engine that Farman had specified. Until then, the only available Dutheil-Chalmers engine was the flat twin used by Santos-Dumont and others to power *Demoiselle*-type microlights, which would have been of no use at all in the big Voisin. The engine Farman was waiting for must have been the 60HP flat six that the Dutheil-Chalmers company was developing, which didn't make its appearance until five months later, in April 1909. Had Voisin been aware that the required power unit was nowhere near ready for delivery, the prospect of selling a built airframe to a paying customer in the knowledge that he could build another in time for the arrival of Farman's new engine must have seemed a legitimate option. Not to Farman, of course. "Therefore coming back from Châlons, you can judge of my stupefaction to find that Voisin had given you my machine built according to my specifications," he told 'Brab'. "I am glad that the machine flies well, but now, you know to whom it is due. [..] I have begun legal proceedings, which I will stop, as Voisin has refunded me the money I paid, in a cheque. I have only been robbed of a few good ideas, but I can do nothing except having no more to do with Voisin."

Voisin's unbusinesslike act infuriated Farman so much that he resolved to build his own aeroplanes from then on, and turned to the drawing board over the winter of 1908. Effectively a simplified Voisin, the resulting Farman box-kite proved very popular (partly because of its Gnome Oméga rotary engine, but mainly because of the famous name it bore), and it was soon adopted as the standard primary training aircraft all over the world. The rest – the wartime machines and the Farmans big and small that did so much to pioneer civil aviation between the wars – is history.

When Farman and his brother Maurice were understandably accused of plagiarising the Voisin for their respective first cellular biplanes (indeed, Voisin was still fighting them through the courts three years later), Henry vigorously defended himself on the grounds that it was he who deserved the real design and engineering credit for making the Voisin a flyable proposition in the first place, and somewhat disingenuously, that insofar as some of his modifications were later incorporated in the standard production 10-metre biplane, Gabriel Voisin had copied *him*.

The final rift with Voisin was exacerbated by the *Flying Fish* debacle. In *Flight* magazine of January 1909, Farman is quoted as saying that one of the three machines he had under construction was "a revolutionary monoplane" he had already patented. Since no such patent exists (and the first Farman monoplane didn't appear until 18 months later), this must refer to the *Flying Fish* still languishing half-built at the Quai du Point du Jour works, where the *American Aeronaut* hailed it as "nothing less than a marvel in the way of simplicity and construction." The distinguished Viennese aerodynamicist Edmund Rumpler was less sanguine. On inspecting the 14-metre airframe, with its five seven-metre planes - the front pair pivoting, as elevators – he concluded that even with 100HP, the *Flying Fish* would hardly have left the ground; with the heavy 35HP Renault V8 Farman planned, the 650-kilo device never stood a chance.In fact, the design had by then been patented by Voisin, not Farman – a mere seven days after the kilometre prize. Despite being a monoplane rather than a cellular biplane, the elegant banana-shaped fuselage, the undercarriage and the steering controls all look like Voisin designs. Indeed, Gabriel Voisin later recycled the *Flying Fish* fuselage to create the first Voisin *canard*, and the same fuselage formed the basis of the triplanes he built for Ambroise Goupy and Sergei de Bolotoff's putative cross-Channel flyer, and the factory's subsequent Voisin-engined tractor biplane. If the basic concept had really been Farman's – and, judging by his statements to the press since early in 1908 about developing a fast new type of machine combining the virtues of his biplane with those of a monoplane, it may well have been – Gabriel Voisin's decision to lodge the patent under his own name can only have been a cynically opportunistic response to the sudden realisation that Farman's sudden global celebrity would inevitably lead to a parting of the ways in which the customer rather than the maker would take the high road.

What is certain is that at the time and in later years, Voisin fulsomely praised Farman's abilities, both as a sportsman and as someone with an instinctive feel for machinery. Writing in *La Revue de l'Aviation* soon after the kilometre, he attributed part of his client's success to his nationality: "After all, let us not forget that our record holder is an Englishman. His level-headed coolness is a quality common to most Englishmen, whereas in France it is all too rare."

In Farman's obituary in 1958, WF Bradley agreed that his unflappable temperament (which the Wrights shared) contributed to his success: "Farman displayed a quiet self-control, calm reasoning and lack of ebullition that gave him an advantage over the rival aviators of his period."

"A decidedly interesting personality," *Scientific American* concluded. "An artist by profession [..] with the essential qualities of a successful engineer and inventor. The inventor should have a strong dash of the imaginative quality; but to be successful, this quality should be mated to a keen logical and discriminative faculty. The most successful engineers have had the ability to pick out the essentials from the nonessentials, and Mr Farman is gifted with this quality to an unusual degree."

As Robert Wohl has pointed out, for all their differences of temperament, the brothers Voisin, Farman and Wright were all described at the time as having the defining qualities generally ascribed to aeronauts. As well as bird-like physical characteristics (sharp features, quick movements, wiry frames and penetrating eyes), they were said to exhibit exceptional self-reliance, determination and attention to detail, along with "extraordinary patience, an artisan-like dedication to work, solitariness, indifference to the superficial emotions of the masses, imperturbability and distance from the ordinary run of human beings."

At Auvours, a French reporter described Wilbur thus: "This man is strange and cold, but his coldness is sympathetic. He is tall, thin, severe – a man tempered like steel. The countenance is remarkable, curious, with the head of a bird, long and bony, and a long beak-like nose. The eyes are blue-grey, with tints of gold that bespeak an ardent fire, for Wilbur Wright is a fanatic."

There were even hints of the Noble Savage in contemporary depictions; he was described as living "like an Iroquois" in a way that ignored the norms of polite society and was implacably hostile to

The recreation of Farman's Voisin built by the factory for the first *Exposition Internationale de l'Aéronautique* in December 1908 bore only a passing resemblance to the kilometre machine, and was probably a customer aeroplane dressed up for the purpose. Its prime location on the balcony overlooking the main exhibition hall of the Grand Palais was the result of an ill-tempered row in which an enraged Charles Voisin threatened to withdraw from the exhibition altogether unless the Voisin took pride of place instead of the Wright the organisers had originally envisaged. He got his way.

242

everything worldly. Despite stories in the popular press designed to soften this harsh image – about Wilbur adopting a stray dog at Auvours (and naming him *Flyer*, of course), and how well he got on with children (who were generally the only locals who pronounced his name correctly), the dominant impression was of inscrutable otherness.

Painlevé's take was couched in the language of Orientalism. "This man's face is widely known. But what neither caricatures nor photographs can reveal is the look in his eyes, both indomitable and candid. He has needed an invincible will and faith and ten years of unremitting daily effort to overcome the caprices and perils of the fleeting, elastic fluid element that surrounds us. He has something of the tireless patience of the Chinese..."

Pseudo-academic conjecture about the physical otherness of the aeronaut went to absurd lengths. The *New York Times* reported on "a certain London phrenologist who declares himself to be the discoverer of the 'bicycle face' and the 'automobile face' has now unmasked the 'aeroplane face'. He has for some time contemplated the features of Messrs. Wright, Farman, Delagrange, Blériot and Santos-Dumont and has tabulated certain characteristics common to all, tapering off into neat distinctions and vagaries of heart and mind. He finds that all have 'the uncertain glance which denotes a vain search for physical balance, the breadth above the eyebrows which reveals constructive ability, the rise over the eyebrows which shows daring, courage and concentrated nervous energy, while all have in general expression benevolent, emotional and imaginative qualities strongly marked – not unlike those on the faces of evangelists, but more deeply accentuated and intellectual.' From these data, the phrenologist deduces that those indulging in aviation may expect to have 'a brain massed unusually above the eyebrows and suffering shrinking and neglect in other directions.'" Although "a strong believer in aeroplanes", the reporter found these claims to be "not absolutely convincing".

More prosaically, the aeroplanists were all described as being intractably obsessive – aware of their reliance on others for what had to be a collaborative enterprise, but unwilling to relinquish control (reasonably so, given the attendant physical dangers). Or to share credit. As with anyone prepared to risk all on an uncertain and inherently perilous endeavour, these were big egos.

To this factor must be added the different ideologies that framed their approaches. French thinking was informed by the fraternal spirit of the French Revolution, prizing communal solidarity above individualism; by contrast, the Americans' spirit of innovation was rooted in the post-Enlightment ideas of the Industrial Revolution in the UK, with its capitalist emphasis on private finance and the protection of intellectual property for commercial gain.

But whatever the true cause of the rift between Farman and Voisin, it brought to an end one of the most productive collaborations in the early history of aviation – one that resulted in Europe's first proper aeroplane. "The achievement suddenly brought the renown of the Voisin brothers to enthusiasts for progress the world over," said *Omnia* a month after the kilometre. "It seems to us, however, that in all the accounts published hitherto of the great event of January 13th 1908, the constructors of the victorious aeroplane have been overshadowed. The ferocity of their quest to discover the secret of flight, their determination to overcome setbacks, ridicule and petty betrayals, their tenacity to win through by their own limited means, revealed truly original characters of great intelligence – men of the calibre that this new industry demands. It would be an injustice to deny them the limelight they deserve, and which they all too readily avoid."

Writing in *Flight* after Gabriel Voisin's death in 1973, Roger Bacon pondered the high success rate of pairs of brothers in early aviation and concluded that "it must be something to do with the thickness of blood needed to overcome the deep despairs of aviation pioneering, which can turn ordinary friendships into hate and make men quit. Each brother keeps the other going."

The story of how these three very different sets of brothers, united only by a stubbornness born of disarming self-belief, liberated us from our servitude to gravity is a tale of stability versus instability, of the phlegmatic versus the mercurial, and of the Old World versus the New. And as with all good stories, it has always been coloured by the prejudices of those who recount it. Like a racehorse compared to a Percheron, the Wright was a high performance machine in a way that the Voisin was never intended to be; but as is always the case, its speed and agility were achieved at the expense of everyday utility. The Wrights were intuitive engineers whose creations were far in advance of those of Langley, Maxim, Ader *et al.* Their greatest achievement was the solution to the problem of three-axis control embodied in their 1902 glider; the knowledge of lift and drag gained in the wind tunnel, which they applied to both wings and propellers, also conferred a big advantage over the French.

Voisin's case for his own place in the history of powered flight ultimately rested on the question of legacy: whose design subsequently became the model for the vast majority of aircraft to follow. He argued that the Wright configuration had no successor; by contrast, the 10-metre Voisin, with its enclosed cockpit, forward main planes and an airframe extending backwards into a horizontal tail plane and vertical rudder, provided the basic template for the vast majority of subsequent flying machines, much as the *système Panhard* had done for the motor car.

For Voisin, it was essentially the tale of a tail. The tail marked the French school of early design much more than the American, and it was for a long time a matter of bitter controversy, but there's no escaping the fact that the Wrights ended up fitting a tail and wheeled undercarriage. Both ditched the front elevator, and wing warping soon fell by the wayside.

Though different in conception and ideological approach, both Voisin and Wright machines influenced all subsequent aeroplanes, of course – the best of each was assimilated into mainstream aircraft design. But they generally looked more like Voisins or Blériots than Wrights. In terms of configuration and form, France won. And just as Blériot was the first to cross the Channel in a heavier-than-air machine, the Voisin design, flawed as it was, notched up an impressive array of 'firsts'. The first aviatrix, Elise Deroche, made her name in the production version, and in the machine initially ordered by Farman, Moore-Brabazon was the first Briton to fly in the UK. In the hands of Legagneux, Farman's 1[-bis] was the first aeroplane to fly in Austria. In May 1908, Delagrange's Voisin was the first to fly in Italy. The 10-metre Voisin was the first to fly in Sweden (Legagneux again, in July 1909), Russia (Alexis Van den Schkrouff, in the same month), North Africa (René Metrot in November 1909), South Africa (Albert Kimmerling in December 1909), Mexico (Alberto Braniff in January 1910), South America (Henri Brégi in Argentina, February 1910), Denmark (Robert Svendsen in July 1910) and Australia (Harry Houdini in March 1910).

Soleil, Tour, Aéroplane – Robert Delaunay, 1913.

246

What unites the French and American designs, however, is the depth and extent of their cultural repercussions, beyond any commercial, recreational or military applications of flight. Images of human ascension that permeated Western culture for thousands of years had hitherto been based on the natural forms of flying creatures. Similarly, the Impressionism that predominated at the turn of the century made the banalities of the real world shimmer with colour and light; in the decorative arts, the florid organic curves of Art Nouveau reigned supreme. But insofar as technology manifests the aspirations of the human spirit as eloquently as the plastic arts, the perceived beauty of these flying machines defiantly rebutted this gentle aesthetic. Stark, stripped to the functionally essential and brutally rectilinear, they were Modernism writ inescapably large.

Their machines were new in a way that nothing else was. Automobiles resembled the phaetons, charettes, landaus and fiacres crowding the streets of previous centuries. Bicycles didn't look that different from hobbyhorses. Powerboats looked like boats have always done since the Phoenicians. But unlike the *Éole* and their other biomorphic 19th century antecedents, the two most successful aeroplanes in the world looked unlike anything else; geometric, with flat planes and right angles, and devoid of all ornament, they had no external referents in either the manmade or natural world.

Think Bauhaus. De Stijl. Le Corbusier. Malevich. Delaunay. Marinetti *et al*. Heralding the advent of a new dimension for human experience, these areonautical creations were marvellously of their time, and informed it accordingly.

Despite the rivalry between both sides of the Atlantic, nothing in the story of the brothers Voisin and Farman in any way diminishes the remarkable feats of the pair from Ohio. Like all great leaps of technology, the achievement of powered flight was a gradual process of learning from the experience of contemporaries as well as precursors, illuminated by flashes of insight, theoretical brilliance, practical ingenuity, physical courage and, most of all, years of dogged experiment. But it would be equally foolish to deny that what Gabriel Voisin and Farman achieved was a cardinal milestone of this journey, and as such, and as a symbol of the optimism of this particularly heroic and productive period in the history of human endeavour, it deserves wider recognition.

LES HOMMES VOLANTS
Les Ailes d'Icare et l'Aéroplane d'Henri Farman

248

Appendices

Dramatis personae:

Perspectives:

References:

250

1. The makers: Gabriel & Charles Voisin

Gabriel Voisin was above all a maker. From childhood to the end of his long life, he never stopped building things with his own hands. As teenagers, exercising the freedom that came from growing up fatherless in their grandfather's bourgeois provincial household, Gabriel and Charles taught themselves to build a bicycle, a rifle, several kites and sailing boats. Before the century ended, a small legacy had allowed them to equip their home workshop with an anvil, a forge, a pillar drill and three vices; with access to the band saw of a neighbouring cabinetmaker, they constructed a steam boat.

The early experiments with cellular box kites led them to discover the kinetic importance of centres of pressure and gravity, which informed all their subsequent creations (including the primitive but pleasingly rakish underslung motor car they constructed in three months from an Aster engine and a motley collection of Audibert & Lavirotte parts in 1900).

Gabriel studied architecture at the École des Beaux Arts in Paris, while Charles - an adventurer by nature, as if to compensate for being somewhat overshadowed by his mercurial elder brother - went off to study hydrography. Thereafter, Gabriel worked as a draughtsman on the great Exposition Universelle of 1900, where he was profoundly moved by the gloriously chiropteric form of Clément Ader's Avion, with its exquisitely wrought lightweight steam engine, feathery propellers and retractable batwings. Having secured an introduction via the ageing pioneer's foreman, Espinosa, Voisin had the opportunity to discuss his youthful aeronautical ideas with its (by then somewhat discredited) creator. There followed a brief diversion from aeronautics when, on coming of age in 1901, Gabriel Voisin frittered away much of the 50,000 francs he inherited on setting up a less than successful travelling theatre company. A second car was built soon after.

When he eventually gained access to the inner circle of French experimenters, Voisin's facility for making things work in the course of realising all these boyhood projects manifested itself in a more pragmatic approach to aeroplane design and construction than most of his peers. At a time when aeronautics in France was dominated by theory, with learned pamphlets and articles copiously embellished with graphs and equations, he had more practical nous.

Gabriel (*left*) and Charles Voisin installing the new Antoinette V8 in the nacelle of Delagrange N° I in the courtyard of the rue de la Ferme in February 1907. Shortly afterwards, Chanute described Gabriel as "the cleverest of the French flying machine pilots."

It's not that he was daunted by theory, but his thinking was led by hands-on experiment, informed by an intuitive understanding of dynamics and mechanical systems and the unshakeable self-confidence to believe he could make them work better. Although an accomplished draughtsman (his design method was always to resolve problems on paper first), his was a world of blue overalls and calloused hands.

His short fuse is illustrated by an incident that occurred in front of a small crowd of onlookers during Farman's tests on the *champ de manœuvres* in the frustrating days of November 1907, when a young reporter innocently approached Voisin with an offer to report on all the test flights for the Grand Prix itself, in return for 1000-franc fee. Slapping his own forehead and clenching his jaw, the veins on Voisin's neck distended as he shrieked his reply: "What makes you think that I, who am penniless, would waste a thousand francs greasing your palm? I know full well that when Farman wins the kilometre prize, his portrait and life story will be splashed across all your pages, whereas a conspiracy of silence will surround the name Voisin!

"I already know the report you'll write, listen: 'Title: Henry Farman's Magnificent Exploit'. Copy: The celebrated and sympathetic pilot has just flown the closed circuit kilometre on a biplane to win the Deutsch-Archdeacon prize.' (At this point you'll take good care to avoid mentioning the constructors, Les Frères Voisin.) You'll then add: 'The aeroplane on which Farman has found fame flies at 13 metres a second, nearly 47km/h; it was built in France,' (to appeal to the national sentiments of your readers), and is fitted with a French eight-cylinder engine.'

"Here again you will refrain from mentioning the word 'Antoinette' and Levavasseur, its creator, unless he had been stupid enough to line the coffers of your miserable rag. Or maybe Levavasseur still believes in the value of publicity, or rather that positive press coverage might help to create a favourable impression of his wretched engine, which everyone has seen Farman battling with every day for three months, and which I am certain isn't even as light as he claims. I've a good mind to weigh it one day and sue Levavasseur for fraud. You, gentlemen of the press, will sing the praises of 'the musclepower that made the flight possible'; in the meantime, if I had anything else to fit to my machine, Farman would have long since won the Grand Prix."

At the height of their respective careers, Henry Farman and Gabriel Voisin flank Alberto Santos-Dumont (*centre*) in front of the monument erected to mark the 20th anniversary of the closed circuit kilometre, whose trajectory is engraved on the plinth behind them.

'Driven' is how Voisin would be described today. Single-minded, energetic and intransigent to the point of arrogance, many said. Not motivated by money, though he knew how to spend it with panache – indeed, he was financially inept. Quick-tempered and intolerant of officialdom and red tape, he was paradoxical in many ways: a rigorous rationalist all too often in thrall to his emotions; a snob who nevertheless preferred the company of those with dirt under their fingernails. He inspired either fierce loyalty or loathing; indifference, never.

He certainly demanded as much from his longsuffering collaborators as from himself. He was tirelessly prolific – apart from all the automotive and aeronautical inventions, the 180-odd patents he lodged between 1908 and 1966 range from designs for prefabricated housing and low-pressure inflatable structures to mopeds, two-stroke engines, industrial dairy equipment, armaments, amphibious vehicles, gas fittings, locomotive controls and a coffee machine. He even patented a better nail.

Interviewed 25 years after the event, the pioneer constructor Antoine Odier recalled that "of us all, Gabriel Voisin and his right-hand man Colliex were the best at combining the theory and practice of the new discipline. They built some 160 of their flying chicken coops, and in proportion to this astonishing output of new aeroplanes, they did so with the fewest accidents."

Like all creative minds, he suffered from the impatience of one whose ideas were generally ahead of their time or of the technologies available to realise them fully. His was a life spent looking forward, not back; when towards the end he eventually he did allow himself retrospection, the past was often seen through the prism of the present, with all that implies for the accuracy of the three autobiographical volumes he dictated in his eighties: *Mes Dix Mille Cerfs Volants* (translated as *Men, Women and 10,000 Kites*), *Mes Mille et Une Voitures* (*My 1001 Cars*) and *Nos Etonnantes Chasses*.

Gabriel Voisin was a canny, practically minded autocrat with a total belief in himself and his ideas and precious little regard for what others thought of either. As such, at a time when it was still possible for one individual to create a complex machine, everything he ever made or helped to make bears the distinctive imprimatur of his personality and thinking just as surely as if it were signed.

II. The flyer: Henry Farman

Describing him as "an extraordinarily clever man" and "the model of the athlete and scientist", the English pioneer (and future customer) Claude Grahame White concluded in 1911 that "what George Stephenson did for the locomotive, Farman has done for the aeroplane."

Born Harry Edgar Mudford Farman, his first flight was not in fact at the helm of his Voisin in 1907. Five years earlier, he had accompanied his younger brother Maurice (an accomplished balloonist) for an astonishing ascent of no less than five kilometres; in 1904 he had made the world's first nocturnal flight, in the military dirigible *Lebaudy*. Even more spectacularly, in the Auvergne in 1905, he left terra firma aboard a 70HP Panhard. On the first 137-kilometre lap of the eliminating rounds for the Gordon Bennett Cup, he negotiated a particularly treacherous bend of the twisting descent into Clermont at such an ambitious speed that the big Panhard flew off the road and propelled Henry and his mechanician high into a tree as a ton and a half of Avenue d'Ivry's finest plummeted into the ravine far below. According to WF Bradley, Farman calmly withdrew a Player's Navy Cut from its case, turned to his hapless mechanic spread-eagled on a nearby branch, sighed, and then coolly murmured, "Pass me a match, Jules."

This 'off' was one of the few occasions when Farman failed to achieve what he set out to. Reserved, modest and courteous, he was nevertheless a stubbornly determined and competitive character. Ferber described him in 1909 as combining a profound knowledge of engines "with a cold, calculating bravery and a tenaciously methodical patience that he owed to his Anglo-Saxon origins."

Six years older than Gabriel Voisin, Farman's background was far more privileged. As the middle of three sons of Thomas Farman, the Paris correspondent of *The Daily Telegraph* and the *Standard*, the family was wealthy enough to employ tutors to home educate the boys – an education in which the better portion of each day was devoted to open-air exercise. From an early age, Farman was therefore at liberty to pursue his own interests and sporting inclinations. Like his father before him, Henry's first passion was for the most glamorous sport of the 1890s: cycling. Racing cyclists were then

of course the fastest men on earth, and their feats attracted widespread publicity. The young Farman duly made his racing début in a 40-kilometre race along the banks of the Seine in April 1892. He rode a tactical race, keeping close to the back wheel of the favourite Cottereau until they were within 150 metres of the finishing line, when the determined young pretender broke free and sprinted to cross the line 10 metres ahead. He went on to beat 75 crack riders to win the gruelling 400-kilometre Paris-Clermont Ferrand race sponsored by Michelin (who scattered nails around various sections of the route to demonstrate the ease of changing their pneumatics) in a record time of 17 hours 38 minutes. A month later, he snatched victory from the then champion Cassignard in the 100-kilometre race for the French championship. He was still only 18, at which age French law allowed him to claim British nationality; although he always regarded himself as French, Farman only acquired French citizenship in 1937.

That he won every race he entered in his first year of competition testifies to Farman's fitness, self-confidence and physical grit. In 1893, with the poet and journalist Edouard de Perrodil, he rode a Gladiator in record-breaking time over the 1440 kilometres from Paris to Madrid, where he was greeted on arrival by some 100,000 enthusiastic Madrileños. His fame was already spreading. The following year, he began tandem racing with Maurice on pillion. Competing as *Equipe Vierge*, they proved unbeatable, setting outright and one-hour world speed records for tandems and three-rider machines and defeating both UK and US champions at the Vélodrome d'hiver in February 1894 to clinch the world championship. During his cycling career, Farman beat all the champions of the day and competed against many who were later to become fellow aeronauts, such as Selwyn Edge, Léon Bathiat, Roger Sommer, Hans Grade, Eddie Audemars, Édouard Nieuport and Alessandro Anzani. Farman was also a member of the French bicycle polo team, with another great cycling champion and future Voisin pilot, Edmond Jacquelin.

There were other strings to Farman's bow while he was pursuing his exploits on two wheels. Following in his mother's footsteps, he also trained as a painter under Gustave Cormon at the École des Beaux Arts, and then in the Académie Colarossi and the Académie Julian. His mentor, the genre painter Gustave Courtois, eventually presented the young Farman with an ultimatum: either to

Farman's glittering competition debut on two wheels as a young man was followed by an equally successful career as a racing driver in the works teams of some of the many marques sold by his family dealerships in Paris and London - including Phébus (*top left*), Darracq, and from 1902, Panhard et Levassor (*top right*).

Above left, in the 1903 80HP Paris-Madrid Panhard in which he finished third in the Gordon Bennett Cup in Ireland.

Above right, in the following year's 100HP works team car.

give up racing or his artistic career. The clincher came when the Salon jury rejected a canvas he had submitted, which prompted Farman to set his brushes aside. By 1898, he had joined his elder brother Dick in the motor business, eventually retailing Panhard, Renault, Mors, Serpollet, Darracq, Decauville, Argyll, FIAT, Prunel, Victrix and Martini cars in Paris and Long Acre; Dick was also involved in the Farman et Micot voiturette shown at that year's Salon.

In the circumstances, motor racing was the obvious next step for one who combined a yen for speed, a fiercely competitive spirit and an undoubted mechanical aptitude. His driving debut was on a Phébus trike at Chanteloup in 1898; his first on four wheels was conducting a 1.9-litre Darracq twin to first place in the light car class of the Grand Prix de Pau in February 1901 (second overall behind his brother Maurice's Panhard) – but only after contesting the initial result on the grounds that it failed to take into account time lost waiting at level crossings. Gentleman or not, Henry was out to win, which he did once again in the Circuit du Sud Ouest three days later. The following month, the little Darracq trounced all other light cars in the Nice-Salon-Nice event. MMC built a car for Farman to drive in the 1901 Gordon Bennett Paris-Bordeaux race, but withdrew it at the last moment because traffic congestion around the Coventry factory (!) had made it impossible to stage a full road trial; Farman drove a Panhard instead, like his brother, and brought it home a creditable seventh. In June he drove the same car to fifth place in the Paris-Berlin trial.

Amazingly, the Farman brothers were still the men to beat in cycling, taking their Whitworth tandem to victory at the Vélodrome d'hiver in March 1902. Back on four wheels a little later, having come fourth in the Paris-Arras-Paris Circuit du Nord, Henry triumphed in the third Gordon Bennett Trophy, his Panhard covering the 615 miles between Paris and Vienna in 16 hours. Again, Farman claimed victory on a technicality, as Zborowski's Mercédès was retrospectively penalised for not observing customs formalities. Henry and Maurice contested the infamous Paris-Madrid of 1903. Maurice abandoned the race to attend to the dying Marcel Renault immediately after his crash, and never raced a car again. According to Henry, his own mount "broke absolutely in halves while I was going at only walking speed through a village." Six weeks later, after the government banned racing on open roads in France, Farman drove a 13.7-litre 80HP Panhard to third place behind

Top, within days of winning the kilometre prize, the showrooms of Automobiles Farman near the Arc de Triomphe proudly proclaimed the victory for all to see.

Above, the first boxkites Farman manufactured under his own name at Châlons (this is N°3) were simplified versions of the 10-metre Voisin.

de Knyff's similar car in the fourth Gordon Bennett race in Ireland. He was beaten in his next event, the Eliminatoires Françaises at Argonne in May 1904, by Henri Rougier (a future Voisin pilot), who wrestled his Turcat-Méry to third place. Although Farman's Panhard only finished eighth, he drove the fastest lap - the first in the world to average more than 100km/h. Two months later, he finished seventh in the Circuit des Ardennes In 1905, he competed with equal distinction on water, at the helm of the Tellier-designed *Palaisoto I* (named after the brothers' firm) – a 40-footer whose 180-horse Panhard six powered the big hull to nearly 50km/h. This gave Farman the taste for fast boating which he later satisfied by building the first of a long series of Farman *hydroglisseurs*. By then, Automobiles Farman had established glossy new showrooms in a prime location in the rue de la Grande Armée (next door to Roland Garros, who was selling Grégoires) in addition to running the biggest garage in Paris, the Palais de l'Automobile, in the nearby boulevard Pereire. With demand for automobiles vastly outstripping supply, this was a highly lucrative concern – especially for someone like Farman, with the personal prestige to attract the right clientele. By 1907, Henry had accrued a personal fortune of more than half a million gold francs.

But the arboreal excursion in the Auvergne dampened his enthusiasm for competitive driving, and he only entered two more races. In July 1907, while his Voisin was being built, he agreed to drive a Renault AK in the Grand Prix de l'ACF at the personal behest of Louis Renault, as a last-minute replacement for the works driver who had fallen ill just before the race; he retired after 336 miles. The following year, five months after the closed kilometre triumph that brought him worldwide fame, Farman returned to Dieppe to drive his last race. His Panhard was the last to finish the ten 48-mile laps, fully two hours behind Lautenschlager's winning Mercédès. With the death of Cissac, it marked the end of motor racing for both Panhard and Farman. By then of course, all Farman's energies were concentrated on aviation. He only returned to four wheels after hostilities ceased, as the manufacturer of the sophisticated (and fabulously expensive) Charles Waseige-designed Farman ohc six-cylinder A6 and its derivatives, which sold even fewer than the equivalent luxury Voisins. Far more significant was the pivotal role Farman played during these years in the development of European air transport; as his tombstone declares with some justification, "he gave the world wings."

Post-war, Farman (*left*) presided over a manufacturing empire that encompassed some of the world's costliest motorcars, as well as recreational and commercial aircraft of every conceivable type.

265

266

III. The assistant: Maurice Herbster

"He's that rare thing: an engineer willing to get his hands dirty," said Henry Farman to an American journalist when questioned in 1908 about the unusually generous remuneration paid to his stalwart mechanician Maurice Herbster.

But Herbster was no ordinary mechanic. A natural sportsman, he had as a young man competed with some distinction at amateur level in the events for which his stocky build and phlegmatic temperament were best suited: boxing, wrestling and shot putting.

He served his engineering apprenticeship for three years with one of the most important figures in the history of the bicycle: Jules Truffault, who in 1875 revolutionised bicycle design with the invention not only of hollow front forks (originally adapted from steel sabre scabbards, it is said), but also wire wheels – initially, with no fewer than 304 spokes. Truffault also patented the first automotive shock absorber (sold worldwide as the Hartford) in 1898, before going on to manufacture bicycles and belt-driven voiturettes under his own name.

It was while working for Truffault that Herbster first met the Farmans, in the long distance cycling events of the 1890s. Whichever of the brothers it was who first recognised his talent, Herbster was recruited in 1901 to help run their nascent motor business and to support the young Maurice Farman's ballooning exploits. He did so with aplomb, inventing an ingenious anemometer that indicated a balloon's direction of travel, and his meteorological kite of 1901 won first prize in a prestigious public competition. He was chosen by Count Henri de la Vaux as his partner in balloon cycling races, in which the hapless passenger completed part of the course on two wheels. By then moving in the rarefied circles of wealthy gentleman amateurs with a taste for glamour and speed, Herbster also took part in the 1903 Monaco powerboat racing championships, at the helm of the Farmans' fast Panhard-powered *Palaisoto*.

His progression from ballooning to heavier-than-air flight was inevitable. Herbster was experimenting with Hargrave cells as early as 1901, as the Voisin brothers had done. In 1903 he built and exhibited a working scale model of a rubber band-powered twin-prop cellular biplane, a modified version of

Left, Maurice Herbster attending to the down-only 'Farman flaps' on I‑bis in Farman's hangar at Châlons in the autumn of 1908, and (*above*) being observed tending the Antoinette.

which competed against the Voisin Archdeacon entry in the in 1905 Aéro Club competition in the Galerie des Machines. A March 1904 report in *Aérophile* observes that he was also working on a full-scale version, which came to naught for lack of funds.

By 1906, at the age of 36, Herbster was chief engineer of the Farmans' motor emporium, the Palais de l'Automobile; his combination of skills, experience and personal loyalty made him the ideal collaborator for the kilometre attempt.

Thereafter, he was appointed general manager and chief pilot of Aéroplanes Farman from 1908 to 1910 and gave many budding aviators the benefit of his experience, first as chief instructor at the Farman flying schools at Bouy and Etampes, and then for Deutsch and Surcouf's Astra company, who were then making Wrights under licence alongside the dirigibles. It was at the controls of a Maurice Farman biplane fitted with floats that Herbster operated the world's first aerial taxi, across Lake Lucerne, where he also piloted Henry Kapférer's *Ville de Lucerne* dirigible service and test flew the first Astra-Wright seaplanes.

Herbster was by then a highly accomplished aviator, with more than 3000 flights to his credit; *Flight* observed in 1912 that by acquiring his dirigible pilot's certificate, he had joined the select ranks of 'triple certified' pilots qualified to fly aeroplanes (in 1910), balloons (in 1911) and airships – a distinction shared by only Santos-Dumont and the military Voisin pilot Captain Albert Etève.

After spending the Great War as test pilot for the propeller, airframe and model manufacturer Les Fils de Regy Frères (whose props equipped many Voisin light bombers) Herbster represented the Levasseur propeller company in the 1920s; by the following decade, he was working with the young engineer Fernand Picard (who years later designed the postwar Renault 4CV and Dauphine) on submersible craft, for which he lodged a number of patents.

Despite having a boss as dourly dogmatic as the machine's creator was autocratic, Maurice Herbster's practical engineering talents and indomitable grit played a significant role in the development of Europe's first usable aeroplane. He died in 1951.

Maurice Colliex poses proudly at the controls of the big Voisin *canard* he tested at Issy-les-Moulineaux in 1911.

IV. The loyal lieutenant: Maurice Colliex

Although usually relegated to a footnote in the history of early aviation, Maurice Colliex made an important contribution to the genesis and evolution of Farman's Voisin.

With hindsight, Colliex was destined to fly since first meeting Gabriel Voisin in class at the Lycée Ampère in Lyon when they were both 16. A talented amateur climber among his other athletic accomplishments, it was studying the soaring of Alpine eagles that ignited his initial interest in flight. Like the Voisin brothers, he began experimenting with kites and gliders made of bamboo and bedsheets, and was introduced to the literature of flight theory through the unlikely offices of the Lyon dentist they shared, Jean-Claude Pompéien-Piraud. A proponent of the ornithopter, this eccentric former designer of mechanical stage props had turned his waiting room into a library on the subject, which the boys avidly devoured.

These studies of the work of Mouillard, Lilienthal, Langley, Chanute *et al* continued until Colliex graduated in physics and mathematics in 1901. While working as an engineer, he pursued further experiments with cellular gliders on the banks of the Rhône at Vassieux until invited by Gabriel Voisin to join the Blériot-Voisin company at the rue de la Ferme in 1906, where he remained his right-hand man as draughtsman, chief engineer and, later, test pilot - in effect, the world's first.

It was Colliex who set up the Voisin flying school at Mourmelon in 1909. As chief instructor, his pupils included Louis Paulhan, Etienne Bunau-Varilla, Henry Fournier and Jean Gobron. He must have been confident of his tutorial abilities, because he allowed Gobron to take Mme Colliex aloft.

The following year (when he was awarded his official pilot's licence) he oversaw the manufacture and delivery of the first all-metal 13.5-metre Voisin light bombers to the military as well as leading the team responsible for both terrestrial and amphibious versions of the Voisin *canard*. It was Colliex who flew the prototype – arguably the first seaplane in the world – along the Seine in October 1910, and concentrated on the further development of this innovative machine throughout

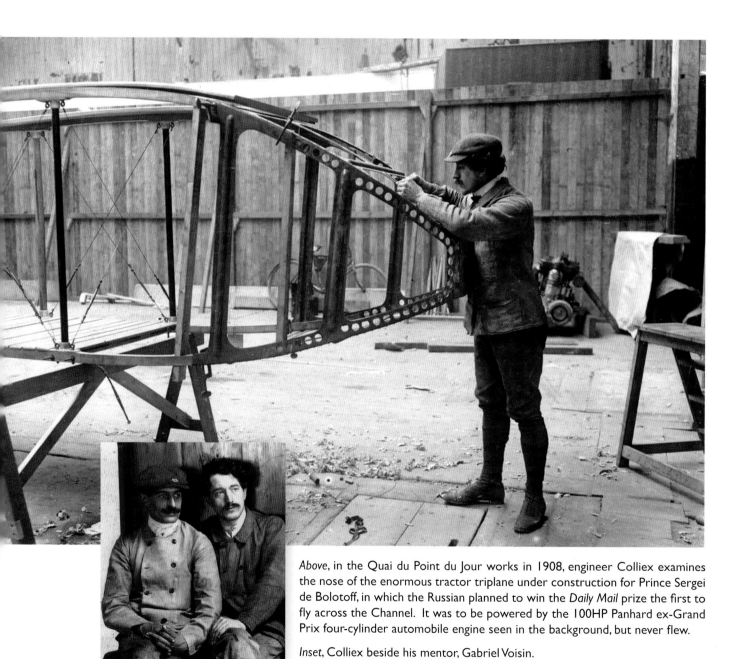

Above, in the Quai du Point du Jour works in 1908, engineer Colliex examines the nose of the enormous tractor triplane under construction for Prince Sergei de Bolotoff, in which the Russian planned to win the *Daily Mail* prize the first to fly across the Channel. It was to be powered by the 100HP Panhard ex-Grand Prix four-cylinder automobile engine seen in the background, but never flew.

Inset, Colliex beside his mentor, Gabriel Voisin.

the first half of 1911 until its delivery to the French Navy aboard the hastily converted seaplane carrier *Foudre* – another world first. He also pioneered a programme of audacious night flying experiments for the military, and oversaw the design and construction of the first and only Voisin four-cylinder aero engine.

These experiences equipped Colliex – still only 32, like his mentor – to strike out on his own in 1912, with an ambitious attempt to build a 24-metre wingspan double biplane flying boat with the engineer Maurice Jeanson. Jointly financed by the army and the Aéro-Club, with two 21-litre 200HP Chenu AH6 airship engines on a common crankcase driving a 4.4-metre propeller and weighing nearly five tonnes with ten people aboard, the Jeanson-Colliex was by far the largest and heaviest aircraft in Europe. The three-kilometre maiden flight of this giant machine took place from the Seine in May 1913, but it suffered irreparable damage when the Despujols hull parted company with the wings on touching down on the river.

A second version with a 600HP Salmson engine and a two-tonne payload was aborted with the outbreak of war, when Colliex was called up – initially into squadron V.14, and then as pilot instructor at the Voisin training schools at Pau, Avord and Ambérieu, where he oversaw the training of some 2500 military pilots between 1915 and 1918, in addition to being responsible for the repair and maintenance of the Voisin bombers stationed there.

On demobilisation, Adjutant Colliex had accumulated 3400 flight hours and was awarded the Military Medal and the Médaille de l'Aéronautique as well as being appointed an officer of the Légion d'Honneur. He joined Société Continentale, the company formed by Pierre Prier and Louis Paulhan to commercialise Parkerisation, the American phosphate conversion coating process, for the aviation industry.

In terms of theoretical and practical knowledge, engineering talent, loyalty and moral support, Maurice Colliex was a prime mover in Gabriel Voisin's endeavour. As unassuming as he was courageous, he was the safe pair of hands his mercurial school friend required.

He died in 1954.

Proselytising as always, Ernest Archdeacon (*left*) makes his views known to Franz Reichel of *Le Figaro* (see p.187)

V. The catalyst: Ernest Archdeacon

In matters of technology, innovation needs a stimulus in the form of political or commercial funding, and public prizes have for centuries been an effective mechanism for incentivising the new.

France's position in the vanguard of automobile and aeronautic progress from the 1890s to the Great War was in no small part due to the vision, energy and generosity of Ernest Archdeacon, who played such a pivotal role in Voisin's early career. Born in 1863, he devoted most of his life to research in applied sciences – and as the scion of an immensely wealthy Irish stockbroking family, his enthusiasm was motivated by a mixture of idealism and intellectual curiosity rather than commercial self-interest.

As with Farman and many of his contemporaries, Archdeacon's progression from racing bicycles to powerboats to cars to aeroplanes was a natural one for anyone intoxicated by speed and driven by the desire to break down barriers. In the latter respect, it can be no coincidence that both Archdeacon and Farman were passionate advocates of Esperanto. Ultimately, he viewed the prospect of air travel as an instrument for attaining world peace – "a revolution which will, at a stroke, transform relations between the peoples of the world".

Soon after qualifying as a lawyer at the Court of Appeal, Archdeacon threw himself into cycling and ballooning, convinced of the latter's potential for gathering meteorological, biological and topographical data. He achieved noteworthy flights in his spherical hot air craft *Courant d'Air* and *Pionnier* in 1885 and narrowly cheated death two years later, in November 1887, when he took part in L'Hoste and Mangot's ill-fated third cross-Channel balloon flight. Fortunately for Archdeacon, damage sustained during take-off in Paris led to his being set down before crossing the coast. Within hours, the craft fell victim to gale force winds, and neither it nor its occupants were ever seen again. Undaunted, Archdeacon went on to make one of the most heroic, not to say reckless, balloon flights of all. In March 1895, accompanied by his friend Léon Serpollet and the blue-blooded engineer Count Henri de la Valette, he took off in hurricane force winds from Paris and landed two hours later some 240 kilometres away in Charleville-Mézières – a world record average speed of 120km/h.

Archdeacon was an ardent sponsor of every type of locomotion.

Above, conducting the 6HP 2.5 litre works Delahaye which he drove to 7th place in the 1896 Paris–Marseille–Paris race.

Left, beside his old friend Léon Serpollet in the Peugeot-Serpollet steam tricycle before their epic drive from Paris to Lyon in 1890.

Far left, in Sarcia and Moussette's electric phaeton in 1898.

He had met Serpollet (holder of French driving licence N°·1) in the late 1880s, when he became the financial backer and first customer of the newly formed Société des Moteurs Serpollet Frères, whose revolutionary steam engines he used to power several high speed launches. So it was that in January 1890, he accompanied Serpollet to drive the latter's Peugeot-Serpollet steam tricycle from Paris to the factory where they were to be manufactured in Lyon – in effect, the first ever long distance journey by motor car in what many regard as the first ever proper automobile.

The 286 miles were covered in ten days - an average speed of around half walking pace, much to the delight of the nay-sayers against whom he railed all his life – yet their arrival in Lyon was nevertheless met with cheering crowds. They brought the car home by train, nursing the many injuries they had sustained during the trip. But far from being discouraged, the intrepid pair embarked on a second expedition to the Ardèche soon after, followed by a third to England. He went on to compete in the great road races of the nineties, driving a more powerful Serpollet to 17th place in 1894 Paris-Rouen trial, and as a shareholder and representative for Delahaye, he drove works cars in the Paris-Marseilles-Paris, Paris-Dieppe and Nice-Castellane-Nice events of 1896, 1897 and 1899.

Archdeacon acquired the Rouxel & Dubois engineering works in 1895, which merged with Paris Singer Ltd to build automobiles and bicycles in London and Suresnes from 1898-1902, patenting several designs for racing machines. Like Santos, he made a point of not exploiting his 15 *brevets* – his passion lay in researching and developing new ideas rather than their commercial exploitation.

In 1895, he co-founded the Automobile Club de France; three years later, he joined Henry de la Vaulx, Deutsch de la Meurthe, Count Albert de Dion and Gustave Eiffel to form the world's first aeronautical association, the Aéro Club de France, and personally endowed several prizes to encourage ballooning. Subsequently recognising the limits of lighter-than-air technology, he set up the Aéro Club's Aviation Committee in April 1903 and was hugely influential in attracting investment to aeronautics in France.

He proselytised endlessly, advancing his theories on aviation in innumerable scientific and popular journals of the time. In the month he founded the Aviation Committee, he reported in *La Locomotion* on the influential Aéro Club seminar in which Chanute set out the principles of the cellular biplane

Left, the fearsome *aéro-motocyclette* Archdeacon commissioned from Farcot for Alessandro Anzani, with its transversely mounted 6HP V-twin and sturdy belt drive to the large pulley on the propeller shaft from whose housing the engine was suspended. The starting wheel was later removed, and the engine started by cord by Archdeacon's chauffeur. The bag at the front contained the battery ignition. The purpose of this 70kg machine was to attract publicity more than for serious research, in which it succeeded. Although never intended as a means of transport, the *Revue Olympique* declared that, once equipped with vestigial planes, the machine presaged the advent of low-flying aerial motorcycles for all.

Below, September 11th, 1906: Archdeacon beside his Milanese protégé, apparently unfazed by his less than pedestrian-friendly mount, just before the timed 50mph run across the Parc d'Achères, where Jenatzy had taken the land speed record in *La Jamais Contente* seven years before. Despite the wide aluminium prop blades being extensively drilled to reduce centrifugal stress, the brazing soon gave way. Archdeacon's pleas to halt the tests fell on deaf ears as Anzani (a future Voisin pilot) carried on regardless.

(although in a letter to the Wrights, Chanute himself dismissed Archdeacon as "a lightweight"). Alongside the gliding experiments conducted from land and water by Gabriel Voisin, Archdeacon pursued his own researches into the efficiency of marine propellers and airscrews – most notably in 1906, with the help of Buchet's chief engineer Ambroise Farcot and Alessandro Anzani, the fiery Milanese ex-European champion gymnast, bicycle racer and world champion motorcyclist whose early manufacturing ventures Archdeacon had personally financed. With a giant two-litre V-twin fitted transversely in a lightweight racing Alcyon-Buchet frame, and a 1.5-metre belt driving an exposed aluminium-bladed propeller, Anzani reached nearly 80km/h over a measured kilometre on Archdeacon's *aéro-motocyclette*. No one else was ever foolhardy enough to ride it again – but thanks to the demands of a cycling trainer who wanted a more powerful pacemaking machine, the engine is said to have evolved into the famous fan configuration triple that later became widely used in aeronautical circles, including by Blériot for his cross-Channel flight.

By offering the 5600-franc *Concours du Vol Plané* as well as the Grand Prix de l'Aviation in 1904, Archdeacon provided a powerful incentive for France's aspiring aeronauts. If Archdeacon was the Maecenas of European aviation, his achievements were more than merely philanthropic; he was an imaginative thinker of considerable prescience. An ardent protagonist of the automobile, the telephone and photography in addition to heavier-than-air flight, he was always coming up with new ideas of his own (including the Archdeacon bedside reader, an electrically controlled variable rate projector of printed text onto the ceiling to facilitate continued study while lying down).

He also invented an automobile speedometer, a complicated mechanism involving a centrifugal governor, which he commissioned from a sceptical Batignolles clockmaker. Under the pseudonym Paul Géry, he even found time to write a play (*La Conquête de l'Air*), which flopped in 1905. Later, in 1926, he was one of the founders of the International Radio Association.

Despite his great wealth, and despite having acted as midwife to one of the defining technologies of the century, decades of supporting others financially while being hounded by the tax authorities left Archdeacon with only modest means, and he died, undeservedly forgotten, in 1950.

Captain Ferber in his experimental *aérovoiturette*, the rolling testbed he constructed from bamboo in 1906, with a 12/16HP Peugeot engine driving two large coaxial propellers.

VI. The proselytiser: Ferdinand Ferber

Captain Ferdinand Ferber's premature death at the age of 47 – the only man ever to lose his life in a civilian Voisin aeroplane – accounts in part for the fact that he is not better remembered as one of the pivotal figures in the early development of aviation.

Tragedy struck on the evening of September 21st 1909 when, while practicing for a planned cross-Channel attempt, the wheels of his machine fell into an overgrown drainage ditch as he was taxiing to a halt after a rough landing on wasteland just outside Boulogne-sur-Mer, pitching the craft onto its nose and pinning him fatally beneath the dislodged Antoinette. By then, Ferber had spent ten years tirelessly advocating the cause of heavier-than-air flight by organising public conferences, publishing papers in the many aviation journals, maintaining personal contact with all the leading practitioners (notably Ader, Chanute and the Wrights) and conducting public experiments with his own designs.

Inspired to study maths by the adventures of Jules Verne, the 15 year-old Ferber was academically gifted enough to secure a place at the Ecole Polytechnique, and subsequently took a science degree as Captain of Artillery; it was in the Fontainebleau library of the Artillery regiment in 1895 that he discovered in *Illustrierte Zeitung* accounts of Otto Lilienthal's meticulously conducted flight experiments in Germany four years earlier. As the first in France to appreciate the value of these trials to flight theory, Ferber determined to devote his energies single-mindedly to promoting aviation – a process he always saw as incremental by nature. The closing years of the century he therefore spent undertaking trials of his own bamboo and silk gliders; it wasn't until 1901 that he read of the Lilienthal-inspired gliders of Chanute in Chicago, and his influential 1894 publication *Progress in Flying Machines*.

In the Alpes Maritimes in 1902, Ferber's glider flew so well that he began searching for suitable motive power. In its absence, he erected by the Promenade des Anglais in Nice what he termed his *Aérodrome* – an 18-metre pylon around which a counterweighted 30-metre horizontal arm could support his motorised gliders for stability tests.

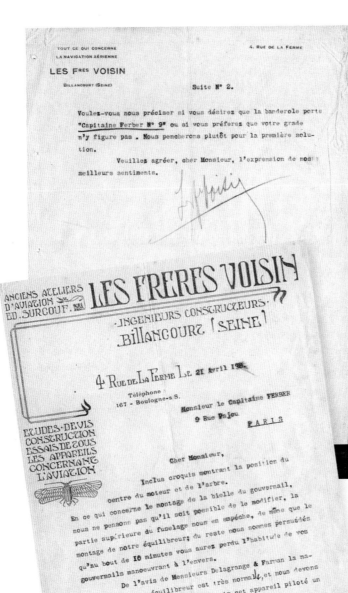

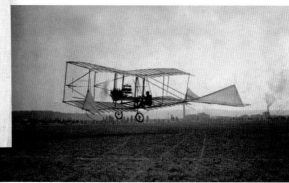

Top, Ferber's effective 1904 glider and (*above*) his less successful 1908 tractor biplane.

Left, a letter to Ferber from Charles Voisin in April 1908, regarding modifications Ferber had requested to the Voisin 10-metre he had ordered.

It was in this machine that Ferber lost his life 18 months later while preparing for a cross-Channel attempt – the only non-military fatality in a Voisin.

Note the Voisin scarab motif on the letterhead, which is often erroneously said to date from the company's participation in the Heliopolis aviation meeting in Cairo in 1910.

No fewer than 260 experiments were conducted with this improbable device – even the Wrights, to whom Ferber first wrote in August 1903, were impressed by its practicality.

Later that month, Ferber was giving a lecture on aviation at the behest of the Aéro-Club du Rhône when he was joined on the podium by "a young man with bright, intelligent eyes" who declared that, having understood every single thing Ferber had described, he had decided thenceforth to devote himself entirely to aviation. Despite the difference in their ages, the two must have struck a chord, as Ferber later recalled that it was the young Voisin who had most completely understood the aeronautical ideas and practical advice he had sought to present.

Over Easter in 1904, Archdeacon summoned Ferber from Nice to join his team for the glider trials from the dunes at Berck, but his attempts proved less successful than those of the younger (and considerably lighter) Voisin. Thereafter, the two remained in close contact, regularly exchanging technical information on both theoretical and practical aspects of design and construction. Ferber was also present at the momentous towed glide down the Seine in 1905.

The full account of Ferber's experiments in the *Revue d'Artillerie* in March 1904 was seized upon by Archdeacon, who further publicised his findings; although he was invited by Colonel Renard to join the research team at Chalais-Meudon, much of his subsequent work there was financed at his own expense, rather than the government's. There, Ferber constructed a system of pylons supporting a 40-metre cable at an angle of 33° for further trials of his gradually evolving tractor biplane prototypes; he published the results of those with the Buchet-powered Ferber N°6 in *Scientific American* in the spring of 1905. In the *Revue d'Artillerie* in August (having in the interim ordered a 24HP Antoinette from Levavasseur after fruitless tests with an asthmatic 12HP Peugeot unit), he made public such information as he had received from Chanute about the Wrights' 1904 flights, but by then, with the death of Charles Renard, he found himself out of step with the lighter-than-air predilections of the military establishment. Dispirited, he negotiated a three-year sabbatical from the army to join the Antoinette company in June 1906 as a consultant to the board, while continuing to work on the ninth of his own prototypes.

Ferber in his Voisin at Boulogne-sur-Mer shortly before his fatal accident in September 1909. Note the front-mounted fuel tank, large enough for his intended cross-Channel flight.

It was Ferber who led the press campaign against the decision to prohibit any more aviation experiments at the *champ de manœuvres* in July 1908, but he paid the price for such public dissent by being recalled to resume (mainly bureaucratic) military duties. For this reason, his flights from this point onwards were made under the pseudonym De Rue.

The magnum opus he began in 1905 appeared that month as *L'Aviation, ses débuts, son développement*. In it, the visionary side of Ferber emerges as clearly as the technologist. He forecast average speeds of 300km/h and cruising altitudes of 8000 metres; beyond that, he reasoned, the thinness of the atmosphere would require rocket or jet propulsion, with the occupants in pressurised cabins. He predicted flight from Paris to Beijing in 48 hours, and considered the profound psychological effect of flying the Channel on British insularity – as with so many of his contemporaries, flight's inevitable erosion of the concept of national borders is a strong theme. He foresaw aeroplanes in regular use by politicians and business types as well as for valuable or urgent freight (not to mention smugglers of contraband and fleers from justice). His general tenor is however optimistic, seeing the new technology primarily as a means of bringing peoples together rather than as a weapon of war.

When René Quinton founded the Ligue Nationale Aérienne in September 1908, he asked Ferber to join the enterprise as chief instructor, which he accepted. Awaiting completion of his *Ferber X* by his mechanician-cum-designer Marius Burdin, the captain bought the ill-fated 10-metre standard biplane from Voisin Frères, in which he competed with some success at the inaugural meetings at Reims and Port Aviation, as well as at Belfort and Wimereux before the catastrophe at Boulogne.

As per his obituary, Ferber "dedicated to the cause of aviation all his intelligence, his scientific abilities and his bravery. He was at the same time the apostle, the prophet and the craftsman. To this endeavour, he sacrificed his career – and like Lilienthal, whose first French disciple he was, his life. At least he had the satisfaction of seeing the realisation of the great idea he had so nobly and unstintingly served."

Below, Henry Kapférer chatting to Wilbur Wright during the sensational demonstration flights at Auvours.

In stark contrast to the Voisin's lightweight bicycle wheels, the hefty dolly required to manhandle the Dayton machine on terra firma had wooden cart wheels better suited to the primitive 5HP Prétot forecarriage in which Kapférer had competed in the world's first hillclimb event at Chanteloup-les-Vignes ten years earlier (*left*).

VII. The friend: Henry Kapférer

The eldest son of the industrialist Jean Kapférer and favourite nephew of the oil tycoon Henri Deutsch de la Meurthe, Henry Kapférer was born with the proverbial silver spoon – but he made excellent use of it.

Graduating as a civil engineer from the Ecole Supérieure des Mines, his early career was spent at his uncle's company, which later became Shell Oil. He sailed the 85m tanker *Le Lion* across the Atlantic in 1893, and went exploring for, and negotiating the rights to, new wells in the USA, the Caucasas, Japan and Indonesia, where he was the first to cross Sumatra by automobile, in a 3.5CV Renault in 1901.

Like Archdeacon, Kapférer was a founder member of the Automobile Club de France and co-founder of the Aéro Club, although still in his twenties. Attracted by the fledgling aviation industry on his return home after the globetrotting years, he joined his uncle's balloon and dirigible manufacturing firm Astra in 1902, where he worked on stability systems, propeller design and model gliders.

At the giant Astra works at Issy-les-Moulineaux and Surcouf's hangar at Sartrouville, Kapférer oversaw the construction of the groundbreaking 62-metre dirigible *La Ville de Paris Nᵒ2,* which his uncle had commissioned in 1906 at a cost of more than a million francs. With Voisin's 6-metre Renard propeller driven at 180rpm by a 70HP Chenu engine, the airship had its maiden flight in Kapférer's hands in October 1906. By the end of 1907, it had made nearly 30 flights, including cross-country sorties of up to 125 miles, breaking national aerial endurance and speed records in the process; it enjoyed a brilliant subsequent career giving domestic and foreign dignitaries and celebrities (including Delagrange) their first taste of air travel.

Over a 15-year period, Kapférer was involved in building and piloting 44 dirigibles including France's first military airship, the *Clément-Bayard Nᵒ1* of 1908. Ten years Gabriel Voisin's senior, he remained a close friend from 1906 onwards, and as a commissaire of the Aéro Club, he wrote the official report on Farman's closed kilometre flight; his habitual bowler hat was a familiar sight at all the

As a commissaire of the Aéro Club, Kapférer witnessed most of the landmark events of the period in both lighter- and heavier-than-air machines.

Left above, on March 26th 1905, as Gabriel Voisin unrolls the tow line and an assistant greases the launch rails on the *champ de manœuvres* prior to testing Archdeacon's second glider as the bowler-hatted Kapférer watches the machine's owner take wind speed readings on his Jules Richard anemometer, then the standard instrument for the purpose.

Left below, at the same place a year later, on the morning of March 16th 1908, Kapférer grimly measures out the course for yet another record attempt. Gabriel Voisin (*far right*) seems equally glum at the sight of the snow-dusted and lumpily frozen terrain. The eminent journalist and author François Peyrey, an ardent supporter of the Wrights, trudges along behind the bicycle; for the local lads, despite the cold, the prospect of yet another flight by the daredevil *avionneurs* was clearly more fun than attending Sunday Mass.

officially observed flight trials on the Issy parade ground. After the disappointing experiences with his own Voisin, Kapférer went on to construct three REP-engined tandem-wing monoplanes to Louis Paulhan's design at Astra. Though ingenious, these were no more successful.

After being almost scalped by a car crash when driving his brother and the engine manufacturer Chenu in 1909, Kapférer endowed the University of Paris's Institut de l'Aérotechnique at St. Cyr the next year, when he also founded the Compagnie Générale Transaérienne. The CGT supplied the non-rigid *Ville de Lucerne* airship Kapférer designed for the world's second scheduled air service, Aero Association Lucerne, initially flown by Maurice Herbster as CGT's chief pilot.

'Kap' was a director on many other company boards and served on innumerable industry bodies; a well-known figure in Parisian society, he was even rumoured to be one of the Dutch spy Mata Hari's paramours.

Thereafter, along with Santos-Dumont, he became a mover and shaker in the worlds of skiing, camping and sailing, and in the 1920s he invented and marketed a successful range of self-steering trailers (also known as Kaps) and various other automobile accessories with his brother Marcel - a business he had been involved in since the early years of the century, as the agent for Vinet detachable rims.

Curiously, he patented several low-pressure inflatable structures – hangars, temporary shelters and masts – in the 1930s, many of which bear strong similarities to several designs by Gabriel Voisin from 15 years earlier.

A man of the arts as well as of science, he is probably best known today for the formidable collection of Symbolist, Impressionist and Postimpressionist paintings he assembled with Marcel – indeed, Vuillard famously painted the two brothers at home in 1912, as well as Henry's wife and children.

Perhaps indicative of Kapférer's adventurous character is that in 1950, not long before his eightieth birthday, he rode 500 kilometres from Paris to his country house near Périgueux by *Vélosolex*...

Wilbur (1867–1912)

290

VIII. The opposition: Orville & Wilbur Wright

Asked by a US journalist to sum up his impressions of France in August 1909, Wilbur withdrew the wheat stalk from his mouth and replied: "I don't know as they like me, nor me them. But that doesn't matter. I've got something I want to sell, and they want to try it if it's all wool and a yard wide…"

Together with the Wrights' understandable concern for monetising their invention, this brisk mutual antipathy runs throughout the story of the homespun Ohioans and their cosmopolitan French competitors, for whom even their surname, with its bafflingly unvoiced Anglo-Saxon consonants, seemed alien - it was generally pronounced 'Vrikt'. Not that lucre in itself was the brothers' main motivation: "We want to get enough from the sale of the first flyer to make us independent of work," Wilbur confided to the *Herald*, "so that we shall have leisure to pursue our investigations without having to be constantly pressed for funds or hampered by the necessity of devoting our time to the control of a great manufacturing business."

To that end, they had no interest in selling machines to private individuals for sport, entertainment or any commercial purpose. Since they always saw flying machines as offering a decisive advantage in time of war, for dropping high explosives as well as for reconnaissance, their priority was to conduct negotiations at government level. "Our neighbours don't hide the fact that they want to be masters of the air at all costs, not so much for scientific reasons as military ones," tut-tutted *L'Aérophile*. In France, resentment of their secrecy and perceived avarice was stoked by the Wrights' behaviour. By their own admission, they hadn't flown for two years, since October 1905. Why not? In London and Berlin as well as in Paris, the niggling doubt as to whether the Wrights were 'flyers or liars' made caution the wisest course for any authority wishing to avoid appearing foolishly gullible. Even at Le Mans, their draconian stipulations raised hackles. Having sold the rights to photographs of his first flight outside the USA to an American publication, for example, Wilbur banned French press photographers from taking shots of the long-awaited machine. The ban was implemented with such vigour that the authorised photographers were required to organise themselves into security squads to confiscate the cameras of amateurs hoping to take snaps of the machine.

Orville (1871–1948)

There were fundamental differences in temperament, too. Although Farman's half-British parentage and upbringing made him seem coolly detached to fellow experimenters in France, if not downright stand-offish, the Wrights remained phlegmatic to a degree that seemed culturally alien, and Wilbur's dry sarcasm was misread as humourlessness. Not that he was uncultured. Although sensitive about not being university educated, Wilbur had taught himself Latin and Greek; when he first visited Paris in the summer of 1907, he went straight to see Notre Dame and the Louvre rather than the Folies Bergère, and enjoyed meeting cultural giants such as Auguste Rodin and Henri Bergson.

Motor described Wilbur as "essentially a Yankee, with no speck of sentimentality in his character." Even US journalists noted the disconnect. "[The French] are disappointed that he will not show any emotion," observed *The American* in its report of the triumphant Auvours flights. "They would like to see a tear or a blush, or an eye shining in triumph, but instead Wilbur leans up against his shed and begins whittling a stick of wood, or twirling a piece of string in one hand while he assures the French aerial experts of what they ought to see when he really tries. Nor do feminine blandishments have more effect on this quiet young man from Ohio, who walks around his tented field many times a day in his shirtsleeves, giving orders to cut away a tree here or a tall bush there, keeping waiting the bevies of charming young French and American women, who come all the way from the distant Brittany coast to witness his sensational performances."

"They have no right here," whined the ungallant Wilbur. "I don't invade their homes, why should they come over my field?" The report continues: "In the shed on the race course, where he sleeps beside his machine, one sees piled in a corner with hammers, a lathe, files and rusty chains, unopened bottles of Champagne, bunches of flowers and all sorts of such delicate presents, for which the austere Wright, who has been raised in a strictly religious atmosphere, has no use. He does not allow his men to drink or smoke either, nor to work on the Sabbath – indeed, one man has already been discharged for painting over the machine with metallic paint on a Sunday."

The incomprehensibility of these attitudes to the French prevented them from taking the Wrights to their hearts. Wilbur can't have been entirely abstemious though, because a discussion of payloads in *L'Aérophile* observed that by the end of his stay in France, he had put on no less than eight kilos...

Temperamental differences aside, Wilbur's closing remarks to the Aéro Club in November 1908 reveal how much his attitude to France and the French had mellowed during his stay: "If I had been born in your beautiful country and had grown up among you, I could not have expected a warmer welcome than has just been given me. When we did not know each other, we had no confidence in each other; today, when we are acquainted it is otherwise: we believe each other, and we are friends.

"I confess that in 1901 I said to my brother Orville that men would not fly for 50 years. Two years later, we ourselves were making flights. This demonstration of my inability as a prophet gave me such a shock that I have ever since distrusted myself and refrained from all prediction. But it is no longer necessary to look to far into the future – we see enough already to know that it will be magnificent. Only let us hurry and open the roads. Once again, I thank you with all my heart, and in thanking you, I am thanking all of France."

Brabazon described Wilbur as "curious, gaunt, polite, aloof, ready to talk to genuinely interested people but chilly and off-hand with those who treated him as a curiosity. Wilbur and his friend Griffith Brewer greatly enjoyed each other's company," he added. "Their idea of happiness was to be in each other's presence, with neither speaking a word."

The brothers themselves had always remained resolutely matter-of-fact about their own achievements; writing to the Aéro Club in Paris from Dayton in November 1906, Wilbur explained: "When we began in 1900, men already knew how to build wings, screws and motors capable of lifting from the ground. Maxim had six years before reported that he had succeeded in supporting an 8000lb machine over a distance of 300ft (a misapprehension, as Maxim's *Leviathan* never flew). But he found himself confronted by such appalling difficulties in the matter of equilibrium that he decided to abandon the attempt to go further. We determined to take up the work where he left off and to try and solve the problem of equilibrium. During six years we overcame one difficulty after another, only to be confronted each time with fresh troubles whose very existence had never been suspected. It was only in 1905 that we finally reached the point of full control under all circumstances. At first we glided for the sake of cheapness, and afterwards used motors hastily improvised over the winter.

"We learned early on that a really practical flyer must possess great structural strength to avoid the shocks of bad landings, and that it would be necessary to improve the dynamic efficiency of wings and screws till much more than ten kilos per horsepower can be carried. When the complex problem of equilibrium had been solved, we saw that for practical use it would be necessary to secure motors equal to automobile motors for durability and reliability, but if possible a trifle lighter. We aimed at reliability rather than lightness." And, he might have added, manoeuvrability rather than stability, because stability by nature impedes the ability to change direction. But for military applications, it didn't matter to the Wrights that the Model A they flew in France was almost as tricky to master as the original Flyer, nor that lengthy periods of pilot training would be required, nor even that it was also inherently more dangerous and less forgiving of human error.

But like Voisin, Wilbur was not one to forgive human error easily, and it was a standard he applied equally strictly to himself. And also like Voisin, he was a practical man who took pride in what he made with his own hands. Both felt more at ease in working clothes, and both ascribed moral value to manual labour well executed. Although Bollée initially shared the general scepticism of the French press, it was this aspect of Wilbur's fiercely independent character that soon won him over.

"This man is no bluffer," Bollée insisted. "He is shy and modest, working hard from morning till night and never making promises he can't keep. He's as punctual as the best of my workers (Wilbur was reported as scrupulously obeying the factory sirens) and works with real skill. He has confidence only in himself and his machine, on which there's not a single bolt, screw or stitch that has not been the object of his personal attention. Even though he had everything he could possibly need in my factory, he came fully equipped. One senses that he is a man used to counting on himself, and himself alone. When he broke a big needle while sewing the canvas for his machine, instead of sending out for a replacement, he quickly fashioned a new one with his own hands, and very well made it was, too."

Speaking at the dinner in his honour at the Aéro Club de la Sarthe after securing the new world records on September 21st, Wilbur famously joked "I know of only one bird that talks – the parrot, and he can't fly very high."

These were men for whom actions spoke louder than words.

Punctilious, pious and puritanical, Wilbur Wright was portrayed in the popular press as impervious to the hedonistic charms of France, in the person of Marianne. The Charles Leandré caricature adorning the cover of the satirical weekly *Le Rire* (*opposite*) shows him as a bird/man automaton perched on a cone bearing the legend "God helps those who help themselves." The caption beneath alludes to his scathing disregard of the brickbats from his French doubters and critics: "He flies as well as one of our chickens, but he must have a far more leathery hide."

297

54243

298

IX. The conduit: Octave Chanute

The French-born self-taught former railway engineer Octave Chanute (well into his seventies at the time in question) provided the only direct link between the French and the American aeronauts. Having returned to Europe in 1875 to acquaint himself with progress in mechanical flight by Le Bris and others, Chanute retired from his engineering business in 1890 to embark on a second career as a champion of aviation (a word he is credited with coining).

His experiments with Lilienthal-type gliders in 1896/97 having convinced him that Francis Wenham's stacked wing concept offered the best way to achieve extra lift without increasing weight, Chanute applied his experience of using the Pratt truss in bridge building to develop the wire-braced fixed wing structure that was so widely used by subsequent biplane constructors.

It was Chanute who collated and analysed all known data on the theory of powered flight, which he published as *Progress in Flying Machines* in 1894. Although the gliders he built relied on the pilot's body movements for controlling equilibrium in flight, he concluded that automatic stability was the goal - a characteristic of the Voisin, not the Wright.

A Boswellian figure, the tireless Chanute began corresponding with the Wrights in 1899, when Wilbur wrote to him as they started serious work on their machine after reading his text. Thereafter, Chanute helped to publicise the brothers' endeavours, visiting Kitty Hawk between 1901 and 1903 and exchanging hundreds of letters. Ferber first wrote to Chanute in 1901, and thereby became one of the first Europeans to read first-hand accounts of the Wrights' piloted glides.

Over the subsequent years, the continuing correspondence between the two was the main medium through which the French learned of the Wrights' progress, though Chanute was vague about the details, especially regarding lateral control. But as the Wrights' busy-bodying confidant and mentor, and as a tireless proselytiser of the future of flying on both sides of the Atlantic, he played a vital catalytic role in the advancement of aviation during the pioneer years. He died in 1910.

Dandy, idealist and socialite, Santos-Dumont's courageous, internationally publicised exploits and endearing personal eccentricities earned him folk hero status in the golden years of aerial experimentation in Paris.

300

X. The dilettante: Alberto Santos-Dumont

When Alberto Santos-Dumont famously piloted his personal dirigible from his château west of Paris to his town house on the corner of the Champs-Elysées and rue Washington, he tethered the blimp to the railings of a first floor balcony and took tea on furniture he had designed to teeter so high that it had to be accessed by pearwood steps, in order to aid his acclimatisation to altitude. The antithesis of the Wrights in every way bar a shared lack of formal engineering education, Santos had little time for flight theory: "I have never worked seriously on abstract data," he admitted. "I have perfected my inventions through a series of tests, fortified by common sense and experience."

Heir to a vast coffee fortune and imbued with the spirit of Captain Nemo and Phileas Fogg, he was the archetypical early adopter. On his first visit to Paris in 1891, he bought one of the first Peugeot automobiles - one of only two built that year. He led a colourful and eccentric life of privilege, in which he set his sights high in everything from his dandyism to his lofty humanitarian ideals. Like so many others who feel themselves to be above hoi polloi, he was also a chronic depressive.

A tilter at convention and received wisdom, his flyers were his *Roçinantes*. Inspired like so many of his generation by Verne and Henri Giffard, Santos commissioned his first airship in 1898, a spherical 13m^3 balloon of silk and bamboo weighing only 20 kilos, which he fitted with a 3.4HP Wolfert engine – one of the first petrol-powered dirigibles. Three years later, he achieved worldwide celebrity by winning the 100,000-franc prize that Deutsch had offered for the first to fly the 11 kilometres from the Aéro Club at St. Cloud to the Eiffel Tower and back in half an hour. This escapade had all the drama of a space walk, with Santos clambering out along the skeletal nacelle to effect engine repairs in full view of the breathless throng beneath, as the unbalanced craft adopted an ever more alarming angle. With his usual generosity, Santos gave a third of his winnings to his mechanics and the remainder for distribution to the homeless of his adoptive city. Equipped with Blériot lighting, he made the world's first nocturnal balloon ascent in 1903. There followed a series of airships of varying sizes and complexity - even a helicopter inspired by Charles Renard's - until he witnessed Voisin's towed flights along the Seine in Archdeacon's glider.

Never knowingly underdressed, Santos-Dumont in his short-lived N°.15 at St.Cyr on March 22nd, 1907. Flanked by tiny condenser tubes and with 50-odd kilos of Antoinette perched precariously above, his habitual *chapeau melon* seems an alarmingly modest concession to pilot safety.

Santos-Dumont's subsequent cellular biplanes, the ungainly and fragile 14-bis and the oddly configured tractor N°.15, stood little chance of winning the Deutsch-Archdeacon Grand Prix, and Voisin knew it. But what followed – the dainty *Demoiselle* – posed a real threat. With Dutheil & Chalmers or 24HP Antoinette power, this elegantly compact 56-kilo bamboo and silk microlight proved itself to be both fast and manoeuvrable as it zipped to and fro across the Issy parade ground.

Santos prided himself on not protecting his intellectual property, in line with his passionate belief in the free exchange of ideas – a position he could of course afford to indulge. The *Demoiselle* was duly built in considerable numbers by several well-known manufacturers for a reasonable price, thereby bringing aviation within reach of a slightly broader section of society.

On the Wrights, he took a characteristically principled stance: "I would not like to undermine the Wright Brothers' merit. I admire them very much. However, I insist that only after our achievements did they come with a more advanced machine, boasting that it was a copy of one they had built prior to ours. What would Thomas Edison, Graham Bell or Guillermo Marconi say if, after publicly exhibiting the electric lamp, the telephone and the wireless, another inventor claimed a better electric lamp, a better telephone and a better telegraph, stating that he had invented them prior to the above gentlemen?"

"Who does mankind honour with heavier-than-air navigation? Shall it be the experiences of the Wright Brothers, hidden from all (they themselves said that they had done everything in silence so that the results of their experiments would not be published abroad) and unknown to everybody, to the point that everyone characterised my 250 metres as the 'most memorable minute in the history of aviation', or shall it be to Farman, Blériot and me, who demonstrated our inventions in front of scientific committees and in broad daylight?"

As it turned out, despite having been one of the most famous men in the world – and certainly the only one to drive himself by ostrich-drawn trap – Santos-Dumont was to be remembered outside South America mainly for the wristwatch the Cartier company made to his specification. After being refused the hand in marriage of Gabriel Voisin's 17 year-old daughter in 1926, he returned to Brazil, where he took his own life in 1932.

304

XI. The brains: Robert Esnault-Pelterie

The most brilliant, the most high-minded and the most technologically ambitious of Farman's rivals was a striking young man seven years his junior: Robert Esnault-Pelterie. Although best known today as the inventor of the joystick (in 1906), and the pre-eminent European pioneer of space travel, he possessed a formidable array of artistic and intellectual talents.

The son of a wealthy cotton industrialist in Geneva, REP had a gilded education and the native wit to exploit its advantages and connections to the full. On leaving military service at 22 in 1903, he set up his first research lab in the family home in rue des Abondances, Boulogne Billancourt, where he built the Wright/Chanute glider he tested unsuccessfully while Voisin was experimenting with the Archdeacon glider at Berck Plage. He is generally credited as being the first to fly with ailerons, in 1904 - some 36 years after the concept was patented by Matthew Boulton. (Although Colonel Renard had similarly equipped his 1873 machine, it never flew.) In 1906, he moved to larger premises in nearby rue de Silly, where the Farman factory was later sited, to begin constructing prototypes of his distinctive tractor monoplanes; by the time Farman was making the first hops in his Voisin a year later, Esnault-Pelterie was flying the first of these at Toussus-le-Noble, and radically advanced it was too. Clad in taut scarlet muslin, the entire machine was gracefully streamlined; the inverse dihedral wings were internally braced to eliminate the enormous drag created by the usual lattice of exposed wires. It was the first aeroplane in the world to have a fully enclosed fuselage and an airframe constructed from welded steel tubing; to save weight, its undercarriage comprised a single large wheel, with smaller wheels at the end of each wing tip and the tail.

REP also confected his own lightweight engines - all fantails with an odd number of cylinders. The best, with seven cylinders, yielded 35HP for a weight of only 52 kilos and drove a four-bladed screw of his own design. A notorious perfectionist, self-confident to the point of being overbearing, it was this insistence on designing and manufacturing every aspect of his futuristic aeroplane himself that inevitably slowed his progress in the race to the Archdeacon prize.

Light, compact, aerodynamically efficient and unmistakeable in scarlet, Robert Esnault-Pelterie's eponymous REP tractor monoplanes were object lessons of intelligent design; that they failed to achieve commensurate success was more a result of the extent of their novelty than any conceptual shortcomings.

Inset, REP's 1904 copy of the Wright glider, which he tested at Cap Blanc-Nez in January 1905. Chanute had told Wilbur that REP's researches were conducted "in the most painstaking and rational manner", but when Kapférer took Wright to meet REP in June 1908, the homespun autodidact and the wealthy intellectual did not get on. Wilbur remarked that REP's ailerons infringed their patent, and REP in turn dismissed the Wrights as "mere acrobats".

306

It's safe to assume he didn't really care, because 'futuristic' is the key to REP's character. His drive to innovate far exceeded the technologies available to realise his ideas. By the time he first took off in 1907, he already had 15 patents to his name, including one for a jet turbine engine; by the end of 1908, REPs already sported oleopneumatic landing gear. Between 1902 and 1918, he averaged one patent every six weeks (excluding depositions abroad). No wonder he rose at four every morning.

Esnault-Pelterie held the fourth French pilot's licence, which he was awarded in 1908. After being left comatose by a high speed crash landing in June of that year after one of his many test flights at Buc, he left the piloting to others. REP was arguably the world's second commercial aeroplane manufacturer, after Voisin, in which capacity he co-founded the Chambre Syndicale des Industries Aéronautiques, of which, in its later Association des Industriels de la Locomotion Aérienne guise, he remained president until 1919. He also organised the inaugural Salon de l'Aéronautique at the Grand Palais in December 1908.

By then, his restless mind was already exploring spheres far beyond the mere practicality of getting an aeroplane to fly properly. He had set his sights beyond just navigating the atmosphere. In a 1912 paper to the Physics Society of France, he presented one of the world's first scientific discussions of space travel, in which he suggested that atomic energy would hold the key to the problem. As early as 1929, he postulated aero-braking, using atmospheric drag to decelerate spacecraft sufficiently to allow gravitational capture by a planet.

The publication of Esnault-Pelterie's *Astronautics* in 1930 was a landmark in the history of the discipline, and by the early 1930s, the potential of rocketry (experiments with which cost him four fingers) had convinced him that nuclear propulsion would not be required to reach the Moon. Besides an astonishing variety of patented inventions, he continued to work on interplanetary travel until his death in 1957.

If the other pioneer aeronauts were pedalling away at the end of the velocipede generation, Robert Esnault-Pelterie was the first and most meteoric son of the Space Age.

308

XII. The rival: Louis Blériot

Like Otto Lilienthal and the other great precursors, the Wrights applied scientific methods to the experiments they conducted. Santos-Dumont created around himself an atmosphere so rarefied as to dissipate any obstacle that might prevent the fruits of his unfettered imagination from being implemented. Esnault-Pelterie's startling innovations were the product of a visionary intelligence attacking the problem from the academic high ground; and though relatively uneducated in matters scientific, Gabriel Voisin combined a genius for fettling with an empirically-derived certainty about where the solution lay.

Although one of the most successful of the pioneers, Louis Blériot was like none of these, but he borrowed from them all. Just as his 1902/03 batwing ornithopter was inspired by seeing Ader's *Avion N°. III* at the 1900 Paris Exhibition, the Blériot V *canard* was a conflation of Santos' 14-bis and Esnault-Pelterie's plans for his first REP; Blériot's Type VI *Libellule* of 1907, with two sets of wings one behind the other, was modelled on Langley's machine, and his first tractor monoplane, the Blériot VII of later that year, was arguably derived from Traian Vuia's.

Blériot's was a visceral engagement with aeroplaning, and he always tested his own machines. Free of preconceptions of his own and propelled by nothing much more than a fierce will to succeed, the brilliant engineering graduate of the Ecole Centrale des Arts et Manufactures, as a successful entrepreneur who started his business at the age of 25, had the self-confidence to jump impulsively from one concept to another until he found something that worked. This trial and error approach inevitably led to a high tally of the latter, whose perilous consequences he was lucky enough to survive. In Gabriel Voisin, he found a persuasive, practically skilled collaborator with strong ideas about heavier-than-air flight, which Blériot found contagious. Significantly, his own version of the Archdeacon glider performed lamentably. And in the machines he subsequently commissioned during their brief partnership, it's clear that Blériot's fanciful but theoretically unsound ideas, such as the elliptical wing configuration, held sway over Voisin's. He paid the piper, after all.

Blériot was disarmingly promiscuous in his aeronautical ideas. So impressed was he at the sight of Wilbur flying at Le Mans that he promptly suspended his pursuit of the monoplane configuration he had made his own to construct the distinctly Wright-like Blériot X two-seater, seen here just before completion in November 1908. The huge chain driven four-bladed pusher propeller has yet to be fitted. In lieu of warping the 12-metre main planes, he replaced the elevator with three vertical rudders, aided by a sizeable elevator plane carried on triangular trusses (the outermost of which were fabric clad) aft of each wing tip. Blériot's own steering wheel-cum-joystick provided the flight controls – sideways for turning, fore and aft for climbing and descending, with the steering wheel actuating the forward rudders. It was equipped with three disproportionately small wheels with fat, low pressure tyres. A pair of huge, gossamer-like vertical radiators cooled the 50HP V8. As such, it combined many different approaches in one splendidly idiosyncratic, but flawed, machine.

310

Blériot made the monoplane his own. Beginning with an audacious fully-enclosed little rear-engined *canard*, he doggedly pursued different iterations of this configuration until he found one that didn't break and could fly.

After the failure of the stubby little *Libellule*, boasting independent wing-tip ailerons to the front pair of tandem wings set at a steep dihedral, he settled on the sturdy, long-tailed, fully-enclosed tractor design with efficient undercarriage, which became the basis of most subsequent Blériot machines. With its low cantilevered wings, and a large tail whose two parts could be moved jointly to act as elevators or independently as ailerons, the Type VII marked a milestone in flight design. Aviators are also indebted to Blériot as well as Esnault-Pelterie for establishing the template for aeroplane ergonomics, with a central joystick and foot controls.

Above all, Blériot had a surfeit of gumption. Taciturn and authoritarian, he had the sheer grit to overcome more setbacks and obstacles than most have to face. He was brave or single-minded enough not to be deterred by physical injury – nor by impending bankruptcy, to which his huge expenditure on aviation activities threatened to drive the profitable acetylene lighting enterprise he had so skilfully built up over the preceding decade.

When Farman pipped him to the post as the first person in the world to fly from one town to another, Blériot not only did the same thing the next day, but he also flew back to his starting point; making the world's first return cross-country flight, however, doesn't carry quite the same cachet, any more than his being the first to take up two passengers (Santos-Dumont and André Fournier).

So it must have been with frenetic enthusiasm that the irrepressible Blériot contemplated his last throw of the dice: to be the first to fly the Channel in a heavier-than-air machine. It was a world-beater, quite apart from the £1000 it paid. Despite competition from languid Latham in his elegant Antoinette monoplane, it was Blériot who succeeded, and won enduring worldwide fame as a result.

The rest is history – a good war, SPAD, post-war civil aviation, and the early death of an ambitious man who made a difference. He was still active in aviation when he died in 1936.

Right, Léon Levavasseur poses at his drawing board in Puteaux.

Above, dated February 1908, a note from Levavasseur to Hans-Jacob Reissner, who had installed the first V16 Antoinette in the prototype cellular biplane that Voisin had built to his specifications.

312

XIII. The motorist: Léon Levavasseur

With the sole exception of the Wrights', every significant achievement in powered heavier-than-air flight from the turn of the century to the end of 1908 was made possible by the Antoinette engine.

A masterpiece of engineering elegance and precision, it powered the record-breaking 1906 flight of Santos-Dumont's 14-bis, Paul Cornu's first helicopter ascent in November 1907 and Blériot's ill-fated monoplane the following month, as well as Farman's Voisin. As the company's advertisements of June 1907 boldly proclaimed: "To win the 50,000 franc Deutsch-Archdeacon prize, simply buy an Antoinette engine and propeller, add some fabric, a tail, a wheel and a rudder, then sit down, keep calm and see what happens!"

The first commercially available purpose-built aero engine, there was no fat on an Antoinette; it was incomparably lighter and more compact than the contemporary car-derived engines by Buchet, Chénu, Rossel-Peugeot, Clément Bayard and Panhard that were adapted for dirigibles. Its power to weight ratio was only equalled in 1909, by the groundbreaking Gnome rotary.

As its creator, Léon Levavasseur is therefore a central protagonist in this tale. Born in 1863, his early training as a painter was short-circuited by the new science of electricity, to which he applied his creative energies with such gusto that he became chief engineer of the Ferranti-Patin company at the age of 28. He was seconded to Algeria, where he designed the world's first tramway system powered by alternating current.

An ardent apostle of new technologies, his interest in internal combustion was sparked by seeing Gottlieb Daimler demonstrate his motorboat on the Seine in 1887. Determined to build his own – and by then, enthused by the prospect of powered flight – he started work in 1901 on an engine designed to yield one horsepower per kilogram. Without capital (Levavasseur was always complaining he never had enough money even to patent his ideas), progress was slow until a benefactor appeared in the form of Jules Gastambide. A wealthy industrialist, Gastambide had met Levavasseur in Algeria, where his rotund and irascible compatriot had sorted out the troublesome

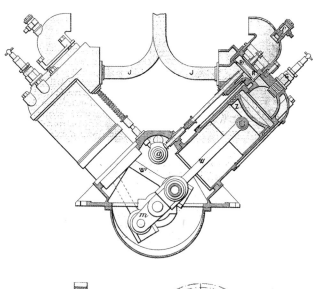

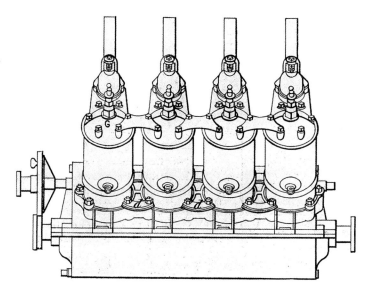

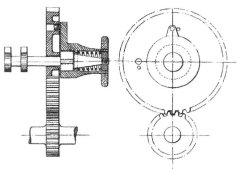

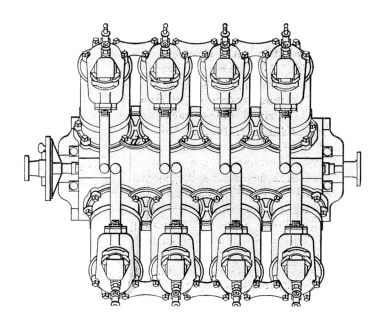

Above, in a bid to emulate the flexibility of a steam engine, the Antoinette boasted a unique feature: its direction of rotation could be manually reversed in seconds. All that was required was to disengage the camshaft from its pinion by pulling the knob provided for the purpose and advance its position by 90 degrees relative to the crankshaft. The ignition timing remained the same. According to Ferber (who sat on the company's board), this facility would prove invaluable for manoeuvring dirigibles into position when docking.

314

generators of his electricity supply company. In the summer of 1902, Gastambide agreed to finance the construction of the revolutionary lightweight power unit Levavasseur proposed. A lathe and two milling machines were duly installed in a rented workshop in Puteaux, along with Levavasseur's brother-in-law Charles Wachter and no fewer than four Welfèringer brothers. Within three short months, the first engine was being bench tested.

Boosted by this rapid progress, Levavasseur made the mistake of prematurely fitting his new unit to an airframe of his own design, which crashed heavily on its first trial flight. A great row ensued when the army, which Gastambide was courting as the main potential customer, contested the claimed power output. Although the promised development subsidy was officially refused, it is said that General André withdrew twenty crisp 1000-franc notes from the safe at Chalais Meudon and pressed them into Levavasseur's grateful palm.

Frustrated, he installed his second engine in a light eight-metre hull, which he christened *Antoinette 1*, after Gastambide's daughter. It proved an immediate and resounding success, outpacing the best that Fiat, Mercédès, Renault and Panhard had to offer (including Farman's *Palaisoto*). Antoinettes ran for four hours at full power in powerboat endurance races, and by the end of 1905 had secured the world water speed record for every distance from one to 150 miles. The engines had flanges at both ends of the crankshaft to allow two or more to be mounted in series, so 16-, 24- and even 32-cylinder variants made their appearance (although the latter promptly sunk the hull into which it was lowered), and Antoinette powerboats were consistently successful at Monaco and other events.

The Antoinette company itself was established in May 1906, with Capt. Ferber as a founder member of the board when he resigned his commission. Realising the value of the engine for his own experiments, Louis Blériot invested heavily in the new enterprise, and was appointed vice president.

Right from the start, Levavasseur opted for at least eight cylinders arranged in two banks at 90 degrees to each other, on the basis that the inherent balance of this arrangement and the number of firing strokes per revolution would obviate the need for a flywheel. It was not the first V8; Clément Ader had experimented with two V4s mounted in tandem as early as 1897.

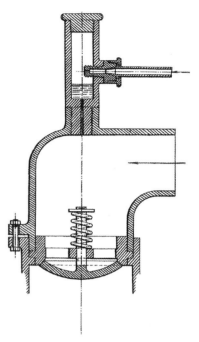

Above, Levavasseur's ingenious but notoriously tricky *mouche* injector. Mounted directly on the bend of the inlet tract immediately above the automatic inlet valve, the fuel was pumped into a small chamber above a tiny (and easily blocked) capillary tube. When the valve opened on the inlet cycle, the consequent depression was sufficient to draw fuel down the capillary tube to be vaporised before entering the combustion chamber.

Its flat plane five-bearing crankshaft ran in a webbed aluminium crankcase with each steel cylinder enclosed in a separate water jacket – initially of spun brass, and then of copper, electrolytically deposited in a lost wax process. This arrangement allowed the cylinders to be individually machined to a thickness of little more than a millimetre. Unsurprisingly, Antoinettes were deafeningly loud.

Although the tiny capacity of these delicate water jackets (little more than 200cc per cylinder) proved adequate on water, where a free flow cooling system was used, it presented a considerable challenge in the air. The water boiled in the jackets was channelled into an aluminium condenser then returned to the engine by a small belt-driven pump on the end of the crankshaft through manifolds to each row of cylinders. Unlike Farman's Voisin, the later Antoinette aeroplanes had large tubular copper radiators on either side of the fuselage to dissipate the heat. Two generously sized valves per cylinder were located one above the other at the side of each combustion chamber, the inlets being automatic and the exhausts actuated by a central camshaft.

Levavasseur's ingenious direct delivery fuel system - there was no injection as such - nevertheless did away with heavy induction pipes, and claimed to render the engine immune from fluctuations in ambient temperature or dew point. Individual plunger pumps operated by variable throw eccentrics fed fuel directly into separate inlet ports, where it was vaporised by the aspirated air. The flow rate was regulated by altering the travel of the eccentrics, but being designed to run at a constant speed, the engine was less than responsive to fine adjustments of fuel flow and ignition timing.

The Antoinette is nevertheless rightly considered an engineering tour de force, without which early aviation in Europe, and Farman's 1908 achievements in particular, would have taken a slower course.

Short, stout, with coarse black hair and a dense ginger beard, Levavasseur was affectionately known as 'Nounours' (the colloquial term for a Teddy bear) by his assistants when he was out of earshot. Face to face, he had a reputation for being anything but cuddly, but this may have been a matter of not suffering fools gladly. A few days before its before delivery to the rue de la Ferme, a reporter from the magazine *Fulmicoton* went to the Antoinette works to see Farman's engine being tested, and his account reveals a more amiable side to Levavasseur's character.

Above, the portly Levavasseur surveys his pretty Antoinette at Puteaux.
Right, looking every one of his 45 years, beside Gabriel Voisin in 1908.

318

"It [*the engine*] was mounted on a stout timber frame bolted to the floor, with a small fuel tank suspended above the exhausts. An experienced assistant swung the large steel and aluminium propeller several times to actuate the mechanical pump sufficiently to prime to the injectors. Everyone then stood clear apart from Levavasseur. At his cry of 'Contact!', a switch was thrown and the propeller was swung another quarter turn. The machine roared thunderously into life, whipping up a sudden whirlwind of dust and dead leaves.

"We all grabbed our hats, but we'd seen nothing yet – the engine was ticking over just enough to reach its operating temperature before full throttle could be attempted. When the *patron* judged this to be the case, he made a hand signal for the power lever to be applied more and more, and we were engulfed in a veritable cyclone of rushing air and screaming machinery.

"The machine ran faultlessly at full power for nearly five minutes before ignition problems interrupted this mechanical symphony. Suddenly, with an imperious gesture, he ordered the ignition to be cut and as the propeller spluttered to an uneven halt, the racket stopped as suddenly as it had begun.

"Dazed and deafened, we spectators were speechless until Levavasseur interrupted the silence.

"'Well, do you like my engine? How many shall I put you down for?'

"'If they were eggs, I'd take a dozen - but I'd like to know the price first,' I replied.

"'For a dozen, we could perhaps come to some arrangement, but normally it costs a trifling 10,000 francs.' (more than the average annual wage at the time)

"'Well, if I emptied my piggy bank I might just about manage a nut or two.'

"'In that case, as such a good client, I'll give you a couple for free,' he chuckled, taking a couple of nuts from the pocket of his weatherbeaten blue cotton jacket and slipping them into my hand. That day, I was enchanted as much by the warmth of Levavasseur's welcome and the kindliness of his humour as his technical competence. Our country is fortunate to have such a genius; when the world gains its wings, it will be thanks to France and Léon Levavasseur…"

Above, Hargrave beside his boxkite at Woollahra Point

Left, although never progressed beyond this sketch, Hargrave's 1895 proposal presages the Voisin Archdeacon float glider and the *biplans à queue* that followed. The only significant differences are Hargrave's ineffectually small cruciform front elevator/rudder and the configuration of the longerons connecting the two main wing cells.

XIV. The precursor: Lawrence Hargrave

"If there be one man, more than another, who deserves to succeed in flying through the air, that man is Lawrence Hargrave, of Sydney, New South Wales," wrote Chanute in his 1893 monograph, *Progress in Flying Machines* - the publication which, together with James Means's aviation annuals, gave the Wrights access to Hargrave's researches. Gabriel Voisin often referred to his 10-metre biplanes, from the Seine float glider for Archdeacon onwards, as 'Hargraves'.

An English-born gentleman scientist of independent means thanks to his father's mining interests, Hargrave began working on the problem of flight in the 1880s, when he was in his forties. As a passionate Darwinist, his inclination "to follow in the footsteps of nature" led him to pursue the impractical ornithopter principle, but after reading what Sir George Cayley's triple paper of 1809 had to say about cambered aerofoils, he undertook his own research into the shape of supporting surfaces and their gliding characteristics in different wind conditions. Although much of his time was spent developing a formidable array of steam, petrol and compressed air engines for his various flappers (including the world's first rotary in 1889, with three cylinders revolving around a stationary crankshaft), he began a correspondence with Chanute in 1891 about his own experiments with curved surfaces with thick leading edges. This led to the invention for which Hargrave is best known – the cellular box kite, which he was convinced offered greater stability and lift than monoplanes. The results of the experiments he ran early in 1893 were presented at that year's International Conference on Aerial Navigation at Chicago's World Exposition, after which Chanute wrote: "He uses exceeding care in determining the different elements which compose the flight of his models. He has carefully registered the sizes of all the parts, the power consumed in each performance, and the length of the flight, together with its trajectory. He states that he has always kept his work in such shape that it could be taken up and continued by any person at any time; so that a stranger, if an expert, could come into his shop, study his notes and drawings, pick up his tools and continue his work, and thus no portion of it would be lost." For the altruistic Hargrave (who admittedly had little need to earn his daily crust), a patentee was "nothing but a legal robber."

322

XV. The engineer: Frederick Lanchester

Respected for his two seminal but impenetrable texts (*Aerodynamics* in 1907 and *Aerodonetics* in 1908), Lanchester delivered a detailed analysis of Farman's Voisin and the Wright at Le Mans to the Royal Aeronautical Society in December 1908.

He felt that the extra heft of the Voisin undercarriage was justified: "If the runners of the Wright would do all that can be done by the Voisin mounting, this additional weight would not be justified, but they will not. The Voisin can rise by itself from any reasonably smooth surface, the Wright is unable to take flight without its launching gear, hence it is not legitimate to attribute its relative lightness to the superiority of its design." (It was not until late 1909 that Wrights gained wheels.)

He deemed the Voisin to be the inferior glider (because of its greater surface friction and the lesser aspect ratio of its wings), but, inefficient as it was, he saw the Voisin propeller as "immeasurably superior from the mechanical standpoint to the chain drive and the wooden propellers of Wright. Since the simple arrangement adopted by Messieurs Voisin is paid for at the price of about a 15 per cent tax on the transmitted horsepower, the question is one of the balance of advantages and disadvantages of entirely different kinds. [..] I consider the Wright disposition of propellers to be a source of danger. If one fails, whether Mr Wright can save himself I do not know." At the time, the first fatality in powered aviation was fresh in his audience's memory, with the death of Lieutenant Selfridge when the machine Orville was demonstrating split a blade of its starboard screw. No other manufacturer of note ever drove more than one prop remotely from a single engine.

"The Wright machine is astonishing in its apparent crudity of detail, he continued. "It is almost a matter of surprise that it holds together at all. By contrast, the Voisin has at least some pretensions to being considered an engineering job." This superiority was evident in a number of ways. Unlike the Wright, the bracing wires of the Voisin could be individually tensioned, for example - a feature which, in conjunction with the cast aluminium strut sockets, allowed it to be rapidly dismantled for storage and transport. But the most important difference he explored was the question of control and both longitudinal and lateral stability - for Lanchester, the Voisin was simply safer.

Above, two weeks after his long flight with Wilbur, Paul Painlevé strikes a pose with Farman in the cramped cockpit of I[-bis] at Châlons in October 1908. As a member of the Stockholm Academy, he officially proposed to the Nobel committee in December that the 1908 prize for Physics be split between the Wrights and Farman and Voisin, but political considerations intervened.

XV. The scientist: Paul Painlevé

One of the lesser known aspects of this story is that both Gabriel Voisin and the Wrights were nominated for Nobel prizes to recognise their achievements in aviation. In December 1908, a week after Farman's final flights at Châlons, the distinguished French mathematician, physicist and future premier Paul Painlevé received a letter at the École Polytechnique from the Swedish mathematician Gösta Mittag-Leffler asking his opinion about awarding the Nobel prize for physics for the invention of the aeroplane to the Wrights, to Farman or to both.

Two caveats were mentioned: that Lord Kelvin had told Mittag-Leffler years ago that Hiram Maxim was the first to have resolved the problem of flight, and that the application must be supported by the respected French polymath Henri Poincaré because no one in Stockholm was competent to pass judgement in such matters.

In his reply three weeks later, Painlevé suggested that the prize be divided into two parts: the first to the Wrights, and the second to the Voisins and Farman, as the only flyers to have mastered changing direction, and that Farman's kilometre preceded the official verification of the Wright flights. Poincaré agreed, and Painlevé marshalled the support of the mathematician Emile Picard, the geometer Jean-Gaston Darboux and the previous year's physics laureate, Gabriel Lippmann.

In January, Painlevé duly submitted a 22-page nomination to the Nobel committee. It was signed only by Painlevé and Poincaré, as Darboux and Lippmann suddenly revealed that they had secretly collected dozens of signatures (including Mittag-Leffler's) to support their nomination of Poincaré. It was an absurd situation, which seemed likely to invalidate both proposals. Politics had intervened – Mittag-Leffler had asked Painlevé to nominate aviation candidates to appease the experimental physicists in the Academy, so they would not oppose Poincaré's candidature.

The ruse failed, because the physicist Svante Arrhenius, a Nobel laureate himself, vetoed the nomination of any candidates from aviation. In his report to the committee, he pointed out that loss of life would ensue from even minor errors in the construction of aeroplanes, and that, in its present state, the invention could hardly be said to benefit mankind. The Academy therefore awarded the 1909 Nobel for physics to Marconi and Braun for their contributions to wireless telegraphy.

Painlevé had for years taken a special interest in aviation, applying his mathematical skills to flight theory. In 1907, he persuaded the Chamber of Deputies to set up a military aviation service, and in 1909 he founded the first university course in aeronautical mechanics.

He was also one of the few to fly as a passenger in both Voisin and Wright machines. At Auvours late in the afternoon of October 11th 1908, with a whopping 45 litres of fuel aboard and surrounded by the usual crowds, he was perched alongside Wilbur when, in the process of retrieving the cap which had been sucked off his head by the propeller draft, Painlevé accidentally yanked the ignition cut-off cord just as the machine hurtled along its launch rail. Powerless, the Model A buried its nose unceremoniously in the sand, snapping a few tensioning wires in the process. Momentarily losing his usual composure, Wilbur was less than amused.

Once repairs had been effected to both the aeroplane and the dignity of its occupants, a second attempt was far more successful: a record flight of some 70 kilometres in 62 minutes, casting long shadows over the autumnal colours of Auvours. It was the most spectacular of Wilbur's many proving flights in France.

Painlevé persuaded Farman to take him up in 1-bis at Châlons two weeks later. His account summarised the French position on the matter: "There are two schools of thought as to how flight is best achieved – the French and the American, as exemplified by Voisin and Wright. [..] The faster an aeroplane goes, the more stable it will be and the more capable of overcoming the caprices of the wind. Such engines will be perfected within a matter of months.

"It is then a matter of ensuring – and herein lies the most serious challenge – that the machine inclines neither towards the front or the rear, nor to the left or right; neither must it deviate from the intended direction. In other words, it must not pitch, yaw or roll excessively, or only do so in a manner whereby the pilot is capable of redressing any resulting imbalance.

"The difference between the two systems lies in the way in which this stability is achieved. Wright prioritises simplicity and lightness above all other factors, but *the stable balance of the machine depends entirely on the pilot*, using three distinct manoeuvres to rectify the three possible conditions, including warping the wings to counteract roll. Thanks to vertical panels between the main planes, like those on a kite, the Voisin is laterally stable. In turns, the machine naturally assumes the appropriate inclination. Two rather than three manoeuvres are required to drive the apparatus: elevator and rudder. Use of the former is furthermore greatly simplified by the addition of a long tail to counteract yaw.

"In terms of power utilisation, there seems little difference between the large slow propellers of the Wright and the smaller high speed Voisin propeller. The Voisin is considerably heavier than the Wright, (650kg as opposed to about 500kg) because of the weight of the tail and because of the undercarriage (80-90kg) required to take off unaided. Bearing these differences in mind, the result of the two approaches is that the Wright holds the outright distance record, both solo and with passenger. It has yet to take off unaided. It will of course be able to do so, but this will be at the cost of adding weight. Farman's Voisin holds the outright speed record, of at least 70km/h, in a machine that has always taken off unaided, thank to its undercarriage."

Painlevé's account of his flight with Wilbur is illuminating: "During the 70 minutes I spent aboard, I was able to observe Wright's gestures very carefully. His left hand, which controls the front elevator via a lever, never rests; by ceaseless tiny movements, it inclines the two small horizontal planes of the elevator in one direction or another. Furthermore, these two planes curve slightly of their own accord as soon as they are inclined, in response to the pressure of the tangential air currents.

"This incessant movement of the elevator is necessitated by the absence of a stabilising tail; like a cyclist maintaining equilibrium via the tiny deflections of the handlebar, the pilot is constantly having to correct the aeroplane's persistent yawing motions. Wright's right hand holds a lever that controls both the vertical rudder at the rear and the warping of the main planes. This hand remains motionless while the aeroplane is flying in a straight line in calm conditions; but in turns, it must simultaneously effect both functions in such a way as to tilt the machine towards the centre of

Above, Paul Painlevé's was the last of some 40-50 flights that Wilbur undertook with passengers at Le Mans (including CS Rolls and Henri Deutsch, who bought 100,000 shares in the French Wright company). Although besieged with offers of large sums to accompany him, he never accepted a sou; the only people he took up were those he personally invited, including Berg's wife and Léon Bollée's 11 year-old nephew.

Inset, unreported at the time, this rare shot reveals that Henry Farman was among the leading lights of France's scientific establishment watching Painlevé's ascents in the Wright at Camp d'Auvours on October 11th, 1908.

the turn, as a bicycle does. One would think that the coordination of these two hand movements would require much practice and independent reflexes in each arm, but with a trained expert at the controls, the Flyer proves remarkably docile – able to make precise tight turns, figures of eight, spirals and so on. Wright seemed able to accomplish these manoeuvres with effortless confidence.

"Only once in the course of our flight did a gust of wind blow us beyond the perimeter of the flying ground; Wright brought his machine to heel as one would an errant horse, making a tight turn and inclining the Flyer towards the horizon. From the cheers that erupted from the spectators beneath, I understood that something exciting had happened, although I had hardly noticed it; had my eyes been closed, I would have sensed nothing. [..] The governing wires are so delicate that they are like extensions of the pilot's nerves. He senses the air through the fabric like a bird with its wings; Mr Wright masters his aircraft like a spirited horse… We turn, we turn, but we are no longer gliding over the camp d'Auvours in the twilight, but across the undefined face of the earth itself."

By contrast, Painlevé's account of his flight with Farman makes the experience sound almost dull: "With my own eyes I have seen Farman undertake the first ever long distance flight, above the field at Châlons and in violent winds; not only did he disappear from the view of the public, but that of the cavalry officers galloping in his wake in a vain attempt to keep up. I have seen him fly his normal circuit several times at altitudes of more than 40 metres.

"Finally, despite the heft of its undercarriage, the machine has taken me as a passenger for a flight of some 1600 metres, accomplishing a turn as perfectly stable as when the pilot alone was on board. In the Voisin, the pilot has but one control to hand: the wheel. Once the aeroplane has attained sufficient speed on its undercarriage, all the pilot has to do is push the steering wheel forwards, which at once makes him an aviator; the elevator plane inclines upwards and the machine is in flight.

"It is much easier to drive than the Wright, but this facility is at the expense of penalties elsewhere. Being heavier, it climbs more slowly and lands less lightly. It is less agile - turns are wider and less precise than in the Wright. Above all, it offers greater resistance to the air, and therefore requires a more powerful engine than the Wright."

XVI. The pilot: John Moore-Brabazon

The only man to have piloted both Voisin and Wright machines was John Moore-Brabazon. After abandoning his trials at Brooklands of the Buchet-engined pusher biplane Howard Wright had converted from the glider built by Short Brothers in Battersea, the ambitious young amateur sportsman and racing driver headed for the centre of European aviation, at Issy-les-Moulineaux – specifically, the Voisin factory, where he agreed to buy the second machine ordered by Farman.

Gabriel Voisin must have taken to the young Englishman four years his junior, because he personally taught his new client to fly at Issy. In May 1909, Brabazon wrote the following for *The Car Illustrated*, and it remains one of the most evocative descriptions of how it actually felt to fly a 10-metre Voisin:

"The type of machine with which I shall deal will be Voisin's bi-plane, similar to that which Farman and Delagrange used, and with which I am more familiar than any other up to now.

"I cannot, however, start without first making it clear that flying machines at present have not reached the stage which the motor car of today has attained. The impression that one only has to buy one, get in and fly is entirely erroneous and my advice to anyone is to approach the subject with respect, and with a firm resolution to see it through. He will have plenty of disappointments, plenty of waiting - sometimes by the week – plenty of hard work, and plenty to learn.

"The whole subject of aeronautics is so empiric that, to those who have some practical experience of its difficulties, the common spectacle of the man who knows all about it is somewhat ludicrous. Let the would-be aviator therefore be prepared to learn, not to teach.

"We now come to our machine, standing ready for its pilot. Its general form is so familiar to the man in the street as to make it unnecessary to describe. The aviator, however, before he gets in (as perhaps his life depends on it) would do well to go round the wiring, feeling every wire to see that all is right. If one wire of two diagonals be slack, do not tighten the slack one; tighten the other till the slack one becomes taut. Having done this, cast your eye over the engine. See that all is in order, and that none of the wire supports to the engine have snapped owing to vibration.

"Next look at your propeller, which in the Voisin has an adjustable pitch. Verify the pitch; this should be done by getting the blades horizontal and then, from a mark, dropping a piece of string with a weight on the end and measuring the horizontal distance from the string to the other side of the blade. This should be the same for each blade, or else the blade has turned slightly in its socket, when it should be reset.

"Having performed this routine work, the aviator gets into his seat, floods the carburettor, and before switching on, sees that there are at least two men holding the machine back. If the engine does not go, a turn of the handle, helped by a man turning the propeller, ought to send her off. The engine once off, the aviator turns round, sits down, and takes hold of the steering wheel, which rotates as well as slides forward and backwards. Rotating the wheel turns the rudder; pushing the wheel forward depresses and elevates the elevating plane.

"The throttle having been three-quarters opened, a signal is given to the men to let go, when, with a bound, the machine leaps forward as if anxious to get away from the earth and everything else. The noise of the engine, the increasing speed, the vibration, and the apparent lack of positive control will instil awe, if not fear, into the stoutest heart (personally, I was terrified); but a few minutes' running along the ground will soon familiarise one to the new sensations.

"After complete 'at homeness' is felt, the throttle is opened a little more and the spark advanced a notch. Instantly the speed increases, and the tail of the machine rises off the ground, giving the driver a feeling that he is going to dive into the earth. This will not happen with the engine set as it is, but the driver can now play with his elevating plane. Depressing it, he will find the tail rising alarmingly; pulling the wheel back and increasing the angle of incidence to the front plane will force the tail down.

"Now the aviator is all impatience to make his first short flight, so the throttle is opened full, the spark advanced, and, remembering his instructions that to fly one must have horizontal speed, the back plane should be so far up in the air as to cause the main planes to make no angle to the horizontal. This is the position for least resistance forward and a very big speed is attained, when suddenly the tail of the machine mounts higher and higher.

"The operator pulls on the front plane to stop this, but with no effect; the front planes dig into the ground, the elevating plane is smashed, and the erstwhile daring aviator is thrown five or six yards into the air. He has made a flight, but not the kind he intended!

"'What ever has happened?' you ask, on picking yourself up. Voisin roars with laughter, and informs you it is nothing; it has happened several times to Farman and Delagrange, and you will soon get over it. I will not endeavour to explain what has happened. The front elevator swings through, let us say, 25 degrees each side of the horizontal when the machine is on the ground. As the tail rises, so the angle you can swing your elevator decreases relative to the true horizontal, until there comes a point, if you allow the tail to get up too much, when the maximum lift you can give to the elevator is to place it horizontal although in its extreme position. In this position it is not trying to lift you in front, and the tail rising still more, you dig into the ground. The only thing to do is to switch off if you have allowed the tail to get too high in this way. Let me tell anyone to whom this has happened that he has done well, as it shows that he appreciates the essence of the question, *i.e.*, that he must have his horizontal speed, and it is his zeal for this that has caused him his accident. The machine is quickly repaired, however; those charming Voisin brothers have foreseen it, and have the new parts waiting.

"Another attempt is now made, the aviator having more respect for his machine than before. The engine is running all out, the back planes get higher and higher, when, before they get too high, a slight pull on the elevating plane is made; when lo!, a jelly-like feeling is felt, and you mount 10 feet into the air. Terrified, you steer for the ground, switch off, and breathe again; still, you have done a flight.

"You have started your apprenticeship. But a word of advice, you pulled your elevator too firmly - just a touch, at first ever so little it must be if you want to sustain the flight. Otherwise you cause the main planes to make too much angle to the horizontal, when the impetus you have gathered will hurl you into the air only to return with a bump to the ground. Therefore, remember to get just off the ground and feel the air pressure on the front plane. Coax her slowly up, never forcing her, gently, gently coaxing the whole time, or else she will come down. Remember that if the resistance forward to the elevator becomes too much in proportion to the lift it gives, you are not helping the machine up, only retarding it, and it will come down. Therefore, be easy with the elevator.

The 25 year-old John Moore-Brabazon made his first flight at Issy in November 1908. A self-confessed 'natural coward' with no head for heights despite his ballooning exploits, he described his first experience as 'like sitting on a jelly in a strong draft'. But he was hooked. He erected a hangar next to Farman's at Châlons, and bought no fewer than four 10-metre Voisins during 1908 and 1909, variously fitted with Vivinus, Métallurgique and ENV engines. Instead of the usual Voisin practice of painting the owner's name beneath the manufacturer's on the tailplane, the fourth bore the name *Bird of Passage*. Exhibited at the first Aero Show at Olympia in March 1909, it was the only machine on display which had ever left the ground. Housed by Short brothers (the Battersea hot-air balloon makers who built the Wright under licence) at Shellbeach, it made the first flight in Britain by a British aviator on May 2nd 1909, two days before Orville and Wilbur arrived with CS Rolls for a tour of inspection. To win the *Daily Mail* prize for first circular mile in all-British machine, Brabazon was later obliged to acquire one of these Short-Wrights.

334

"Now I come to an equally important part of the manipulation of your machine, its lateral stability. As soon as you leave the ground, the machine will take it into its head to turn over sideways, and this must be stopped quickly, or you will dig a wing into the ground and smash your machine up. This is done by the rudder at the back, and I will explain how.

"When in flying you wish to turn, and put your helm over, the arc of the circle described by the exterior of the wing is longer than the arc on the interior of the circle; in other words, if you are turning to the left, the right-hand tip of the aeroplane has to go through more air to get round than the left-hand tip. Consequently it is getting more lift, and the machine will lean over to the left, making, so to speak, its own banking. It is this very peculiarity which you use to balance the machine laterally. If the machine tends to lean to the left, you must steer to the right to pick your balance up. In doing this you cause more air to meet the left wing than the right, consequently the left wing will rise. This sounds very easy, but in practice it is quite the most difficult thing to do of all. As possibly you have already noticed, it is the opposite to a bicycle, and the movements you make on a bicycle become instinctive, so that if you lean to the right you want to turn to the right to pick your balance up, which if done on an aeroplane will lead to disaster. To do an ordinary turn in the air the helm must be held slightly over, and the machine will lean the whole time going round; but, owing to the centre of gravity being below the centre of support, the machine will assume the horizontal by itself after the corner.

"Some final words of advice:

i),   in your initial attempts see that there is no wind, or, if any, get it head on, and on no account attempt to turn;

ii),   never go out in a wind over 12mph until you are an expert;

iii), don't fly too high, never higher than 20 feet.;

iv), don't at first make too long flights, until you are sure that everything is standing up;

v),   the best times to fly are from daybreak till the wind is too strong, and at sunset, when the wind generally goes down.

"All I can tell you, my friend, is that one flight of say half a mile on an aeroplane, driven by yourself, is the most exhilarating, interesting, healthy and sporting amusement it has ever been my wish to experience."

Outside the forge at the Quai du Point du Jour factory late in 1908, the Voisin airscrew used for Farman's closed circuit kilometre machine stands beside that for Count de Lambert's hydroplane (*centre*) and the giant six-metre rotor for Paul Cornu's *Hélicoplane*.

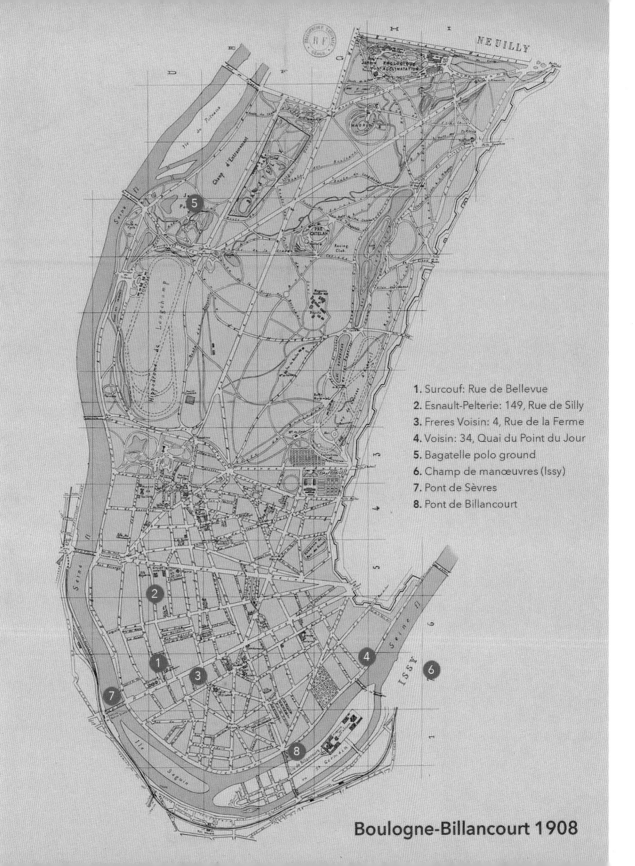

1. Surcouf: Rue de Bellevue
2. Esnault-Pelterie: 149, Rue de Silly
3. Freres Voisin: 4, Rue de la Ferme
4. Voisin: 34, Quai du Point du Jour
5. Bagatelle polo ground
6. Champ de manœuvres (Issy)
7. Pont de Sèvres
8. Pont de Billancourt

Boulogne-Billancourt 1908

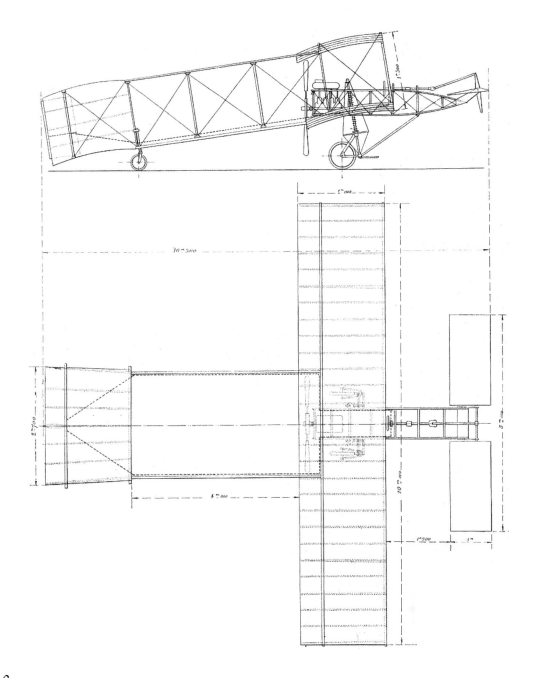

XVII: Technical evolution

August 1907: delivery configuration

Nacelle: Uncovered, with nose 30 per cent shorter than Voisin Kapferer and Delagrange N⁰.1.

Main cell: 10m span, 2m chord with planes set at a slight dihedral 1.5m apart by four pairs of spars on each side, with central horizontal bars bracing the inner four front spars.

Tail cell: 6m span, trapezoidal in elevation, with extended side panels and a single central vertical rudder mounted in line with the leading edge, and controlled via a foot-operated wooden bar in the cockpit. Initially, all lifting surfaces covered in white varnished silk. The legend on the side panel reads HENRI FARMAN N⁰.1' (all in capitals).

Elevator: 5m biplane front elevator actuated by sliding a transverse wooden bar along runners.

Landing gear: Long-travel coil springs on suspension uprights on either side of the pilot parallel to the wing struts, with pairs of castering wheels front and rear (of 70cm & 40cm diameter respectively). The main forks of the landing gear consist of a square-shouldered twin tube assembly.

Engine: Antoinette cooled by radiator of thin copper tubes traversing the nacelle diagonally in front of the pilot. Pointed cylindrical tanks for fuel and water mounted in front of the cockpit.

October 1907: initial modifications

1st-6th — The ignition advance/retard control is relocated to the side of the cockpit beside the pilot.

6th-14th — The large biplane elevator replaced by a two-part single plane (extending 2.1 metres on each side of the nacelle) carried high on the nose by two upwardly curving wooden supports.

The elevator is initially still actuated by a horizontal bar in front of the pilot, linked via parallel wooden members over the nacelle.

16th-18th — The undercarriage assembly is fitted with large spacers beneath the coil springs to increase the machine's overall angle of incidence by 2°, while the angle of the tail plane is reduced by the same amount; the vertical end panes of the tail plane are also shortened.

Bungee cords are added to the top of the springs to act as shock absorbers.

24th — The front elevator is mounted slightly further forward and slightly lowered, as is the engine itself (requiring a cut-out on the upper main plane to clear the tip of the propeller).

November 1907: major modifications

6th-8th

Front elevator actuated by sliding steering wheel column, fitted with a cable and pulley system to operate the rudder in place of the foot bar.

24th-28th

A smaller tail cell replaces the six-metre original; the rudder moves to the extreme rear of the cell, and the long side panels return. The landing gear geometry is also revised, with U-shaped forks replacing the square-shouldered originals and the main suspension uprights inclined backwards relative to the wing spars.

The fuel tank is moved to the upper main plane to avoid vapour lock problems in the fuel pump. A larger 2.3m propeller replaces the 2.1m original, effectively reducing the engine's maximum revs by 200rpm; the diminution of engine power was compensated for by increased thrust. A magneto fitted beneath the pilot's seat replaces the trembler coil and camshaft-driven distributor to overcome problems of humidity.

December 1907: the Grand Prix configuration

18th-24th

The radiator and water tank are replaced by a large condenser tank (conical at the rear) supported above the Antoinette by a large diameter tract rising from each cylinder. The pilot's seat is comprehensively drilled to save weight, and the uncovered main spars on each wing are covered (though Fabre claimed January 7th).

March-July 1908: 1^{-bis} and the Ghent/NY configuration

All lifting surfaces are recovered in rubberized Continental fabric of the type used for dirigibles. On the side panels of the tail, the hand-painted inscription now reads: 'Etudié et construit par les Frères Voisin' (either above or below the owner's name, which is now written 'Henri FARMAN N⁰.1^{-bis}' in lower case). The horizontal bracing bar in front of the pilot is eliminated (although the fixings remain), and aluminium bicycle mudguards with mud flaps are fitted.

The air-cooled dry sump 40HP Renault V8 makes its appearance in place of the Antoinette on March 14th, but fails two days later. By March 19th, it is replaced by the rebuilt Antoinette of the kilometre attempts; the mudguards and mud flaps are also discarded

April 24th-29th   A new 60HP Antoinette is fitted in April in time for the Ghent exhibition flights.

May 25th-June 2nd   At Ghent, vertical panels are fitted on either side of the pilot to protect the engine, with central cut-outs on the leading edge for visibility. A 20-litre expansion chamber is installed above the engine and filled with ice for the attempt on the distance record, and the profiled fuel tank on upper wing is replaced by much smaller cylindrical tank in the same position. Longer induction pipes are fitted, terminating in curved (rather than vertical) intake trumpets.

August-November 1908: Châlons experiments

Re-rigged with no dihedral, the wings are flat; the inner vertical panels with cut-outs on the leading edge first seen at Ghent move to the middle, and outer ones added in a reversion to Hargrave's classic box-kite concept.

Later, large ailerons are fitted the trailing edge of the main planes. These eventually necessitate upper and lower cut-outs to the long end panels to facilitate the ailerons' arc of movement. A movable hoop is fitted to form a canvas windbreak in front of the pilot.

A new Antoinette appears with the fuel tank mounted laterally above the engine immediately behind a large double-matrix radiator with profiled oval neck. Experiments are carried out with intake trumpets set at random heights and directions.

A third upper wing is added and the upper plane of the tail cell extended outwards on November 16th, but by the 28th, 1[-bis] reverts to biplane form, but with the main planes reduced in size for a bearing surface totalling no more than 40m^2. After several such short-lived experimental permutations of the size, profile and number of main planes, 1[-bis] finally reverts to triplane configuration once again for sale to the Austrian syndicate in January 1909.

VOYAGE DE CHALONS A REIMS
FARMAN 1908

COLLECTION ÉDITÉE PAR LEFÈVRE-UTILE

XVIII: Bibliography & acknowledgements

Les Progrès de l'Aviation (Ferber, Berger-Levrault, 1904)

L'Année Scientifique et Industrielle (Hachette, Paris, 1906-08)

Eléments d'Aviation (Victor Tatin, Dunod, 1908)

Le Problème de l'Aviation (Armengaud, Delagrave, 1908)

L'Homme S'Envole (de Forge, Berger-Levrault, 1909)

La Route de l'Air (Berget, Hachette, 1909)

L'Aéroplane Pour Tous (Lelasseux, Lib.Aéronatique, 1909)

Flying Machines (Kennedy, Van Nostrand, New York, 1909)

The Aero Manual (Temple Press, 1909)

L'Aviation - Ses Débuts (Ferber, Berger-Levrault, 1910)

Vehicles of the air (Lougheed, 1910)

The Aviator's Companion (Farman, Mills & Boon, 1910)

L'ABC de l'Aviation (Louis Gastine, Albin Michel, 1911)

Comment Vole un Aéroplane (WH Rolls, Pierre Roger, 1911)

Flying-machine from an Engineering Standpoint (Lanchester 1915)

Les Moteurs d'Aviation (Martinot-Lagarde, Berger-Levrault, 1917)

A History of Aeronautics (EC Vivian, 1920)

The War in the Air, Raleigh, Clarendon press, 1922-28

La Naissance de l'Aéroplane (Voisin, Automobiles Voisin, 1926)

La Gloire des Ailes (Blériot & Ramond, Ed de France, 1927)

L'Envol (Robert Gastambide, Gallimard, 1932)

25 ans d'Aéronautique Française 1907-1932 (Marchis, 1934)

Henry Farman et l'Aviation (Sahel, Bernard Grasset, 1936)

Flight into History (Freudenthal, U of Oklahoma Press, 1949)

The Papers of Orville and Wilbur Wright (McGraw Hill, 1953)

Souvenirs d'une Vieille Tige (Antoine Odier, Fayard, 1955)

Le Cinquantenaire du Premier Kilometre (Voisin, Soulas, 1958)

Etudes (Henri Delgove, January, 1959)

Histoire de L'Aviation Française (Silombra, Laumiere 1960)

Mes 10,000 Cerfs Volants (Voisin, La Table Ronde, 1961)

Débuts Véritables de l'Aviation Française (Ferber, Fayard, 1970)

The Wright Brothers (Gibbs-Smith, Science Museum, 1972)

First Flight (JE Walsh, Allen & Unwin, 1975)

Rebirth of European Aviation (Gibbs-Smith, Science Mus, 1974)

Wright Brothers and the RAS (Pritchard, RAS, 1975)

No longer an Island: Britain and the Wright Brothers (Gollin 1984)

Industrie Aéronautique en France 1900-50 (Chadeau, Fayard, 1987)

Wright Flyer: an Engineering Perspective (Wolko, Smithsonian 1987)

Wilbur and Orville (Howard, Ballantyne, 1988)

Visions of a Flying Machine (Jakab, Smithsonian, 1990)

A Passion for Wings (Robert Wohl, Yale Univ. Press, 1994)

French Aeroplanes before the Great War (Opdycke, Schiffer, 1999)

Blériot - Herald of an Age (Elliott, Tempus, 2000)

Léon Delagrange, le Dandy Volant (Delagrange, Lariviere, 2003)

Wright Brothers and the Birth of the Air Age (Crouch, USAF, 2003)

Taking Flight: Inventing the Aerial Age (Hallion, OUP, 2003)

The Bishop's Boys: (Crouch, Norton, 2003)

Early Automobiles and Airplanes: The Cultural Lag (Bromley, 2004)

Wilbur's Story (Holmes, 2007)

Robert Esnault-Pelterie (Torres & Villain, Ed.Confluences, 2007)

Les Frères Wright et la France (Carlier, Paris, 2008)

La Belle Époque de la Conquète de l'Air (Tison, Le Mans, 2010)

The contemporary remarks cited in this text are from these newspapers and periodicals:

Revue de l'Aviation	*Revue Aérienne*	*L'Aérophile*
Revue Aéronautique	*L'Aéronaute*	*La Revue de d'Artillerie*
La Nature	*L'Illustration*	*La Vie au Grand Air*
Le Sport Universel Illustré	*Fulmicoton*	*L'Eclair*
Le Matin	*Pionniers (Revue des Vieilles Tiges)*	*Omnia*
The Aero	*Flight*	*The Engineer*
Scientific American	*The Times*	*The New York Times*
New York Herald	*Sydney Morning Herald*	*Brisbane Courier*
Brooklyn Daily Eagle	*Aeronautics*	*American Aeronaut*
The Autocar	*The Motor*	*American Magazine of Aeronautics*
The American	*The Chicago Record Herald*	*The Post*
Progress	*Wiener Luftschiffer-Zeitung*	*Berliner Zeitung*

Photographs and illustrations

Most of the photographs reproduced here are from the author's collection or reprinted from contemporary publications. Images from the Rol, Meurisse and Branger press agencies are from the collection of Les Amis de Gabriel Voisin, with others courtesy of the Voisin archive at the Mullin Automotive Museum in California, the Henry Ford collection, the Library of Congress, Wright State University, the National Library of Australia, the municipal archives of Issy-les-Moulineaux and Boulogne-Billancourt, the Royal Aeronautical Society, Getty Images, Fondation Lartigue, Fondation Marius Berliet, Fondation de France and the Bibliothèque Nationale de France.

Acknowledgements

This account would not have been possible without the generous help of knowledgeable friends, notably Philippe Ladure, Stefan Ittner and other members of Les Amis de Gabriel Voisin, Jacques Hauvette, Nigel Mills, Jacques Daireaux, Laurent Friry and members of The Aerodrome Forum. For their help with proofreading, design and production, I am indebted to Jonathan Rishton, Sorina Hunter, Derek Todd and Christophe Allirot at West End.

Index

In Memoriam

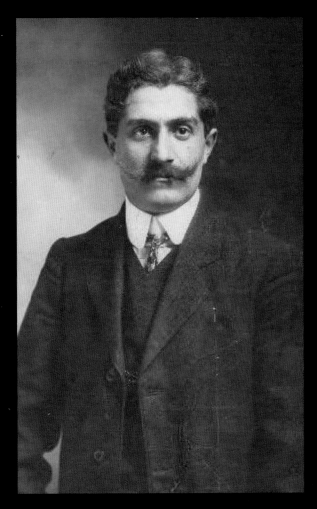

Charles Voisin, 1882-1912

Eugène Gabriel Voisin, 1880-1973

GRAND-PRIX DE L'AVIATION

Henri FARMAN